The
Writer's
Complete
CRIME
Reference
Book

The Writer's Complete CRIME Reference Book

MARTIN ROTH

Cincinnati, Ohio

The Writer's Complete Crime Reference Book. Copyright © 1993 by Martin Roth. Printed and bound in the United States of America. All rights reserved. No part of this book may be reproduced in any form or by any electronic or mechanical means including information storage and retrieval systems without permission in writing from the publisher, except by a reviewer, who may quote brief passages in a review. Published by Writer's Digest Books, an imprint of F&W Publications, Inc., 1507 Dana Ave., Cincinnati, Ohio 45207. Revised edition.

97 96 95 94   5 4 3 2

Library of Congress Cataloging-in-Publication Data

Roth, Martin
    The writer's complete crime reference book / by Martin Roth. — revised.
        p. cm.
    Includes bibliographical references and index.
    ISBN 0-89879-564-8
    1. Detective and mystery stories — Authorship. 2. Detective and mystery stories — Handbooks, manuals, etc. 3. Crime — United States — Handbooks, manuals, etc. 4. Criminal justice, Administration of — United States — Handbooks, manuals, etc. I.   Title.
PN3377.5.D4R6   1993
364 — dc20   93-2889
                                                                          CIP

Design by Joan Jacobus

The charts on pages 36-41 are reprinted with the permission of the Pharmaceutical Manufacturer's Association.

To my wonderful wife, Marjorie, without whose encouragement, patience, support and love, this book might never have seen the light of day.

Acknowledgments

I wish to express my sincere appreciation and gratitude to Barry Fisher, Director of Scientific Services Bureau, Los Angeles County Sheriff's Department; Michael Fooner, international crime expert and author on criminal justice; criminal defense attorney Arthur Lewis; and to the untold number of other experts and specialists from local, state and federal law-enforcement agencies; the U.S. armed forces military justice systems; the private investigators, judges and criminalists who so graciously provided me with much of the invaluable information included in this book.

One last kudo, and that is to my editor, Charles Clark. His knowledge, assistance and contributions to this revised edition are most gratefully appreciated.

Contents

Preface   *1*

Crime ————————————————————————— **4**

Crime and Motive   *4*

General List of Crimes   *5*

Crimes Associated With Politics   *7*

Crimes Associated With Business   *7*

Domestic Crimes   *8*

Crimes Associated With Racketeering   *8*

White-Collar Crimes   *9*

Crimes By Employees   *10*

Means of Escape   *11*

Acts of Violence   *12*

Homicide   *14*

Burglary   *19*

Robbery   *20*

Larceny   *21*

Auto Theft   *21*

Confidence Games   *22*

Trickery   *26*

Sex Offenses   *27*

Computer Crime   *29*

Smuggling   *30*

Arson   *34*

Drugs   *35*

National Crime Information Center   *47*

Where to Go From Here   *48*

Criminals ——————————————————————— **52**

Organized Crime   *52*

Modus Operandi   *60*

Weapons Used by Criminals   *61*

Firearms and Manufacturers   *62*

Weapons Terms   *65*

Explosives   *70*

Where to Go From Here   *70*

Cops ——————————————————————— **74**

    Police Department Organization *74*
    Los Angeles Police Department: Organization and Functions *75*
    Los Angeles County Sheriff's Department *86*
    Office of the District Attorney of Los Angeles *104*
    Office of the City Attorney of Los Angeles *105*
    Cincinnati Police Division *106*
    Department of Justice *109*
    INTERPOL, U.S. National Central Bureau *116*
    Federal Bureau of Investigation *116*
    U.S. Marshall's Service *120*
    Immigration and Naturalization Service *121*
    Drug Enforcement Agency *123*
    Bureau of Alchol, Tobacco and Firearms *124*
    Customs Service Special Investigative Division *124*
    Internal Revenue Service Criminal Investigations *125*
    Coast Guard *126*
    Postal Inspection Service *126*
    Federal Air Marshals *127*
    Bureau of Land Management *128*
    Defense Criminal Investigative Service *128*
    Defense Investigative Service *129*
    Army Criminal Investigative Command *129*
    Naval Investigative Service *129*
    Air Force Office of Special Investigations *130*
    Military Police *130*
    Other Federal Investigative Agencies *131*
    INTERPOL *131*
    Private Investigators *132*
    Where to Go From Here *133*

Investigations ——————————————————— **136**

    Writing About Investigations *136*
    Fundamentals of Investigation *137*
    The Scene of the Crime *142*
    Sources to Investigate *145*
    Missing Persons *147*

Steps in Indentifying a Body *148*
Surveillance *150*
Forensic Sciences *152*
Interrogation *153*
Police Codes *157*
Where to Go From Here *163*

The Courts _____ *165*
The Grand Jury *165*
Rights of Defendants *168*
The Courtroom *170*
Military Justice System *172*
Status of Forces *179*
Courtroom Concepts *179*
Evidence *191*
Where to Go From Here *199*

Prisons _____ *202*
Penal Systems *202*
Rights of Convicted Felons *203*
California Correctional Institutions *203*
Federal Bureau of Prisons *218*
Parole *224*
Capital Punishment *231*
Where to Go From Here *236*

Language _____ *239*
Slang *239*
Legal Terminology *268*
Where to Go From Here *276*

Index _____ *279*

Preface

This second edition of *The Writer's Complete Crime Reference Book* has been reorganized to make it easier to use. The forty short chapters of the first edition have been regrouped into seven longer chapters covering the major topics in crime writing. The chapter contents in the table of contents tell you exactly where to find subtopics, and the index will guide you to shorter discussions of the same topic in different chapters.

Many sections of this book were supplied by the agencies described. This shows not only how the agencies view themselves, but also how you can easily get the same sort of information from virtually any police department or federal law enforcement agency. Just call or write to them, and most will be happy to help you.

New in this edition are sections titled "Where to Go From Here," located at the end of each chapter. These give you a start on the research it will take to make your writing convincing to an increasingly sophisticated audience. Often this research will involve not only direct contact with an authority in the field you're writing about, but also a lot of reading, so each section has a bibliography of the latest books on each topic.

Of course, these books were the "latest" when this manuscript went to press. By the time you read it, a number of new books in each field will have been published, and other changes will have occurred. Be particularly careful when writing about crime detection techniques and slang; they are hard to keep up with. The slang in chapter seven was collected over many years, and much of it is obsolete. The purpose of that section is as much to give you an idea of what the police and criminals have invented slang *about* as to give you the slang itself. For example, a "gun" that was called a "gat" or a "heater" forty years ago might now be called a "piece." The point is to get a feel for words likely to have slang equivalents.

There are few aspects of crime and detection that stay the same over time. This book can point you in the right direction and give you some good clues. But in the end you have to get on the telephone or go to the library to find the details that will make your story grab the reader with its accuracy and authenticity. We hope

The Writer's Complete Crime Reference Book will help you to do that, and that you'll turn to it time and again for the sort of advice you can't get anywhere else.

HOW TO AVOID COMMON MISTAKES

Even the best writers make mistakes. A recent book by an excellent mystery writer had a number of small, but distracting errors about guns. The writer knew that .357 Magnum revolvers can also fire .38 Special ammunition, and that the barrels of Dan Wesson revolvers are easy to change, but some details of how to use this in her story eluded her. Getting the details wrong is the most common error in crime writing.

Admit it! As writers, we often take dramatic license and convince ourselves that the reader or audience isn't going to know the difference. Not true anymore. Crime readers and TV and movie audiences are getting pretty sharp and will pick up on sloppy crime writing. It takes a little longer, but getting it right is well worth the effort—for your sake, as well as for the people reading or watching your story. The following are a few mistakes to watch out for:

- Don't confuse ballistics with firearms identification. Ballistics is the study of the trajectory of a bullet, not the identification of the gun the bullet came from.
- Don't confuse "criminologists" with "criminalists." Criminology is the scientific study of crime and criminals. A criminalist is a specialist in one of the forensic sciences.
- Bodies are seldom outlined in chalk or tape because they may have to be rolled over. Chalk markings or tape may be used when the victim is found outdoors, when someone has been struck by a vehicle, or when the victim has fallen from a great height.
- "Take him downtown for questioning" is a cliché that should be used with care because a suspect can refuse to be questioned. If the suspect refuses to be questioned, there isn't anything the officer can do except detain the suspect while checking for outstanding warrants.
- Use the right police codes. Too often writers use California

codes for stories set in New York City, and vice versa. Codes vary, so if you name the city your story takes place in, check that city's police radio codes.

- Don't confuse bullets with cartridges. The bullet is the projectile at the end of the cartridge or casing. Both bullets and cartridges are valuable clues to the identity of the weapon.
- If you write about a real city, find out the color of its patrol cars. Los Angeles patrol cars are black and white. New York's cars are blue and white. Uniforms and badges also vary from city to city.
- Don't have your investigator pick up a suspect weapon by inserting a pencil into the barrel. Doing so might contaminate any of the victim's blood spatterings inside the barrel and could also affect the rifling, thus compromising later comparisons made in the police lab.
- Don't have your investigator put weapons and similar pieces of evidence into plastic bags—plastic sweats, and any prints on the article could be damaged. In most instances paper bags are used to collect physical evidence.
- Keep crime scene personnel at a minimum. In real life, anyone not essential to processing the scene is kept away. If that is not possible, have your characters use a trail already examined by a criminalist.
- If your story needs red herrings (other suspects to investigate before the perpetrator is caught), develop them so they are not easily dismissed by the reader. Give them good motives, opportunity, no alibis and depth of character.

These are just a few examples. In any story, you have hundreds of details to supply, and for every one of them you have to answer your readers' questions before they ask them. The key to accurate writing is to keep looking for the right answers—not just any answers or even good answers. You need answers that will amaze your readers and keep them asking for more.

Good hunting!

1
Crime

CRIME AND MOTIVE

What makes people commit crimes — especially those that disregard the lives, safety and possessions of others — is the subject of criminal psychology and can only be hinted at here.

There are no rules about why people commit crimes. The motive could be purely psychological, going far back into the individual's childhood. Then again, the criminal act might happen on the spur of the moment. Perpetrators may feel justified, or they may be unaware that what they are doing is unlawful.

People do not commit crimes without a motive, even those who bear no grudge and do not commit a crime out of passion, or for personal gain. Committing a crime for the sheer thrill is itself a motive. The writer must decide the reason before developing the plot, though the criminal's motive may not be revealed until the end of the story.

To determine the motive for the crime, it is important to develop the character of the criminal. The professional writer already knows to flesh out characters as much as possible. It is essential to give the victim a believable background, not only to explain the perpetrator's motive, but also to provide something for the police to delve into during their investigation. Real-life criminal investigators usually go through laborious and often tedious days (and even years) before turning up a lead, so providing more personal and professional background makes the police officer more interesting.

GENERAL LIST OF CRIMES
Abduction
Adultery
Affray
Aiding and abetting
Armed robbery
Arson
Assault
Auto theft
Battery
Bigamy
Blackmail
Bookmaking
Bootlegging
Bribery
Burglary
Compounding a felony
Concealment of birth or death
Conspiracy
Counterfeiting
Disorderly conduct
Disturbing the peace
Drunk driving
Drunkenness
Dueling
Embezzlement
Escape from lawful imprisonment
Extortion
False impersonation

False imprisonment
Forgery
Gambling
Grand larceny
Hijacking
Homicide
Illegal sale of arms
Impersonating an officer
Incest
Indecent exposure
Industrial espionage
Kidnapping
Larceny
Libel and slander
Littering
Loan sharking
Loitering
Manslaughter
Manslaughter, involuntary
Manslaughter, voluntary
Misconduct in office
Murder
Narcotics (possession, sale, smuggling)
Obstruction of justice
Perjury
Piracy
Prostitution
Rape
Rape, statutory
Receiving stolen goods
Resisting arrest
Rioting
Robbery
Sabotage
Slavery
Smuggling
Suicide
Swindling

Tampering with evidence
Trespassing
Unlawful assembly
Vandalism
Weapons (carrying concealed, firing in public)

CRIMES ASSOCIATED WITH POLITICS

Assassination
Blackmail
Bribery
Compounding a felony
Conspiracy
Cover-up
Embezzlement of government funds
Falsifying records
Fraud
Graft
High treason
Libel and slander
Malfeasance in office
Misuse of government funds
Perjury
Treason
Unauthorized destruction of public records

CRIMES ASSOCIATED WITH BUSINESS

Arson
Compounding a felony
Copyright or patent infringement
Counterfeiting
False advertising
False records or books
Hijacking
Illegal stock transactions
Industrial espionage

Insider trading
Mail fraud
Possession of stolen merchandise
Record piracy
Revealing privileged information
Sale of illegal goods
Sexual harassment
Tax fraud
Theft

DOMESTIC CRIMES

Assault
Battery
Child abandonment
Child abuse
Harassment
Husband beating
Incest
Marital rape
Mercy killing
Nonpayment of child support
Parent abuse
Wife beating

CRIMES ASSOCIATED WITH RACKETEERING

Blackmail
Illegal siding business
Illegal stock-and-bond trading
Insurance frauds
Mail-order fraud
Phony accident claims
Phony land promotions
Phony mediums
Phony money-producing schemes
Protection extortion

Quack doctors
Shell games
Skimming
Swindling

WHITE-COLLAR CRIMES

One growing type of crime is that taking place within corporate America, banks and brokerage houses. Much of the investigation of white-collar crime is done by the Federal Bureau of Investigation; the United States' Attorney's Office; the Internal Revenue Service; the Federal Trade Commission; the Postal Inspector's Office; the Securities and Exchange Commission; and the Defense Criminal Investigative Service, which was created in 1982 to investigate corporate corruption in the defense industry. The following are some white-collar crimes:

Antitrust violations
Arson-related insurance frauds
Bank frauds
Boiler-room investment scams
Bribery
Computer thefts
Corporate-raider manipulations
Embezzlement
Excessive interest charges
False or misleading advertising
Fraudulent bankruptcy
Fraudulent billings
Fraudulent loans
Inferior merchandise
Insider trading
Kickbacks
Manufacturing or distributing faulty parts
Medicare and medical insurance frauds
Misappropriation of funds
Overcharging for auto repairs
Overcharging on government contracts

Product substitution on government contracts
Shortchanging in retail stores
Staged accident insurance fraud
Stock manipulations
Tax-shelter frauds

CRIMES BY EMPLOYEES

Not all thefts are committed by professional criminals. Many are committed by employees for a variety of reasons. The employee often feels justified, unlike the criminal who commits his or her act purely out of greed. At times, however, crimes are committed in the office by nonprofessionals with the same motive as that of the common criminal. The following are some of these crimes:

Arson or other property destruction
Assisting professional criminal
Blackmail
Diverting company funds to self
Falsification of company books or records
Forging signatures on checks, letters, etc.
Misappropriating company funds
Padding or falsifying expense accounts
Physically attacking an employer or employee
Sabotaging factory, office, plans, equipment
Selling company secrets
Theft of cash or company checks
Theft of company books, records or documents
Theft of company plans, research, technical information
Theft of company products or merchandise
Theft of computer programs
Theft of equipment or office supplies
Theft of personal possessions
Trading on inside information
Using company equipment for personal gain

Motives for Internal Crimes
Bigoted or prejudiced against employer
Blackmail company for profit or revenge

Disagreement with policies
Disagreement with political ideals
Drug or alcohol addiction
Employee feels grossly underpaid
Employee is deeply in debt
Jealousy or envy
Labor disagreement
Personal dislike of employer
Revenge for firing
Selling company secrets
To control employer or company
To draw attention to a specific issue
Unfair treatment by supervisor

MEANS OF ESCAPE

Airshafts
Commandeered vehicle
Distraction
Driving
Explosives
Fighting
Forged papers
Helicopter
Hiding
Hiking
Impersonation
Key theft
Kicking down
Ladders
Leaping
Ropes
Running
Sawing
Scaling
Sewers
Shooting

Swimming
Taking hostage
Tunneling
Underwater

ACTS OF VIOLENCE

Acid throwing
Amputation
Arm twisting
Axing
Beating
Binding
Blackjacking
Bleeding
Blinding
Boiling oil
Bombing
Bone breaking
Bone crushing
Branding
Bread-and-water diet
Burning at stake
Burning by steam
Burying alive
Castration
Cat-o'-nine-tails lashing
Chain beating
Chaining
Cigarette burning
Crucifixion
Deafening by sound
Decapitating
Depriving of sleep
Disfiguring
Dragging
Dripping water on head

Drowning
Electric shock
Exposing to wild animal
Eye gouging
Fingernail pulling
Flesh-eating ants
Flogging
Forced marching
Forcing to view an atrocity
Freezing
Frightening
Garroting
Gassing
Genital crushing
Genital electrical shocking
Hair extraction
Hanging
Hanging upside down
Head twisting
Hot wax
Immersion in hot water
Impaling
Kicking
Kidnapping
Knifing
Lead-pipe beating
Leg twisting
Mugging
Mutilating
Needles under fingernails
On the rack
Pistol whipping
Poison darts
Powerful light in eyes
Pressing with weights
Rib cracking
Rubber-hose beating
Running over by auto

Salting wound
Sandbagging
Scalping
Setting afire
Shattering kneecap
Shooting
Skull crushing
Slave labor
Slow drowning
Slow poisoning
Snakebite
Sodomy
Standing in confinement
Starving
Stoning
Strangling
Stretching
Suspending by thumbs
Tar-and-feathering
Tearing of flesh
Teeth pulling
Thrown from high place
Thrown to animals
Thrown to sharks
Thumbscrew
Thumb twisting
Whipping

HOMICIDE

Homicide is the killing of a human being. The circumstances of the homicide determine whether or not taking that life is a criminal or an innocent act.

A criminal homicide is neither excusable nor justifiable and falls into two categories: murder and manslaughter. In order to charge murder, there must be premeditation. The person accused of the murder must have intended to commit bodily harm or kill;

engaged in a dangerous act with wanton disregard for human life; or engaged in a felony such as a robbery, burglary, rape or arson. It must also be shown that the victim is dead, and that the death was at the hands of the accused.

Manslaughter is neither murder nor an innocent homicide but rather the unlawful taking of a human life without premeditation or malice aforethought. The terms "voluntary" and "involuntary" indicate whether or not the killing was intended. Taking a human life during the heat of passion, even though there was an intent to kill, is considered voluntary manslaughter. The taking of a life without the intent to kill is considered involuntary manslaughter.

Motives for Homicide

Ambition
Blackmail
Cover another crime
Debt
Employed for the purpose
Fear
Feud
Gain
Jealousy
Love
Mercy
Protecting someone
Rage
Revenge
Rivalry
Sadism
Self-defense
Sex
Thrill
To frame another

Means of Murder

Arson
Automobile crash

Axing
Beating
Bombing
Burning
Burying alive
Cremation
Drowning
Electrocution
Exposing to disease
Exposing to extreme cold or heat
Exposing to wild animal
Frightening
Garroting
Gassing
Hanging
Hit and run
Impaling
Knifing
Overdosing on a drug
Poisoning
Shooting
Stabbing
Starving
Stoning
Strangulation
Suffocation
Throwing from height

Unusual Means of Disposing of Bodies
Acid
At sea
Auto crusher
Buried in woods
Buried under floor
Compactor
Cut into small pieces
Disposed of in trash

Dropped down well
Dropped from plane
Dropped in quicksand
Fed to animal or fish
Incinerator
Placed in existing, marked grave
Sealed in wall

The First Officer on the Scene

The first officer on the scene of a homicide has a wide range of duties. Here is a partial list:

Determine identity of perpetrator or suspect(s).
Note time of arrival.
Prevent anyone from disturbing scene pending arrival of medical examiner and crime lab.
Prevent unauthorized people from entering the crime scene and anyone present from leaving.
Locate and preserve weapon and check for prints.
Take names of anyone present and description of any possible suspect(s).
Separate witnesses to prevent any conversation between them.
Note position of the body, clothing.
Check for bullet holes, shell casings, bloodstains.
Search for clues.
Preserve evidence.
Check with medical examiner for time of death, cause and wounds, and ask if death occurred at location where body was discovered.
Have sketch or photograph made of location, body position.
Take statements of witnesses.
Attempt to learn motive.
Run make on victim to see if prior record exists.
Check for datebooks, diary, letters, addresses and phone numbers belonging to victim.
Learn identity of friends, relatives, enemies.

Serial Murder

According to recent studies, most serial killers suffer more from cultural and sociological problems than from medical problems. Serial killers usually seek celebrity status, venting their aggression and hostile feelings to gain publicity. Serial killers usually act sane, and often are not psychotic, but are generally sociopaths. Studies reveal that most serial killers are white males between the ages of twenty-five to thirty-five and are usually products of working- or lower-middle-class families. Serial killers often seek victims from upper-middle-class backgrounds. Many serial killers are charming, selfish, impulsive and ambitious; many come from broken homes or homes where they were abused. Most serial killers have suffered rejection, which causes them to experience frustration and psychological emasculation. Few serial killers express any feelings of guilt or remorse for their crimes.

Most serial killers target women, using some ruse to gain control of their victims. Their patterns usually call for sexual contact, followed or proceeded by murder and mutilation. One violent act makes it easier for the serial killer to continue seeking, murdering and mutilating victims. Motivations have been broken down by researchers into four major categories.

The first is called the visionary type. These killers claim to hear voices belonging to demons or God ordering them to kill.

The second type is the sociopath. These individuals have a goal, usually the elimination of certain people. They think they help society by purging it of those they believe to be destructive.

A third type finds gratification from exercising power over the victim, having sex with the victim, with the control of the victim bringing greater satisfaction than the sexual act itself.

A fourth type is the pleasure-seeking killer. For these individuals the thrill comes from performing a knowingly perverted act.

In general, most serial killers are sexually motivated even if sex itself is not the ultimate gratification. In a majority of cases, serial killers are responding to a secret fantasy, and the killings may involve cannibalism, torture, mutilation, dismemberment, necrophilia or a combination of these acts.

Episodic aggressive behavior is a common factor among people who later become serial killers. The following are examples of episodic aggressive behavior:

Arson
Chronic drug or alcohol abuse
Cruelty to animals
Deviant sexual behavior
Drastic changes in moods
Hyper- or hyposexuality
Inability to tell the truth
Parental abuse
Religious obsession

BURGLARY

Burglary, the most common form of theft, is the entering of premises to commit a theft. Some jurisdictions distinguish between entering a dwelling at night and housebreaking, the unlawful entering of a building with intent to commit a crime, so the definition of burglary varies in different states. To consider a housebreaking a burglary, the following elements must be established:

Breaking and entering occurred.
The act took place at night.
The dwelling belonged to another person.
The offender's intent was to commit a crime.

Burglaries of Safes

Blow Job: Blowing the safe by using an explosive charge, usually a plastique.

Carry Out: The safe is physically removed.

Chopping: The safe is turned upside down to expose the bottom, the weakest section. A hole is made and a jimmy applied to permit access.

Click Job: Using a stethoscope and listening for the clicks as the combination falls into place.

Punch Job: Using a sledge and center punch, the dial is knocked off with a hammer, and the punch is held against the spindle and hit sharply. If the safe has tumblers at the end of the spindle, the small sockets are broken when the spindle is forced back and the lock is released. Some safes are punchproof when the tumblers are off-spindle.

Rip Job: Using an electric drill and crowbar, a hole is made in upper- or lower-left corner. A bar is placed in the hole and the door is pried open.

ROBBERY

A leading form of major crime is robbery; many robbers specialize in robbing persons, stores or premises. The following are some types of robberies:

Armored cars
Bank messengers
Banks
Cabdrivers
Casual strollers
Gambling games
Gas stations
Payroll clerks
Residences
Restaurants
Stores
Truck drivers

Methods of Robbery

Assault
Beating
Binding
Drugging
Threats

LARCENY

Anyone who steals any article of value of another person is guilty of larceny. The investigator must prove that the suspect has wrongfully obtained and withheld the property. In addition, the value of the property and the intent to permanently withhold it must be confirmed. Among the types of larceny are:

Art frauds
Baggage thieves
Bag stealers or muggers
Computer theft and fraud
Confidence games
Credit card thieves
Embezzlers
Hotel thieves
Loan sharks
Lush workers (those who prey on drunks)
Pickpockets
Securities frauds
Shoplifters
Those receiving stolen goods

AUTO THEFT

When a vehicle is stolen, used and then abandoned, the motive is temporary use, and the charge is temporary appropriation. In most instances, temporary appropriation is done by juveniles, joy riders and professional criminals using a vehicle in a crime.

The professional auto thief steals to profit from the vehicle, either by reselling it or stripping it and selling the parts. Although some thieves jump the ignition, most professionals use a device called a *code cutter*, which makes keys based on the ignition code number. Another device used is a *slapper*. This device pulls out the ignition cylinder, allowing the thief to insert a replacement.

CONFIDENCE GAMES

Con men have a wide variety of swindles, with many more being thought up every day. Many cons might also fall under the categories of fraud, stock manipulation and embezzlement.

One of the oldest swindles is the Money-Making Machine. Cons show the victim a machine that, as they demonstrate, produces dollar bills. The machine is sold to the victim, or the victim is asked to invest in the production of more machines like it.

The Inheritance is a scam in which victims are told they have come into an inheritance of some famous person, but that money is needed for litigation and proving their right to their portion of the estate. The con takes the money and is never heard from again.

In a con involving hot merchandise, the victim is approached to buy something of great value, like a fur or jewels. The victim is led to believe that the merchandise has been stolen. In reality, though, it is fake.

The Just-a-Few-Dollars-More scam is usually performed by a scam artist who is content with picking up some small change. These individuals appear well-groomed and friendly and select an expensive item in a small retail shop. They offer to pay for the merchandise by personal check and ask to have it delivered after the check has cleared. As the salesperson writes up the order, the perpetrators, about to write the check, suddenly realize they have no cash and need $20 or $30 to get through the day. Could the check be for just a little more than the amount of the sale? Because the sale garners a sizable commission and the merchandise won't be shipped until the check clears, the customers' wishes are usually granted. The perps leave the store with the cash, never planning to receive the merchandise anyway, as the shipping address and the check are phony.

Phony airline tickets produce hundreds of millions of dollars in losses to major carriers, and hundreds of millions in profits to the counterfeiters. They easily dispose of the bogus tickets by selling them to travelers who think they're buying discounted legitimate tickets.

The Pyramid is a get-rich-quick scam in which people are promised big gains for a short-term investment. The scam artist develops a reputation for delivering when the first customer gets money plus a substantial profit, thus becoming a walking advertisement for the plot. Once the chain begins, the new investors get back less and less, as the scam artists pocket their money without actually investing a dime, until the pyramid eventually comes tumbling down. The pyramid scam was conceived by Charles Ponzi in the 1920s and is sometimes referred to as the Ponzi Scheme.

Computer scams are becoming more common. As computers become more sophisticated, so do computer crooks, who steal everything from software programs to stocks and bonds. They also alter credit card billings, switch bank accounts, transfer funds illegally, alter records, produce false billings and authorize false loans and payments.

Film and record piracy are also on the upswing. Those usually involved are employees who have access to the original print or master and see an opportunity to pick up extra cash. These individuals make deals with organized crime, who are capable of mass distribution of the pirated films and tapes.

Some of the largest money-producing scams are offers made through mail-order ads placed in the backs of magazines. Some mail-order scams offer products or services that are either not worth the money or are nonexistent.

One of the sickest scams is to prey on those who have just lost a close relative by notifying the bereaved that the deceased ordered a personalized Bible or other article that is now ready for delivery. Naturally, having no way of checking with the deceased about the order, and believing the obligation should be fulfilled, the bereaved accepts the article and usually pays a pretty sum.

In the Badger Game, an attractive woman lets herself be picked up by a married man on the make. Choosing a mark who appears wealthy, she spends several pristine evenings with him before finally agreeing to go to her hotel room. Once in a compromising position, the door bursts open and in comes her wronged husband who threatens to expose the man's doings to his wife. The man quickly offers to make some sort of settlement to keep things quiet. A variation of this is when someone posing as a cop barges in threatening arrest, but instead accepts a bribe.

In the Shirley Temple, a mother or both parents of a child are approached by a supposed talent scout or theatrical manager who claims their child can be a big television or movie star. He offers them a contract, but naturally there will be expenses for photographs. The photographs are actually taken, but the price is highly inflated.

The Miss Lonely Hearts gambit is perpetrated by women who correspond with lonely men seeking romance and marriage. The female con exchanges a series of love letters with the victim, and usually includes a knockout picture (phony). She then tells her victim that if he'll send her the plane fare, she'd like to visit him. Naturally, she never shows up.

In the Spanish Prisoner, a letter from a supposed European, Middle Eastern or Asian businessman is shown to the mark by the roper. The letter says the writer has a sizable foreign bank account but is unable to withdraw money because he is unjustly being held in jail. He needs cash to bribe the guards so he can escape. For this he is willing to pay twice the amount of money needed. Included with the letter is a foreign bank book with the bank's phone number and a signed withdrawal slip to be held as security. A call to the bank confirms the account. In exchange for the cash, the mark gets the worthless bank book and withdrawal slip. Unfortunately, the bank book is fake and the bank the mark called was actually an accomplice at a pay phone.

The Flying Game is also known as the "hot TV hustle." A con artist pretends to be selling a hot stolen item such as a camcorder, packaged in what appears to be the original unopened box. The item looks like it was just whisked off the shelf. Naturally the con man can't stand around while the victim examines the hot merchandise. When the victim gets home and opens the package, the box is empty except for some stones.

Other Scams and Cons

Auto repair gyps
Bad check passers
Bargain sales
Bogus works of art
Carnival games and pitch setups

Counterfeit labels and designer clothing
Counterfeit money
Family tree artists
Finance rackets
Fortune-telling
Going-out-of-business sales
Home improvement scams
Household gimmicks that don't work
Imitation jewelry
Insurance frauds
Land fraud
Learn-at-home courses
Loaded dice
Loan sharks
Mail-order aphrodisiacs
Marked cards
Massage parlors
Mediums
Mind reading
Miracle drugs
Phony auctions
Phony auto accidents
Phony charities
Phony C.O.D. schemes
Pool sharks
Record pirates
Reproductions sold as originals
Rigged gambling equipment
Stock swindles
Tip sheets
Travel contests/free weekends
Weights and measures frauds
Work-at-home scams

Hundreds of scams are perpetrated on the public every day. These are just a few samples of the work of cons and bunco artists. Call or visit your local police department to find out more about scams.

TRICKERY

Many times criminals resort to conning, duping or tricking their opponent or accomplice. The following are some common cons, dupes and tricks:

Convincing another party that he or she is innocent.
Causing another party to believe something has happened that really hasn't occurred.
Convincing another party that he or she has been double-crossed.
Convincing the other party that what he or she has is really counterfeit.
Pretending to be an informer.
Causing the other party to believe an accomplice has talked or has turned against him or her.
Pretending that someone is dead.
Pretending a victim or witness is still alive.
Convincing someone that something counterfeit is real.
Pretending to be someone else.
Pretending to already know another's plan.
Convincing another that he or she has already been defeated.
Causing someone to believe he or she has been betrayed.
Pretending to know another's secret.
Stalling for time.
Causing another to act before he or she had planned.
Pretending to have changed sides.

Devices Used in Trickery

Counterfeits
Doctored photographs
False papers or identification
False reports
Hypnosis
Illusion and special effects
Imitating another's voice
Leaving false prints
Planting false evidence
Playing dead

Playing on emotions
Playing on fears
Theatrical sets

SEX OFFENSES

Any working cop who investigates rape, child molestation, prostitution and pornography will tell you that it's one of the sickest worlds one could possibly enter. Even hardened criminals have no use for sex offenders, especially those who molest children. Sexual assault crimes are crimes of violence and often have little to do with sex. They are about anger and power over the victim.

Most people think that rapists only go after provocative and attractive young women. Not true. Lots of older women are raped. They're easy victims and they may remind the rapist of a hated relative.

There are different types of rapists. Date rapists know their victims. The Gentleman Rapist rapes because he has trouble with his masculinity. Sadistic rapists usually like to record rapes for reviewing and reliving later on. They often kill their victims. Anger-punishing rapists seek to punish victims for what other women have done to them. Serial rapists are usually ritualistic in the rapes they commit.

Rape Victims

Rape victims more often than not feel psychologically dirty and often have a compulsion to wash, bathe, douche, discard clothing—anything to rid themselves of any connection to the incident. Some rape victims are bitten, most if not all are bruised and scratched, many have bruises near the shoulder and upper arms where they've been pinned down. Bruises appear on the inside of the victim's thighs where the legs were forced apart. Black eyes are not uncommon, and some victims bear marks around the throat from choking and throttling.

Rape Investigation

There is no place in modern police procedures for the outmoded attitude that rape victims provoked the rape. Victims should be treated nonjudgmentally and with sensitivity. As much information about the rape, the victim and the suspect should be garnered quickly. Victims appearing calm or who do not easily volunteer sensitive details of the assault should not be treated differently than more cooperative victims. The crime scene should be secured, and the first officer on the scene should arrange for removal of the victim to a hospital emergency room as soon as possible.

At the hospital, the doctor first takes the victim's medical history and the details of the assault. The doctor would then make a thorough examination for evidence of cuts, bruises and lacerations. Photographs should be taken. The victim should also be examined for trace evidence adhering to her body such as grass, soil, semen, blood, hairs, fibers and skin scrapings if the victim scratched her assailant. Vaginal specimens and a vaginal aspirate should be taken. The physical evidence is essential to establish that penetration and nonconsensual intercourse occurred, and to help establish the identity of the rapist.

Pedophilia

Pedophiles, as the word implies, are fascinated by children. They usually begin by taking pictures of children or purchasing child pornography pictures and tapes.

Many pedophiles marry divorcees or widows who have small children. Strangely, many pedophiles actually love and care for children. But some pedophiles are exceptions to that rule. These individuals are not satisfied with the sexual assault, and may torture, mutilate and kill their victims as well.

Pedophiles usually seduce their victims and gain their trust, and they seldom confine their molestations and sexual assaults to one child.

What happens to these victimized children? Most are traumatized for life. In a number of cases, the children are turned into prostitutes with the abuser acting as the pimp, or are sold to another pimp's stable.

Homosexual Sexual Assault

Sodomy and other homosexual assaults can take place in the community at large or in jails and prisons. The same care and investigation should take place with this type of rape as with any other. There are special charges in the case of sodomy.

Sex Crimes Unit

Most major cities have a sex crimes unit that handles the majority of sexual assault cases. If a homicide is involved, the case would then be handled by the homicide division.

Prostitution is usually investigated by the local vice squad. If the prostitution ring is part of organized crime it would be investigated by a city, state or federal organized crime unit.

Pornography is investigated by the local vice squad unless the law enforcement agency has a special section for the investigation of pornography. If pornography involves interstate movement, it then falls into the jurisdiction of the Office of Postal Inspection and the Department of Justice.

COMPUTER CRIME

With the advent of the computer, a new brand of crime has come on the scene. Today's computer criminal can embezzle funds, transfer bank accounts, divert payments, obtain credit, eavesdrop on confidential data, bill for nonexistent merchandise, steal programs, commit sabotage and erase expensive software programs. Offenders commit computer crimes for various reasons: the thrill of pulling it off, greed, profit, industrial or military spying, extortion and blackmail. Computer criminals have even held stolen programs for ransom.

Computer criminals work in a variety of ways. Some gain access to codes simply by experimentation, whereas others scrounge through office trash baskets, or observe an authorized operator at work and note the access code to a program. Computer crime investigators often require the assistance of expert consultants.

SMUGGLING

The smuggling of illegal drugs, weapons, aliens, works of art, currency, jewels, industrial products, antiques, national treasures, stolen or unauthorized documents, food, plants, animals and unauthorized medications into or out of the United States is a serious problem.

Concealment of Objects

Smugglers are extremely creative in their means of hiding and transporting what they are smuggling. Here are some possible hiding places:

Air conditioning ducts
Airplanes
Art objects
Attics
Automobiles
Ballpoint pens
Barrels
Bedposts
Behind paintings
Birdcages
Books
Bottles
Building materials
Buried in garden
Cameras
Cane, cane handle
Canisters
Casts and bandaged areas
Chairs
Cigarette lighter
Cigarette pack

Cleaning equipment
Clocks
Clothing
Coffins
Crates
Cremation urns
Crutches
Cuffs or pleats in shirt, pants
Dead bodies
Dog houses
False teeth
Film canisters
Flashlights
Food
Freezers
Furniture
Hearing aids
Hollowed-out books
Household appliances
Industrial machinery
Jars
Jewelry boxes
Kitchen utensils
Kitty litter boxes
Light fixtures
Lipstick holder
Luggage
Machine parts
Makeup compact
Mattresses
Musical instruments
Paintings
Pendant
Picture frames
Plants
Plaster cast
Radios
Recorders

Religious artifacts
Rings
Shipping containers
Shoes
Shower heads
Sink traps, drains
Sports equipment
Telephones
Televisions
Toilet articles
Toilet tanks or bowls
Toys, dolls
Trucks, vans, campers
Umbrella
Under carpet or tile
Under drawers
Vases
Wall sockets
Wheelchairs

Concealment in Aircraft and at Airfields

Added doors
Boxes
Duffle bags
Extra fuel tanks
Passenger seats
Plastic bags
Trucks, campers, vans
Window frames

Concealment at Marinas or on Boats

Added or modified fuel tanks
Bilges
Concealed compartments
Electronic equipment
Modified bulkheads
Raised decks

Transport trailers

Concealment at Checkpoints

Attached to pet
Baggage with concealed compartments
Bulky clothing
Carried by infant or minor
Inside pet cage or pen
On or in deceased person
Secret coffin compartment
Sewn into garment or in lining

Suspicious Persons

Smugglers, as creative and professional as they may be, often give customs agents a reason to suspect their activities. Some clues include:

A life-style inconsistent with a claimed occupation.

An international carrier employee who seldom takes time off or insists on working the shift coinciding with a particular flight.

Persons who constantly purchase small quantities of gasoline for vehicles; their vehicles might possibly have a modified gas tank used to transport contraband.

Persons requesting hotel rooms with a view of the customs lane.

Persons who appear to be in too much of a hurry.

Persons who have a difficult time looking an agent in the eye.

Individuals who tell their children to board ahead of them.

Persons paying cash for rental vehicles.

Purchasing large amounts of tape or plastic bags.

Private aircraft owners who frequently make trips out of the country.

Persons receiving large amounts of mail from outside the United States, especially from Colombia, Peru, Thailand, Brazil and Pakistan.

Persons operating currency exchanges from private residences or vehicles.

ARSON

Arson is the malicious and willful burning of private property or a business structure. If it endangers lives as well as property, most states provide for additional punishment. The term *burning* need not imply the total destruction of the structure, but merely the ignition of the structure.

If the structure is used as a dwelling, it is classified as inhabited, although it is not necessary that a person occupy the structure at the time the arson is committed. It is essential that malice or criminal intent be shown to conclude that the crime is arson.

In an arson investigation, the investigator looks for physical evidence of a burning, incendiary devices and eyewitnesses. The investigator would try to link the suspect to the scene and find evidence showing intent. Motives such as revenge, economic gain and insurance fraud, as well as pyromania, would be investigated.

Some pyromaniacs derive sexual stimulation by starting fires. Others seek notoriety by setting fires and alerting the fire department. Many of these individuals want to be firefighters and then attempt daring rescues.

Liquid incendiary agents include alcohol, benzol, gasoline, ether and kerosene. Solids with incendiary properties include coal dust and grain. Substances that burn on contact with water are sodium, potassium and calcium carbide. Oxidizing agents that, when decomposing, aid combustion include nitric acid, potassium permanganate in contact with glycerine, quicklime mixed with water, chlorates and metallic peroxides. These are just a few oxidizing agents that cause combustion.

Motives for Arson

Business rivalry
Conceal a previous crime
Defraud an insurance company
Destroy company books or records
Extortion
Intimidation
Murder
Revenge

Sabotage

Thrill

For additional information on arson, contact the arson squad of your local police or fire department.

DRUGS

Trafficking in addictive drugs is an international, multimillion-dollar business. The production and sale of drugs has become the most profitable product of some foreign countries. Other than murder, there have probably been more books, movies and television episodes dealing with drugs than any other area of crime.

Narcs, as most cops working drugs are called, are a special breed. Most can read the action on any street, especially those working undercover. They often fool dealers and other junkies by using mortician's wax on their veins, and add ink and dirt to mimic the look of tracks. They can easily spot coke and heroin addicts, street dealers and junkie whores.

Heroin addicts always shoot up when they wake up in the morning and late at night. Once they've had their fix they're in pretty good shape, except for their sallow complexions, itchiness and jumpiness. Heroin addicts only shoot what they need, as opposed to coke freaks who are progressive users. On the street, heroin is boy, coke is girl. Cocaine addicts tend to commit more crimes than heroin addicts, especially crimes of violence.

Dollars and Dope

By the time a cocaine shipment arrives in the United States, the kilo that may have cost the Colombians $100 is worth $10,000 to $15,000. By the time it's moved to the next city, it's up to $25,000. The dealer who cuts it down to the bag level gets between $3,000 and $5,000 an ounce, and the street dealer gets $25 a bag and sells hundreds of bags a day. Colombian drug lords live like kings; dealers in the United States may buy expensive clothes and drive expensive cars, but many live like pack rats.

Frequently Abused Drugs

Drug	Chemical or Trade Name	Description	How Taken	Typical Dose	Duration of Effect	Initial Signs	Risks of Abuse	Physical Dependence
NARCOTICS								
Opium	*Papaver somniferum*	Dried milk of opium-poppy pod	Smoked or swallowed	Varies	6 hrs.	Euphoria Drowsiness	Loss of appetite Painful withdrawal symptoms	Yes
Morphine	Morphine sulphate	Derivative of opium	Injected	15 mg	6 hrs.	Euphoria Drowsiness	Loss of appetite Painful withdrawal Impaired breathing	Yes
Heroin	Diacetylmorphine	Derivative of morphine	Injected	Varies	4 hrs.	Euphoria Drowsiness	Loss of appetite Painful withdrawal Constipation	Yes
Methadone	Dolophine Amidone	Synthetic analgesic	Swallowed or injected	10 mg	4-6 hrs.	Less acute than opiates	Loss of appetite Painful withdrawal Constipation	Yes
DEPRESSANTS								
Barbiturates	Phenobarbital Seconal Nembutal	Barbituric acid derivative	Swallowed	50-100 mg	4-12 hrs.	Drowsiness Muscle relaxation	Incoherence Depression Withdrawal difficulty	Possible
Meprobromate	Miltown Equanil	Non-barbiturate sedative	Swallowed	Varies	4 hrs.	Drowsiness Muscle relaxation	Incoherence Depression Withdrawal difficulty	No
Methaqualone	Sopor Quaalude	Non-barbiturate sedative	Swallowed	75-100 mg	4 hrs.	Drowsiness Muscle relaxation	Delirium Coma	No

Frequently Abused Drugs (*Continued*)

Drug	Chemical or Trade Name	Description	How Taken	Typical Dose	Duration of Effect	Initial Signs	Risks of Abuse	Physical Dependence
STIMULANTS								
Cocaine	Methyl ester of benzoylecganine	Isolated alkaloid of coca leaf	Sniffed or injected	Varies	Varies	Excitation Talkativeness Tremors	Loss of appetite Irritability Insomnia	No
Amphetamines	Benzedrine Dexedrine Methedrine	Synthetic central-nervous system stimulant	Swallowed	2.5-5 mg	4 hrs.	Alertness Talkativeness Activity	Irritability Confusion Aggressiveness	No
HALLUCINOGENS								
Marijuana	*Cannabis sativa*	Flowering resinous top of female hemp plant	Smoked	1 or 2 cigarettes	4 hrs.	Relaxation Euphoria Vagueness	Altered perception Impaired judgment	No
Peyote	3, 4, 5-trimethoxy-phenethylamine	Dried cactus buttons containing mescaline	Swallowed	350 mcg	12 hrs.	Exhilaration Anxiety Gastric distress	Visual hallucinations Paranoia Possible psychosis	No
LSD	d-lysergic acid diethylamide	Synthetic compound 400 times more powerful than mescaline	Swallowed	100 mcg	10 hrs.	Excitation Exhilaration Vagueness	Visual and auditory hallucinations Possible psychosis	No
DMT	Dimethyltryptamine	Synthetic compound similar to mushroom alkaloid psilocybin	Injected	1 mg	4-6 hrs.	Excitation Exhilaration	Possible psychotic reaction	No

© Pharmaceutical Manufacturers Association. Used by permission.

Some Substances Used For Non-Medical Purposes

SUBSTANCE	COMMON OR SLANG NAMES	ACTIVE INGREDIENT	SOURCE	PHARMACOLOGIC CLASSIFICATION	MEDICAL USE
Alcohol	Booze, Juice, Sauce, Brew, Vino	Ethanol, Ethyl Alcohol	Natural (from fruits, grains, vegetables)	CNS depressant	Solvent antiseptic, sedative
Marijuana	Pot, Grass, Dope, Weed, Home-grown, Sinsemilla Maui-wowie, Thaisticks, Joints, Roaches, Indica: Concentrated resin called Hash or Hashish	Tetrahydrocannabinols (THC)	Cannabis sativa	CNS depressant, hallucinogen	Experimental research only
Amphetamines	Ups, Uppers, Speed, Crank, RX Diet Pills	Amphetamine Dextroamphetamine Methamphetamine (Desoxyephedrine)	Synthetic	CNS stimulant	Control appetite. Narcolepsy—some childhood behavioral disorders; relieve depression
Amphetamine Look-alikes	Legal stimulants, Ups, Uppers, AMS, AKS, RJS	May contain caffeine, Ephedrine, Pseudoephedrine, Phenylpropanglamine	Synthetic/natural	CNS stimulant, decongestant, appetite depressant	None
Cocaine	Coke, Rock, Toot, Blow, Snow, Pearl Flake	Cocaine Hydrochloride Benzoylmethylecgonine	Natural (from coca leaves)	Local or topical anesthesia	Local or topical anesthesia
Cocaine Freebase	Base Freebase	Cocaine base	Natural (prepared from Cocaine Hydrochloride)	Local or topical anesthesia	Topical anesthetic ointments
Barbiturates	Barbs, Bluebirds, Blues, Tooies, Yellow Jackets	Phenobarbital Pentobarbital Secobarbital Amobarbital	Synthetic	Sedative Hypnotic	Sedation, Epilepsy
Methaqualone	Ludes, 714S, Sopor	Methaqualone	Synthetic	Sedative hypnotic	Sedation
Heroin	H, Horse, Junk, Smack, Stuff, Brown Sugar	Diacetyl morphine	Semi-synthetic (from morphine)	Narcotic analgesic	None legally
Morphine	White Stuff, M, More	Morphine Sulphate	Natural (from Opium)	Narcotic analgesic	Pain relief
Codeine	Schoolboy	Methylmorphine	Natural (from Opium) semi-synthetic (from morphine)	Narcotic analgesic	Ease pain & coughing
Oxycodone		14-Hydroxydihydro-Codeinone	Semi-synthetic (Morphine-like)	Narcotic analgesic	Pain relief
Meperidine		Meperidine Hydrochloride	Synthetic	Narcotic analgesic	Pain relief, prevent withdrawal, discomfort
Methadone	Dolly	Methadone Hydrochloride	Synthetic	Narcotic analgesic	Pain relief, prevent withdrawal, discomfort

ABUSE FORM	HOW USED	EFFECTS SOUGHT	LONG TERM POSSIBLE EFFECTS	PHYSICAL DEPENDENCE POTENTIAL	PSYCHOLOGICAL DEPENDENCE POTENTIAL
Liquid	Taken orally, applied topically (rubbing alcohol)	Intoxication, Sense Alteration, Anxiety reduction	Toxic Psychosis, addiction, neurologic damage	Yes	Yes
Plant Particles (dark green or brown)	Smoked or eaten	Euphoria, relaxation, increased perception	Bronchitis, Conjunctivitis, possible birth defects	Possible	Possible
Tablets, Capsules, Liquid, Powder (white)	Taken orally or injected	Alertness, activeness	Loss of appetite, delusions, hallucinations, toxic psychosis	Possible	Yes
Capsules or Tablets	Taken orally	Alertness, activeness, weight loss	Hypertension, stroke, heart problems	Possible	Yes
Powder (white) or Liquid	Snorted or injected	Stimulation, excitation, euphoria (subtle)	Loss of appetite, depression, convulsions, nasal passage injury	No	Yes
White Crystal	Smoked, injected	Intensified Cocaine effects	Weight loss, depression, hypertension, hallucinations, psychosis	Yes	Yes
Tablets or Capsules	Taken orally or injected	Anxiety reduction, euphoria	Severe withdrawal symptoms, possible convulsions, toxic psychosis	Yes	Yes
Tablets	Taken orally or snorted	Euphoria, aphrodisiac	Coma, convulsions	Yes	Yes
Powder (white, grey, brown)	Injected, snorted or smoked	Euphoria	Addiction, constipation, loss of appetite	Yes	Yes
Powder (white), Tablets or Liquid	Taken orally or injected	Euphoria	Addiction, constipation, loss of appetite	Yes	Yes
Tablets or liquid (in cough syrup)	Taken orally or injected	Euphoria	Addiction, constipation, loss of appetite	Yes	Yes
Tablets	Taken orally or injected	Euphoria	Addiction, constipation, loss of appetite	Yes	Yes
Tablets or Liquid	Taken orally or injected	Euphoria	Addiction, constipation, loss of appetite	Yes	Yes
Tablets or Liquid	Taken orally or injected	Euphoria	Addiction, constipation, loss of appetite	Yes	Yes

Some Substances Used For Non-Medical Purposes (*Continued*)

SUBSTANCE	COMMON OR SLANG NAMES	ACTIVE INGREDIENT	SOURCE	PHARMACOLOGIC CLASSIFICATION	MEDICAL USE
Inhalants	Solvents, Glue, Transmission fluid, Toluene	Organic solvents	Synthetic	None	None
Nitrous Oxide	Laughing Gas, Gas, Whippitts, Nitrous, Blue Bottle	Nitrous Oxide	Synthetic	Inhalation anesthetic	Anesthesia
Butyl Nitrite	Liquid Incense, Room Deodorizer, Rush, Locker Room, Locker Popper	Butyl Nitrite	Synthetic	Vasodilator	None (Amyl nitrite used in Angina Pectoris)
LSD	Acid, LSD-25, Blotter Acid, Windowpane, named after pictures on paper, Mesc	D-Lysergic Acid Diethylamide	Semi-synthetic (from Ergot Alkaloids)	Hallucinogen	Experimental research only
Mescaline (Peyote Cactus)	Mesc, Peyote, Peyote Buttons	Mescaline	Natural (from Peyote Cactus)	Hallucinogen	None
MDA, MMDA, MDM	Love Drug, Ecstasy, XTC	34-Methylenedioxy-amphetamine Analogs of MDA	Synthetic	Amphetamine-based hallucinogen	None
DOM	Straserenity Tranquility, Peace	2.5-Dimethoxy-4-methyl-amphetamine	Synthetic	Amphetamine-based hallucinogen	None
Psilocybin	Magic Mushrooms, Shrooms	Psilocybin	Natural (from Psilocybe Fungus—a type of mushroom)	Hallucinogen	None
PCP	Crystal, Tea, THC, Angel Dust	Phencyclidine	Synthetic	Dissociative Anesthetic	Once used as a veterinary anesthetic
Coffee, Tea, Colas	Espresso, Cafe, Natural Stimulant, Guarana, Guaranine	Caffeine	Natural	CNS stimulant	Mild stimulant
Tobacco	Cigs, Smokes, Butts, Cancer Sticks, Coffin Nails	Nicotine	Natural (from Nicotina Tabacum)	CNS Toxin	Emetic

ABUSE FORM	HOW USED	EFFECTS SOUGHT	LONG TERM POSSIBLE EFFECTS	PHYSICAL DEPENDENCE POTENTIAL	PSYCHOLOGICAL DEPENDENCE POTENTIAL
Various	Inhaled or huffed (poured on a rag or towel and inhaled by mouth)	Intoxication	Impaired perception, coordination, judgment; toxicity from solvent impurities	No	Yes
Gas in Pressurized Container	Inhaled	Euphoria, relaxation	Kidney or liver damage, peripheral neuropathy, spontaneous abortion	No	Possible
Liquid	Inhaled	Exhilaration	Damage to heart and blood vessels, may aggravate heart problems	No	Yes
Tablets, Capsules, Liquid, or Paper Squares	Taken orally	Insight, distortion of senses, exhilaration, mystical/religious experience	May intensify existing psychosis, panic reactions	No	Possible
Tablets, Capsules, Raw Drug (Buttons)	Taken orally	Same as LSD	Milder than LSD	No	Possible
Tablets or Capsules	Taken orally	Same as LSD	Milder than LSD	No	Possible
Tablets, Capsules or Liquid	Taken orally	Stronger than LSD effects	Same as LSD	No	Possible
Mushrooms, rarely as Tablets or Capsules	Taken orally	Same as LSD	Milder than LSD	No	Possible
Tablets, Powder in Smoking Mixtures	Smoked, snorted or taken orally	Distortion of senses	Psychotic behavior, violent acts, psychosis	No	Possible
Beverage	Taken orally	Alertness	May aggravate heart problems	Possible	Yes
Snuff, Pipe Cut Particles, Cigars or Cigarettes	Smoked, snorted or chewed	Relaxation	Loss of appetite, habituation, lung cancer	Possible	Yes

© Pharmaceutical Manufacturers Association. Used by permission.

Drug Addiction

Addiction is the state of dependency on drugs, such that they are necessary to function physically and mentally. When addicts are deprived of the substance, they have a physical craving manifested by symptoms of withdrawal that causes severe mental and physical distress.

With habitual use of a drug, the tolerance to that drug is increased, and the user requires progressively increasing dosages to function. As tolerance takes place, the span of time usually decreases between doses of the drug. If addicts become deprived of the drug, they become physically and mentally ill.

Use and Effect

Each drug has its own properties and effect, and the means of administration varies with the type of drug the user is taking. Some narcotics can be taken in more than one way, e.g., ingestion, sniffing or injection. (Please see charts on pages 36-41.)

Possession

Possession of a narcotic or illicit drug is a crime, because it constitutes the probability of use or sale. It is conceivable that a user might also be dealing in drugs to support a habit.

Selling

Selling or dealing in drugs is a more serious offense than possession. Trafficking or dealing in drugs is, in most cases, the domain of the professional criminal connected with a large drug ring or organized crime. Those at the top of the ladder in drug trafficking usually have expertise in evading the law and escaping detection and prosecution, despite the attempts of law enforcement officials to prosecute them.

Trafficking in drugs means the transporting or smuggling of illegal substances for eventual sale. As most illegal drugs are produced outside of the United States, those dealing in drugs employ many creative means of smuggling their contraband into the United States. In most instances, the drug is brought in refined, so it needs only to be cut before it is ready for street sale. The drug may be transported into the United States by boats, cargo vessels, airplanes landing in remote areas or body carriers, sometimes referred to as mules.

Drug traffickers and dealers are powerful people with many connections and an enormous financial empire with which to bribe government officials and police. Those at the very top are usually insulated from those who work beneath them. Their business has many levels of sale and distribution, ranging from the grower or producer to wholesalers, mules, pushers and peddlers. A mule, pusher or peddler could be a member of organized crime or a street gang, a user, a pimp, a prostitute, a student or anyone who sees an opportunity to make a quick buck.

Points of Origin

Cocaine is a white, crystalline powder made from the coca shrub, a plant cultivated by the Andean Indians prior to the Spanish occupation of South America. The major producing countries are Colombia, Chile, Peru and Bolivia, although other countries are also producing the drug in increasing amounts.

Crack, also known as rock cocaine, is the result of changing the structure of cocaine hydrochloride from the salt to the free base. By this method (heating the salt form in the presence of alkali), the cocaine is changed into a form that can be smoked. Ordinary cocaine is inhaled through the nose, whereas crack cocaine, when smoked, goes directly to the lungs. Inhalation does not provide the rush that results from smoking crack.

Opium is derived from the oriental poppy plant, grown mainly in Asia, although the poppy has now been cultivated in other countries such as Mexico, Cuba and the Balkans. The major producers and suppliers of opium are India, Turkey, Thailand, Pakistan, Laos, Mexico and Afghanistan. Although opium was once primarily smoked, it has produced such derivatives as morphine and heroin, which are injected.

Marijuana, one of the most widely used drugs, comes from the hemp plant, which grows wild or can be cultivated. Primary sources are Mexico, Cuba, Turkey, Greece, India, Syria, Africa, the United States and Brazil.

Mescaline or peyote can be found in northern Mexico and the southwestern United States, and is derived from the peyote cactus.

Psilocybin is a hallucinogen extracted from a form of mushroom found in Mexico.

Barbiturates are probably the most abused type of drugs available to the addict. They are readily obtainable from a physician, hospital or local pharmacist if the user has the right connections.

Synthetics carry the effect of a narcotic but have been synthesized and are therefore less expensive. Many of these are listed as narcotics by federal and state regulatory agencies.

PACKAGING AND DISTRIBUTION

Cocaine
Bindles
Casting material
Duct tape
Fiberglass
Heat-seal plastic
Large sealable sandwich bags
Sno-seals
Trash bags
2 × 2 sealable sandwich bags

Tar Heroin
Clear plastic wrap
Sealable sandwich bags
Various tapes

Powdered Heroin
Balloons
Bindles
Blocks (compressed)
Casting materials

Film canisters
Plastic
Plastic wraps

Phencyclidine (PCP)

Cigarettes (tinfoil bindles)
Gallon bottles
Grape juice bottles
Mouthwash bottles
Vanilla extract one-ounce bottles

Marijuana

Bales, plastic encased
Sealable sandwich bags
Trash bags

Psychoactive Drugs

Alcohol
Amanita muscaria
Amphetamines (pep pills)
Amyl nitrite
Atropine
Ayahuasca
Barbiturates (goof balls)
Belladonna
Benzedrine
Betel nut
Bufotenine
Caffeine
Cannabis
Charas
Chloral hydrate
Cocaine
Codeine
Cough syrup
Crack (rock cocaine)
Dagga

Dexedrine
DMT
Ether
Fly agaric
Ganga (Jamaican slang for marijuana)
Glue
Goof balls (barbiturates)
Hashish
Hemp
Heroin
Hydrangea
IT-290 (Tryptamine)
Jimsonweed
Kat (Khat)
Kava
Kef
L.A.D. (a blended acid detergent)
Laudanum
Lotus flower
LSD
Magic mushrooms
Mandrake
Marijuana
Mescaline
Methamphetamine
Methedrine
Morning glory seeds
Morphine
Naline (an opium antagonist)
Nembutal
Nicotine
Oblivion
Opium
Paregoric
PCP
Pep pills (amphetamines)
Percodan
Peyote (mescaline)

Psilocybin
Reefers
Rock cocaine (crack)
Sedatives
Sleeping tablets
Snuff
Speed (methamphetamine)
Tea
Tobacco

For information on obtaining free books and brochures dealing with drugs, write to the Drugs and Crime Data Center & Clearinghouse, 1600 Research Boulevard, Rockville, Maryland 20850, or call 1-800-666-3332.

NATIONAL CRIME INFORMATION CENTER

The National Crime Information Center (NCIC) is a nationwide criminal justice network that provides information to law enforcement agencies. NCIC contains records on stolen property such as vehicles, license plates, guns, securities, boats and serialized articles; persons for whom arrest warrants are outstanding; unidentified persons; missing persons meeting specific criteria; and criminal histories on persons arrested for serious offenses. An NCIC Advisory Policy Board made up of federal, state and local justice officials advises the FBI director on policy matters concerning NCIC operations, which gives the users a voice in overall management of the system. Users of NCIC include the fifty states, all federal law enforcement agencies, the Royal Canadian Mounted Police, and the Police of the Commonwealth of Puerto Rico and the U.S. Virgin Islands—all at no cost to them.

Missing Children File

The juvenile category of the NCIC Missing-Person File responds to inquiries within seconds. A missing-child record may be entered by a parent, legal guardian or next of kin by filing a missing-persons report with any local or state law enforcement agency. The record should contain descriptive and identifying data such as nicknames, birthplace and date, height, weight, scars, marks, blood type and dental information. When a positive identification is made, the record of the child is removed from the system.

Foreign Fugitive File

Implemented in 1987, this file contains Canadian warrants and new wanted-persons records for foreign fugitives entered by the U.S. Central Bureau of the International Police Organization (INTERPOL).

WHERE TO GO FROM HERE

The U.S. Department of Justice, Office of Justice Programs, Bureau of Justice Statistics, offers a variety of free books, brochures and bulletins that can provide you with valuable information dealing with all aspects of crime and justice.

Call 1-800-732-3277 and ask for their free catalog, or write Justice Statistics Clearing House/NCJRS, U.S. Department of Justice, P.O. Box 6000, Rockville, Maryland 20850.

The following books cover a range of subjects in criminal law and related topics, particularly malpractice. Malpractice is included because it often borders on the criminal and can be a rich source of story ideas. These books tend to be more scholarly and technical than those books cited in the other chapters, which is where you'll find the down-and-dirty narratives of real people and real cases. Here you'll find books about law and criminal justice policy, where they've come from and where they're going.

Alderman, Ellen, and Caroline Kennedy. *In Our Own Defense: The Bill of Rights in Action.* New York: William Morrow & Co., 1991. Entertaining popular discussion of the Bill of Rights as applied in recent case law. Many of the cases discussed are criminal.

Benjamin, Daniel, and Roger Miller. *Undoing Drugs: Beyond Legalization.* New York: Basic Books, 1991. Reviews the current problems and policies and proposes leaving the question of legalization to the states.

Buckland, John, ed. *Combating Computer Crime: Prevention, Detection, Investigation*. New York: McGraw-Hill, 1992. Lots of information on how computer crime is committed and detected, including how to determine whether a company is vulnerable.

Epstein, Lee, and Thomas G. Walker. *Constitutional Law for a Changing America: Rights, Liberties and Justice*. Washington, D.C.: CQ Press, 1992. A massive book by two political science professors who attempt a more street-level approach to constitutional issues; that is, they discuss how interest groups, politicians, the media and public opinion influence the selection of justices and the interpretation of the Constitution.

Ewing, Charles. *Battered Women Who Kill: Psychological Self-Defense as Legal Justification*. Lexington, Massachusetts: Lexington Books, 1987. Sometimes highly technical, this is nevertheless a readable discussion of the law of self-defense, particularly its psychological interpretations, as applied to cases of battered women who kill.

Farrell, Harry. *Swift Justice: Murder and Vengeance in a California Town*. New York: St. Martin's, 1992. The story of the lynching of two confessed murderers in San Jose in 1933.

Felkenes, George. *Constitutional Law for Criminal Justice* (2nd ed.). Englewood Cliffs, New Jersey: Prentice Hall, 1988. Textbook on the Constitution and criminal law. Table of cases and general index.

Felthous, Alan. *The Psychotherapist's Duty to Warn or Protect*. Springfield, Illinois: Charles C. Thomas, 1989. Presents the legal ramifications of a therapist's failure to warn those who are threatened by patients and later harmed.

Feuer, William W. *Medical Malpractice Law: A Guide for Health Care Professionals*. Irvine, California: LawPrep Press, 1990. A guide for physicians on avoiding and dealing with malpractice suits. Includes brief sections on how suits are filed, pretrial discovery and what happens during a trial.

Fletcher, George. *A Crime of Self-Defense: Bernhard Goetz and the Law on Trial*. New York: Free Press, 1988. Fletcher, a professor of law at Columbia University, gives a first-hand account of the prosecution of Goetz, the man who shot four teenagers on a New York subway in 1984 and claimed self-defense.

Gilespie, Cynthia. *Justifiable Homicide: Battered Women, Self-Defense and the Law.* Columbus: Ohio State University Press, 1989. Covers the law of self-defense and its application to battered women who kill.

Information Please Almanac. Boston: Houghton Mifflin, annual. Recent editions have covered recidivism, numbers of arrests, numbers of police and crime rates.

Israel, Jerold, and Wayne LaFave. *Criminal Procedure: Constitutional Limitations* (4th ed). St. Paul, Minnesota: West Publishing, 1988. A volume in the famous "Nutshell" series of short handbooks for attorneys. The discussion is technical and uses legal shorthand whenever possible, but it can help answer some of the stickier questions in courtroom and procedural novels.

Kleiman, Mark. *Against Excess: Drug Policy for Results.* New York: Basic Books, 1992. Discusses current policy regarding all recreational drugs, including those that are currently legal, and urges a rational and moderate approach.

Miller, Richard. *The Case for Legalizing Drugs.* New York: Praeger, 1991. Presents the position that most of the social problems associated with drugs are caused by the laws against drugs.

Murdock, Rosamund. *Suffer the Children: A Pediatrician's Reflections on Abuse.* Santa Fe, New Mexico: Health Press, 1992. Covers the history of abuse and current problems, including social service and legal systems.

Schwartz, Bernard. *The Great Rights of Mankind: A History of the American Bill of Rights.* Madison, Wisconsin: Madison House Publishers, 1992. Scholarly discussion of the origins of the Bill of Rights in English and colonial law, its adoption into the Constitution and its application.

The Universal Almanac. Kansas City: Andrews and McMeel, annual. Recent editions have covered crime rates by state and city, arrests and jail populations and expenditures.

Van Duyn, J. *Automated Crime Information Systems.* Blue Ridge

Summit, Pennsylvania: TAB Books, 1991. Basic information on a variety of crime information systems, including automated fingerprint identification systems, stolen property registries and computer-aided dispatch programs.

Wells, Tim, and William Triplett. *Drug Wars: An Oral History From the Trenches*. New York: William Morrow & Co., 1992. Verbatim accounts from dealers, users, cops and others.

Wisotsky, Steven. *Beyond the War on Drugs: Overcoming a Failed Public Policy*. Buffalo, New York: Prometheus Books, 1990. A critical study focusing on the social problems arising from the drug war itself.

World Almanac and Book of Facts. New York: Pharos Books, annual. Recent editions include crime rates and information on prisons and the FBI.

2
Criminals

ORGANIZED CRIME

Organized criminal gangs are structured either in local, state, national or international levels. These gangs include La Cosa Nostra, South American organizations, Mexican networks, the Sicilian Mafia, national outlaw motorcycle gangs and Oriental organized crime groups. Organized crime is involved in corruption of public officials, illegal infiltration of legitimate businesses, gambling, loan sharking, laundering of illicit funds, murder, labor racketeering, extortion, counterfeiting, prostitution and drug trafficking.

The Mafia

The Mafia is probably the most familiar name in organized crime. Sometimes dubbed "the Mob" or "La Cosa Nostra" ("Our Thing"), it is believed to have had its roots in Palermo, Italy, in 1282, when Sicilian Vespers revolted against the French Angevins, who were then ruling Sicily.

Although the Mafia is one of the strongest organized crime groups, it began as a secret society formed to protect the poor, oppressed and mistreated Sicilians from their invading rulers.

Once freed of French domination, however, the Mafia increased both in number and power. In 1417, however, the Italian states again found themselves under foreign domination, this time by the Bourbons, who had spawned the birth of another secret organization in Seville. Called "The Camorra," this organization began with no altruistic ideals. It was composed of out-and-out criminals. Transported to Sicily and neighboring states by the Bourbons, the Camorra and the Mafia soon began to merge, with the Mafia's once altruistic aims now giving way to more profitable ventures: gaining control of all criminal activities. The Camorra maintained headquarters in Naples and the Mafia was based in Sicily. The Mafia reached the pinnacle of its power around the turn of the nineteenth century. It was then that the Mafia and the Camorra began migrating to the United States to prey on Italian immigrants.

Once here, however, bad blood often led to feuds between the Camorra and the Mafia. Although the bonds were often sealed between the two, feuds plagued both organizations. Wars erupted frequently as the two competed for supremacy in the new land. Over the years, the Mafia grew stronger and became the dominant force in the United States. The Camorra still exists to a small extent in this country, but the Camorra N'Drangatta reigns in Naples. The old Mafia continues to be a force in Sicily.

When the Mafia first settled in the United States, they were referred to as "The Black Hand," because their hands were often stained by the tar paper in which they wrapped the remains of those who opposed them.

Members of the Mafia are sworn to obedience to their chief (see organizational chart, page 54). They have no allegiance to the law, only to their own organization. Any offense committed against one member is considered to be against the organization. Members are bound by "Omerta," or the code of silence. It is simply a way of saying, "If you talk, you die."

The Mafia in the United States subverts and infiltrates any branch of the government that might benefit their purpose. It aims to control every profitable area of crime and legitimate business. Members are willing to murder any member or outsider who informs on them or is a threat.

Mafiosi show respect and complete obedience to those of

An Organized Crime Family

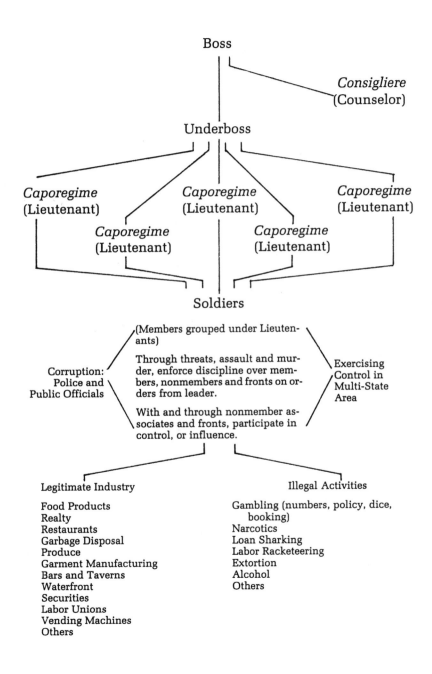

Boss

Consigliere
(Counselor)

Underboss

Caporegime
(Lieutenant)

Caporegime
(Lieutenant)

Caporegime
(Lieutenant)

Caporegime
(Lieutenant)

Caporegime
(Lieutenant)

Soldiers

(Members grouped under Lieutenants)

Corruption:
Police and
Public Officials

Through threats, assault and murder, enforce discipline over members, nonmembers and fronts on orders from leader.

With and through nonmember associates and fronts, participate in control, or influence.

Exercising
Control in
Multi-State
Area

Legitimate Industry

Food Products
Realty
Restaurants
Garbage Disposal
Produce
Garment Manufacturing
Bars and Taverns
Waterfront
Securities
Labor Unions
Vending Machines
Others

Illegal Activities

Gambling (numbers, policy, dice, booking)
Narcotics
Loan Sharking
Labor Racketeering
Extortion
Alcohol
Others

greater authority within their organization. In a dispute, those involved may request a sit-down, where a council determines who is right or wrong and decides ways to restore peace between the opposing parties.

As time passed and Mafia families began to spread out, each family was given its own territory to operate. Soon, the Mafia ensconced itself in almost every major city in the United States. In time, another transition took place—one that transformed the "Mob" and the "Mustache Petes" from pinstriped-suited racketeers and gangsters into black-mohair and gray-flannel-suited "businessmen," who disguised their criminal activities as legitimate businesses and labor unions.

Meyer Lansky, a close personal friend of Mafia mobster Frank Costello, possessed a brilliant criminal mind and envisioned a great criminal empire. He brought the Italian, Jewish, Irish and German criminal gangs together as the National Crime Syndicate in a working agreement that would end gang wars and greatly increase the coffers of organized crime.

The Syndicate stood to gain greater strength in unity as well as greater profits if it expanded its control over prostitution, gambling and other criminal activities. Syndicate members concealed much crime under the guise of legitimate enterprises, but also sought to infiltrate the labor movement. Their profits were often stashed in foreign banks and used to influence foreign government officials. The money was also invested in real estate here and abroad. Of course, this was during the days when drugs were but a small part of organized crime's empire.

This situation soon changed, and so did the meaning of the term *organized crime*. The Korean and Vietnam conflicts introduced drugs as a profitable organized crime activity. Unfortunately for both the Mafia and United States law enforcement agencies, little attention was paid to other organized crime enterprises. However, the effect was soon felt, as Chinese, Japanese, Colombian and Jamaican gangs became more powerful. Although the Mafia still holds a substantial position in drug trafficking, it is no longer the worldwide leader.

Asian Organized Crime

Asian organized crime groups have become a serious problem in the United States and Canada. Police departments have begun to encounter these groups in larger numbers and consider them both dangerous and highly motivated.

Unfortunately, the Asian gangs are difficult to investigate because the police often don't understand the gangs' language and culture. Lately, this has resulted in city, state and federal agencies assembling Asian task forces, using officers acquainted with the Asian population and languages.

Yakuza

The Yakuza, as Japanese organized crime is known, dates back to the seventeenth century. The word "Yakuza" means a worthless hand in a card game. The Yakuza of today refer to themselves as "worthless persons" or social outcasts. The Japanese police refer to them as "Boryokudan," or "the violent ones."

The Yakuza are organized into family and subfamily groups known as "Gumi," each owing its allegiance to an "Oyabun" or boss. Loyalty to Yakuza leaders by their members is expressed in ways such as self-mutilation and tattooing. It is not uncommon to see Yakuza members with tattoos symbolizing some underworld achievement or an expression of loyalty to a boss or family. Nor is it uncommon for members to sever portions of their fingers to express their subservience.

Recently, Yakuza members have become active in the United States in southern California, the San Francisco Bay area and in Nevada, investing their illegal gains from prostitution, narcotics, gambling, pornography, smuggling, gunrunning and extortion rackets in restaurants, jewelry shops, real estate and import/export firms. Another Yakuza criminal activity is the blackmailing of United States-based Japanese company employees who are in personal or financial trouble.

Korean Gangs

Much of Korean organized crime involves prostitution in larger American cities. Like the old "Black Hand" of the American Mafia,

Korean organized crime is also into extortion of Koreans who have emigrated to the United States.

Chinese Gangs

During the American West's gold rush era and the early days of the railroad, many Chinese were imported and used almost exclusively as slave labor. Chinese Tongs began as benevolent associations formed to protect themselves. Although all Tongs are not necessarily involved with the Triad or in criminal activities, a number of Tongs are involved in one or more criminal activities.

The Chinese Triads are among the fastest rising criminal organizations in the United States. Like the Sicilian Mafia, Triads were founded as patriotic secret societies, one of which was "The Eight Trigrams Sect of Fists of Harmony and Justice." They were later referred to as "Boxers" when they led the Boxer Rebellion against the Europeans. The Triads are represented by an equilateral triangle, with each side of the triangle signifying one of the three basic Chinese concepts: Earth, Man and Heaven. Most Triads have long since abandoned their original purpose in favor of criminal endeavors, including murder-for-hire, prostitution, extortion and drug trafficking.

The Chinese organizations control most of the world's supply of heroin from the Golden Triangle, which covers parts of Burma, Thailand and Laos. They earn more in one year than the total of U.S. currency now in circulation. The size and number of Triads is unknown. However, Hong Kong's 14K Triad is only one of fifty Triads in the British Colony, and 14K supposedly has fifty subgroups. Hong Kong has roughly three hundred thousand Triad members; there are only two thousand known members of the American Mafia. The United States is said to have five major Chinese Tongs, the largest of which is New York's On Leong Tong, followed by San Francisco's Hip Sing. The Ying On Tong covers Los Angeles and the southwestern portion of the United States. The Hop Sing and Suey Sing Tongs operate on the Pacific Coast but also have locations on the East Coast. Because many Tong members in the United States are law-abiding citizens, the Tongs give the Triads a deep cover.

Due to the staggering profits of their drug trade, the Triads, like the Mafia, have been able to infiltrate the legitimate business community, permitting them to launder their profits. Chinese street gangs in the United States—most members are sixteen to twenty-eight years old—are almost always members of a Triad sub-group, such as the Wah Ching. This subgroup is supposedly one of the largest Chinese youth gangs on the West Coast; only San Francisco's Hip Sing rivals it in size. In New York, the On Leong use the youth gang known as the Ghost Shadows for their street muscle, and the Flying Dragons work for the Hip Sing Tong.

The Triads' national syndicate in the United States is run to some extent like the Mafia: It has a council based in New York. The Triads have a policy of maintaining a low profile while expanding their criminal horizons. The Tongs now employ newly formed Vietnamese gangs to do their violent and deadly work.

Today, Chinese street gangs have begun to flourish. One of the most visible is the United Bamboo gang, also known as Chu Lien Pang. This gang originated in Taiwan and today boasts over four-teen thousand members worldwide, several hundred of which operate in the United States. The United Bamboo gang is deeply involved in heroin trafficking, gambling, extortion, robbery and murder for hire.

Vietnamese Gangs

The fall of Saigon and the collapse of the Republic of Vietnam caused a massive exodus of Vietnamese to the United States. Some of these individuals were criminals. Unlike the Chinese and Japanese underworld, however, there is little evidence that they operate in organized crime groups. Some Vietnamese refugees have been assimilated into Chinese criminal organizations. The Flying Dragons contingent in New York, also known as the Viet-Ching, are heavily involved in extortion, armed robbery, prostitution, auto theft, arson and gambling.

The Vietnamese gangs are highly mobile and commit criminal acts across the nation, often using safe houses shared by members of other gangs. Because many Asians distrust American banks and keep large amounts of cash in their offices and homes, they are easy targets for these gangs.

Street Gangs

Street gangs were once neighborhood toughs who banded together to protect their neighborhood's turf from members of bordering gangs. Although these gangs stole hubcaps, tires and an occasional car, most of their time was spent warring with rival gangs. But today, primarily due to the tremendous increase in drugs, the term *street gang* has taken on a more sinister meaning. A set of stolen hubcaps brings a few dollars, but drug trafficking can bring millions.

Street gangs now battle over who sells the drugs and where. Whereas the street gangs of bygone days were primarily teenagers, today's street gang members may be as young as ten years old or as old as forty-something. And whereas street gangs once went to war armed with chains, bats, knives and zip guns, today's arsenal includes automatic weapons, machine pistols, shotguns, bazookas and hand grenades. Often their firepower exceeds that of law enforcement.

Street gangs do not necessarily qualify as organized crime because they have no political clout or corrupt connections. They do, however, have leaders and lieutenants and follow orders. Gangs such as California's Crips and Bloods have grown large enough to send cadres to other cities.

Some street gangs have adopted colors—such as the blue for the Crips and red for the Bloods—to distinguish themselves from rival gangs. Others set themselves apart by the clothing they wear or the way they wear it. Many gangs have devised secret codes, handshakes, slang and signals to ensure their individuality.

What was once a neighborhood nuisance is now a national menace. Many of these alien gangs begin by preying solely on their own ethnic groups. But as the profitability of drug trafficking increases, more of these gangs begin to look for greener pastures elsewhere.

Motorcycle Gangs

Although most motorcycle gangs are somewhat organized, they lack discipline, leadership and corrupt connections. Most bikers travel in small packs, although some larger biker gangs have chapters across the United States. One example is the Hell's Angels, who wear their insignia on leather jackets or as tattoos.

Unlike street gangs, motorcycle gangs don't usually carry automatic weapons or claim a specific turf. Bikers claim whatever turf they are on at the time. Bikers carry their women with them, and in most cases their women are treated as virtual slaves, often being passed around from one biker to another. Most illegal motorcycle gangs are involved in drug trafficking, although some have resorted to robbery, rape, murder and other crimes.

Bikers operate clandestine drug labs, often manufacturing methamphetamine (speed).

MODUS OPERANDI

Almost every criminal who commits a particular crime over and over again has an M.O., or modus operandi, a pattern used in the commission of the crime. For example, professional burglars seldom commit other types of crimes, and they often employ the same method to choose a neighborhood and commit their burglaries.

Armed robbers usually select the same targets repeatedly, such as banks or liquor stores. Rapists customarily choose the same type of victim and commit rape the same way time and time again. It is unusual for a criminal to deviate from a chosen pattern even though that pattern leaves evidence for the police.

Police check the age, sex, race, religion, physical appearance and occupation of victims to see if they match the M.O. of any known criminals. They check how, when and where the crime was committed, and look for any special technique or trademark. This may or may not pinpoint a particular suspect, but it might connect one crime with another.

Major crime M.O.s can often be found in the files of the National Crime Center.

WEAPONS USED BY CRIMINALS

Acid
Air gun
Ax
Bayonet
Bazooka
Billy club
Blackjack
Bola
Bomb
Bow and arrow
Brass knuckles
Broadsword
Chain
Cutlass
Dart
Drug overdose
Fire
Flame thrower
Gaff
Garrote
Gasoline
Grenade
Hammer
Hook
Ice pick
Javelin
Knife
Machine gun
Molotov cocktail
Pistol
Poison
Revolver
Rifle
Rock
Rope
Shotgun

Six-shooter
Slingshot
Sword
Tomahawk
Vehicle
Zip gun

FIREARMS AND MANUFACTURERS

There are literally thousands of types, calibers and manufacturers of handguns and shoulder weapons, but law enforcement agencies rely primarily on handguns and automatic weapons. Criminals, though, use a much wider variety of weapons, many of which are listed here.

Most handguns are either revolvers, which have a rotating cylinder containing from four to twelve cartridges, or semiautomatic pistols, which have a magazine containing from five to fifteen cartridges, though magazines holding up to thirty are available for many pistols.

Automatic weapons fire as long as the trigger is depressed and there are cartridges in the ammo clip or magazine. The semiautomatic fires one shot each time the trigger is pulled.

Almost all small arms are rifled, meaning that the barrel of the weapon has spiraled grooves that give the bullet a stable trajectory when fired. Shotguns are smooth bored, having no spiraled grooves in the barrel.

In rimfire ammunition, the primer is in the rim of the base of the cartridge, whereas in centerfire ammunition the primer is in the center of the base. The only modern weapons that use rimfire ammunition are .22 caliber. The rest use centerfire ammunition.

Most law enforcement agencies use standard weapons issued to their department or agency, but criminals use whatever type of weapon they prefer. If you write about the weapons used by a particular law enforcement agency, contact that agency to check out what weapons are issued and under what circumstances.

A sample of weapons available to criminals include:

Revolvers

Charter Undercover .38 Special
Colt Anaconda .44 Magnum
Colt Model 1917 Army .45 ACP
Freedom Arms .454 Casull
North American Arms (NAA) Model 22S .22 short
Ruger GP-100 .357 Magnum
Ruger Super Blackhawk .44 Magnum
Smith & Wesson Ladysmith .38 Special
Smith & Wesson Model 16-4 .32 Magnum
Smith & Wesson Model 627 .357 Magnum
Smith & Wesson Model 686 .357 Magnum
Dan Wesson Model 15 .357 Magnum
Dan Wesson Model 41V .41 Magnum

Semiautomatic Pistols

Beretta Cougar .32 auto
Beretta Minx .22 short
Beretta Model 92 9mm Parabellum
Browning Baby .25 auto
Browning BDA .38 Super Auto
Browning Hi-Power 9mm Parabellum
Charter Arms Model 79K .380 auto
Colt Model 1911 .45 ACP
Colt Mustang .380 auto
Coonan .357 Magnum
Glock Model 20 10mm
Heckler & Koch HK-4 .380 auto
Heckler & Koch P7-M13 9mm Parabellum
Interarms Model 43 Firestar 9mm Parabellum
Magnum Research Desert Eagle .357 Magnum
Mauser Bolo 7.63mm
Mauser HSc Super .32 auto
Mauser Luger 7.65mm Parabellum
Mauser Luger 9mm Parabellum
Sauer H.38 .32 auto
Sauer Pocket 25 .25 auto

SIG-Hammerli P240 .38 Special
SIG-Sauer P226 9mm
Springfield Armory Model 1911 A1 .45 ACP
Walther GSP .22 LR
Walther PP .380 auto
Walther PPK .380 auto
Walther P.38 9mm Parabellum
Webley Mark IV Police .32 Smith & Wesson

Machine Guns and Assault Rifles

Heckler & Koch HK53 5.56mm
Kalashnikov AK47 7.62mm
M-16 5.56mm
Thompson Model 1928A1 .45 ACP
Uzi Submachine Gun 9mm Parabellum

Rifles and Carbines

Armalite AR-15 .223
Browning Autoloader .22
Browning BAR .300 Winchester Magnum
Enfield EMI Semiautomatic .280
Harrington & Richardson Model 155 Shikari .45-70
Harrington & Richardson Reising Model 60 .45 ACP
Harrington & Richardson Ultra Model 370 6mm Remington
Mauser Model 66 SP Match .308 Winchester
Plainfield M-1 Carbine .30 M-1
Remington Model 742 .30/06
Ruger Model 44 .44 Magnum
Weatherby Fibermark .340 Weatherby Magnum
Winchester Model 100 .243 Winchester

Shotguns

Browning Auto-5 12-gauge Magnum
Harrington & Richardson Model 400 12-gauge
High Standard Flite-King Brush 12-gauge
Ithaca Mag 10 Supreme 10-gauge Magnum
Ljutic Space Gun 12-gauge

Marlin Model 55 Hunter 20-gauge
Mossberg Model 500ATP8 12-gauge
Remington Model 11R Riot Gun 12-gauge
Savage Model 720 12-gauge
Winchester Model 1300 XTR Deer Gun 12-gauge

WEAPONS TERMS

Although not all criminals are experts on weapons, many are. The following are some of the more important terms used to describe guns. For more information, see Michael Newton's *Armed and Dangerous*, listed at the end of this chapter.

Accuracy: Depends on several factors. The barrel must be as near perfect as possible. The bore must be of uniform size its entire length, and the grooves of the rifling must be uniform throughout. The fit of the bullet is of utmost importance. The bullet must be of the correct diameter, hardness and density.

Bluing: Colored finish of the metal parts of guns; can be black, blue or brown.

Bolt: Part of the breech-loading rifle that pushes the cartridge into position and locks the mechanism to prevent its opening on discharge.

Breech: Rear part of a firearm, behind the bore.

Breech Block: Section of the breech-loading mechanism that closes the breech and receives the backward pressure of the explosion.

Buckshot: Large shot used in shot shells, often for crowd control.

Bullet, cannelured: Elongated bullet with grooves around it. These grooves are used for holding the lubricant or for crimping purposes.

Bullet, hollow-point: Has a hollow point to increase the mushrooming effect on impact.

Bullet, metal jacket: Has a jacket of metal that completely encases the nose.

Bullet, soft-point: Metal-cased bullet with a tip of lead that mushrooms on impact, increasing the striking energy.

Bullet, wad-cutter: Bullet with a flat tip, most often used for target shooting.

Bull's-eye: Center of the target; a shot that hits the center.

Butt: Rear portion of the gunstock.

Caliber: Diameter of the bore in the barrel, and in rifled arms, diameter of this hole before rifling, expressed in decimal fractions of an inch.

Cannon: Ordnance or artillery.

Carbine: Short-barreled rifle.

Cartridge: Container for an explosive charge, which may or may not include the bullet. The modern cartridge is ready to fire. Early cartridges were broken, with the contents emptied into the chamber or barrel.

Cartridge case: Metal container for the explosive charge.

Catch: Part of the mechanism for holding another part in a desired position, such as the bayonet catch, safety catch or locking catch.

Center-fire cartridge: One in which the priming composition is in a cap in the center of the cartridge base.

Chamber: Rear end of the barrel; this end receives the shell or cartridge.

Clip: Device for holding several cartridges together so that they may be loaded simultaneously in the gun.

Cock: Movable portions of the firing mechanism; to make the mechanism ready to fire.

Crimping: A mechanical operation used in making cartridges; done by compressing the mouth of the metallic shell or case to hold the bullet in place. Applied also to shot shells.

Cylinder: Chambered, breech part of a gun that revolves around an axis to expose the cartridges successively for firing.

Double-action: Handgun that is cocked and fired when the trigger is pressed.

Drift: Lateral deviation of the flight of a bullet.

Ejector: Device that throws out the fixed cartridge case, or a firearm equipped with such a device.

Firearms identification: Branch of forensic science. Every firearm has individual characteristics imprinted on the bullets and shells. Characteristics can be established by comparison with a test bullet or shell fired from the weapon.

Firing pin: Part of the firing mechanism that strikes the cap or primer to explode the powder charge.

Flare pistol: Large pistol used to fire flares for illumination or signaling.

Fulminate: Explosive substance or compound that ignites when struck, such as fulminate of mercury.

Gauge: Diameter of the bore of a gun, expressed in the number of balls of that diameter required to make a pound. Thus, a 12-gauge has a diameter of such size that twelve balls of lead, each fitting the bore, weigh one pound. Usually used in regard to shotguns.

Grooves: Cavities inside a rifle barrel, usually spiral, by which a bullet receives a spinning motion, giving it an accurate flight.

Hair trigger: Trigger requiring only a light touch for firing.

Hammer: Part of the mechanism that strikes the primer directly, or strikes the firing pin. In flintlocks, the frizzen was sometimes called a hammer.

Handgun: Handheld firearm such as a pistol or revolver.

Ignition: Setting the powder on fire.

Impact: Force of a bullet striking an object.

Jacket: Covering for a bullet.

Lock: Firing mechanism; to set the safety to prevent firing.

Machine gun: Automatic gun firing small-arms ammunition. In the U.S. military sense, it refers to weapons fired from a mount, such as a bipod or a tripod; Europeans tend to include automatic rifles under this classification.

Magazine: Part of a repeating firearm that holds cartridges to be fed into the action.

Muzzle: Mouth, or forward end, of a gun.

Muzzle velocity: Velocity of a bullet at the muzzle.

Oval-bore rifling: Bore that is oval shaped, the oval being twisted to give the bullet a spinning motion. This was developed to take the place of lands and grooves. Most rifles with this feature were made by Lancaster of London around 1850.

Percentage of pattern: Number of pellet marks in a thirty-inch circle over a forty-yard range, divided by the number of pellets in the load.

Percussion cap: Small metal cup holding fulminate placed on the tube or nipple of a percussion gun. When struck, the sparks enter the barrel through a hole and fire the charge.

Pins: Pieces of iron or steel used to hold the barrel and stock together.

Pistol: Handgun in which the cartridge is inserted in the chamber at the back of the barrel; in the autoloading type, the cartridges are inserted in a magazine in the butt or handle.

Pistol carbine: Pistol that has a detachable shoulder stock so that it can be fired either from the hand or from the shoulder.

Powder: Used in cartridges are either black, semi-smokeless or smokeless. Smokeless powders are either bulk, meaning that its charge roughly equals the charge of black powder, or dense, which is denser and of much less bulk.

Pressure: Force exerted in the cartridge chamber and bore of the barrel by the powder gasses. Usually described in pounds per square inch.

Primer: Percussion cap used to ignite the powder charge.

Priming powder: Gunpowder in the pan used to set off the main charge.

Range: Distance to the target; the maximum distance a bullet will travel.

Recoil: Backward motion of a gun when fired, commonly called kick.

Repeater: Gun that can be fired several times without reloading; usually applied to rifles and carbines.

Rest: Any support to steady the gun during aiming and firing.

Revolver: Firearm, usually a handgun, with cylinder of several chambers that revolves on an axis. A firearm with several barrels revolving about a common axis.

Rifle: Shoulder firearm having spiral grooves cut in its bore to give the bullet a spinning motion and thus, greater accuracy.

Self-loading: Semiautomatic; the fired cartridge is extracted and ejected, and another cartridge is placed in position ready to fire.

Shell: Case for holding the charge.

Shocking power: Force delivered to the target on impact.

Shot: A projectile; small pellets; the number of bullets that can be fired without reloading.

Shotgun: Firearm with shells that normally contain a number of small pellets, though they can also fire single bullets called rifled slugs.

Sight: Aiming device.

Slide action: Loading and cocking mechanism operated by the manual movement of a slide under and parallel to the barrel.

Spiral rifling: Spiral grooves in the bore of the gun's barrel.

Stock: Portion of a firearm that fits against the shoulder in firing.

Striker: Hammer or firing pin.

Stud: Projection on a gun for holding another part, such as the bayonet stud or the sight stud.

Swivel gun: One fired from a swivel mount.

Takedown rifle: A firearm in which the barrel can be taken from the action; employed for compactness.

Trajectory: Path of the bullet through the air.

Trigger: Part of the lock pulled by the finger to release the cock or hammer and fire the piece.

Trigger guard: Metal loop or rectangle protecting the trigger.

Trigger plate: Portion of the mechanism through which the trigger enters.

Trigger pull: Amount of pressure necessary to release the trigger.

Velocity: Speed of a projectile in flight, usually expressed in feet per second.

Wad: Yielding substance, usually made of felt, placed over the powder of a shot shell to control the gas blast.

Windage: Allowance made for drift of a bullet.

Wobble: Unsteady rotation or spin of a bullet; usually caused by insufficient twist in the rifle barrel.

EXPLOSIVES
Alarm-clock bomb
Bangalore torpedo
Blasting gelatin
Dynamite
Grenade
Incendiary bomb
Magnifying-glass bomb
Molotov cocktail
Nitroglycerin
Plastique
Time bomb
T.N.T.

WHERE TO GO FROM HERE

A good place to go for information about criminals is the police agency responsible for catching them. Explain why you want the information, be polite but persistent, and be ready to produce your credentials. That is, don't tell a cop that you're doing a piece for *Time* unless you're actually doing a piece for *Time*, or that you've published five crime novels unless you have them ready to put on your contact's desk at the police station.

The following books are about a variety of criminals, groups and issues:

Abrahamsen, David. *Murder and Madness: The Secret Life of Jack the Ripper*. New York: Donald I. Fine, 1992. A psychiatrist pins the Ripper's crimes on a member of the Royal Family and his tutor.

Ayoob, Massad. *Fundamentals of Modern Police Impact Weapons*. New York: Thomas, 1978. Discusses nightsticks, kubotans, police flashlights and improvised weapons.

Catanzaro, Raimondo. *Men of Respect: A Social History of the Sicilian Mafia*. New York: Free Press, 1992. The story of the modern Mafia's beginnings in loose bands of Sicilian bandits in the early 1800s to the organization's current extensive influence on Italian society.

Cooper, Sydney C., and Anne Scott. *Home Security*. New York: Consumers Union, 1988. Reliable information on how thieves operate and prevention techniques and devices.

Franzese, Michael, and Dary Matera. *Quitting the Mob: How the "Yuppie Don" Left the Mafia and Lived to Tell His Story*. New York: HarperCollins, 1992. How one of the most successful Mafia dons ever was convinced by his wife to cooperate with prosecutors and leave the mob.

Giancana, Sam, and Chuck Giancana. *Double Cross: The Explosive, Inside Story of the Mobster Who Controlled America*. New York: Warner Books, 1992. This is what Sam Giancana's brother reports the mob boss told him about, among other things, the deaths of Marilyn Monroe and John Kennedy.

Lewis, Jack. *The Gun Digest Book of Modern Gun Values*. Northbrook, Illinois: DBI Books. Published every two to three years. Particularly useful because it has specifications and pictures (generally photos) of a wide variety of guns, and tells what one might expect to pay for them at the local gun or pawn shop.

Lewis, Jack. *Handguns*. Northbrook, Illinois: DBI Books, annual. Articles on and tests of what's new, or at least relatively new.

Niehaus, Joseph. *The Sixth Sense: Practical Tips for Everyday Safety*. Tempe, Arizona: Blue Bird Publishing, 1990. Written by a cop, this contains some good ideas on writing about crime and getting the protagonist out of tight situations.

Newton, Michael. *Armed and Dangerous: A Writer's Guide to Weapons*. Cincinnati: Writer's Digest Books, 1990. A top adventure novelist tells all about guns.

Provost, Gary. *Perfect Husband: The True Story of the Trusting Bride Who Discovered Her Husband Was a Cold-blooded Killer*. New York: Pocket Books, 1991. The story of a man who marries a successful woman, opens a front business for petty crimes, commits a murder and tries several times to have his wife killed.

Quigley, Paxton. *Armed and Female*. New York: Dutton, 1989. Thorough and readable book on the arguments surrounding owning and using guns from a woman's perspective. Good chapters on buying guns and self-defense.

Schwartz, Anne. *The Man Who Could Not Kill Enough: The Secret Murders of Milwaukee's Jeffrey Dahmer*. New York: Carol Publishing Group, 1992. The story of the Dahmer case by the first reporter on the scene after Dahmer was arrested in July 1991.

Stevens, Serita Deborah, and Anne Klarner. *Deadly Doses: A Writer's Guide to Poisons*. Cincinnati: Writer's Digest Books, 1990. How to poison your characters and get away with it.

Stewart, James. *Den of Thieves*. New York: Simon & Schuster, 1991. The story of Michael Milken, Ivan Boesky, Martin Siegel and Dennis Levine, the central figures in the junk bond and arbitrage scandal that shook Wall Street in the 1980s.

Vaksberg, Arkady. *The Soviet Mafia*. New York: St. Martin's, 1991. "Soviet investigative reporter" may sound like an oxymoron, but that's what Vaksberg was. Published just as the Soviet Union fell apart, the book details how the increasing openness in Soviet society increased opportunities for crime.

Weissberg, Michael. *The First Sin of Ross Michael Carlson: A Psychiatrist's Personal Account of Murder, Multiple Personal-*

ity Disorder and Modern Justice. New York: Delacorte Press, 1992. The story of a young man who killed his parents by a psychiatrist who testified in the case.

Wilson, Colin. *A Criminal History of Mankind*. New York: Carroll & Graff, 1983. Puts social control and crime in historical perspective.

3

Cops

POLICE DEPARTMENT ORGANIZATION

Two large metropolitan police departments and a variety of other local and federal agencies described in this chapter illustrate how such agencies are organized. Contact the agency you are writing about to research the specifics more fully.

The differences in police departments can be major. The Los Angeles Police Department (LAPD) and the New York Police Department (NYPD) are two of the largest police departments in the nation. Although they share the same areas of responsibility in their communities, their organizational structures differ in many ways. For example, both police departments function under police commissioners with a chief of police in charge of the force, but the structure of their bureaus, departments and special units differ in many respects. Whereas the LAPD operates out of divisions, the NYPD operates out of station houses often referred to as precincts. Neither the LAPD nor the NYPD uses the police title lieutenant colonel, but the Cincinnati Police Department does. These are only a few examples, so before you write about a particular agency, check it out.

LOS ANGELES POLICE DEPARTMENT: ORGANIZATION AND FUNCTIONS

The following information was provided by the LAPD:

The Detective Support Division is responsible for investigating suspected conspiracies directed toward educational institutions; investigating specified bomb-related crimes; investigating, arresting and processing certain felony fugitives and out-of-state misdemeanor fugitive suspects; monitoring gang-related activities and gang-related crimes; maintaining surveillance of known criminals engaged in unlawful activities; and responding to subpoenas and legal processes that are directed to sections of the Detective Support Division.

The Criminal Conspiracy Section is responsible for investigating criminal conspiracies directed toward the various educational institutions in the city; all bombings, attempted bombings and bomb threats; extortion or threats of extortion not investigated by Robbery-Homicide Divisions, involving adult and juvenile victims or suspects, and when extortion elements involve or imply an explosive device or nuclear material; investigating all written and verbal threats against the mayor, city council members, city attorney, city comptroller and persons designated by the commanding officer, Detective Services, Headquarters Bureau; and maintaining records of all incidents motivated by hatred or prejudice in the city.

The Fugitive Section investigates, arrests and processes felony fugitives, out-of-state misdemeanor fugitive suspects and out-of-state juveniles wanted on criminal charges.

The Gang Activities Section is responsible for investigative patrols monitoring gang-related activities, including those who are gang members, as well as photos and vehicles of gang members.

The Special Investigations Section maintains a mobile force of investigators to assist other divisions in locating and maintaining surveillance of active, known criminals and to effect arrests.

Bunco-Forgery is responsible for investigating auto repair frauds; offers of bribes; consumer frauds; Corporate Securities Act violations; any crime committed through use of computer-stored information or sabotage of same; manufacturing, distribution or wholesaling of pirated recordings; capping; fraudulently printed

Organization of the Los Angeles Police Department

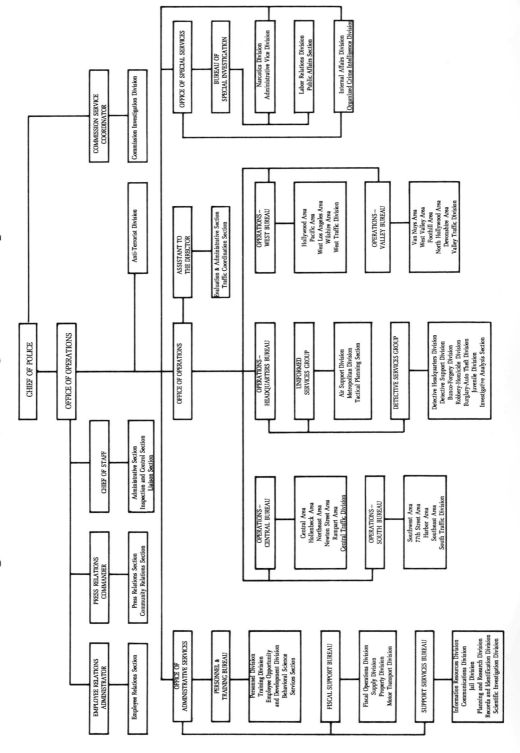

checks; counterfeit currency; forged airline tickets; burglaries and thefts of blank checks and checkwriting equipment; fraud by worthless checks or credit cards, or forgery; and forged prescriptions. Bunco-Forgery also maintains a Pickpocket Detail.

Headquarters Detective Services Group, Robbery/Homicide Division is composed of a Robbery Special Section, Bank Robbery, Hijack-Cargo Theft Section, Homicide Special Section, Rape and Domestic Violence Section, Major Crimes Section and Officer-Involved Shooting Section.

The Robbery Special Section is responsible for investigating extortions or threats of extortion when a prolonged investigation is required, when the extortion does not involve a juvenile as a victim or suspect and when the suspect has threatened to do unlawful injury to the person or property. This section investigates selected kidnappings used as a means of robbery.

The Bank Robbery, Hijack-Cargo Theft Section investigates robberies of banks, bank employees and messengers, insured credit unions, savings and loans and armored cars; thefts of commercial vehicles transporting merchandise when cargo is the object of attack; and extortions by any means, including explosives when directed against a bank, employee, etc.

Homicide Special Section is responsible for investigating abortions, certain major homicide cases, attending coroner's autopsies involving homicide or suspected homicide victims and reviewing all deaths, arrests and crime reports pertaining to homicides.

Major Crimes Investigation Section is responsible for investigating major selected crimes at the direction of the commanding officer, and for providing personnel to accompany VIPs who are visiting the city.

Officer-Involved Shooting Section is responsible for investigations when an officer has discharged a firearm, causing a gunshot wound to be inflicted on any person; when an officer receives a gunshot wound; when a staff or command officer is involved in a shooting in which no gunshot wound was inflicted on any person; when death or serious injury results from an officer-related incident (except those involving traffic officers); and in incidents involving the death of a person in department custody.

Rape and Domestic Violence Section is responsible for investigating selected sex crimes and insuring proper collection of evidence in sexual assault cases.

The Burglary/Auto Theft Division is responsible for investigating all vault and safe burglaries except where the safe has been removed from the premises or the case lacks evidence of forced entry; burglaries where business machines are the primary object of the theft and reported loss is in excess of $20,000; all burglaries or thefts where fine art is the objective; hotel-room thefts and burglaries in major hotels; telephone-booth burglars; shoplifters; and major receivers of stolen property.

Commercial Auto Theft Section investigates stolen trucks (in excess of five tons); thefts of commercial trailers, tractors and heavy-duty equipment; secondhand auto-parts dealers; car, truck and motorcycle thieves.

Pawn Shop Section investigates and ensures compliance with laws, rules and permits pertaining to antique dealers, junk collectors and dealers, pawnbrokers, secondhand stores and swap meets.

Headquarters, Detective Services Group, Juvenile Division is composed of a commanding officer, administrative section, operations section, juvenile narcotics section and child protection section. It provides information, training and evaluations of juvenile policies and procedures; implements modifications of same; ensures that departmental policies are being followed; audits and processes all juvenile arrest dispositions; conducts follow-up investigations of cases in which a parent, stepparent, legal guardian or common-law spouse appears responsible for depriving a child of the necessities of life to the extent of physical impairment; physical or sexual abuse of a child; homicide when the victim is under eleven years of age.

This division conducts any child-abuse case directed by the commanding officer of the Juvenile Division; investigates violations of state and federal laws pertaining to sexual or commercial exploitation of children under sixteen years of age (e.g., child prostitution rings); assists fire department in processing of juvenile arson cases; investigates narcotics cases when suspect or victim is a juvenile; conducts counseling and provides dispositions for juvenile narcotics violators; conducts undercover juvenile narcotics investigations; and maintains liaison with the juvenile justice system's probation department, youth authority, juvenile court, district attorney and public defender in the processing of juvenile cases.

Office of Operations

The Office of Operations is responsible for stimulating mutual understanding between the police and the community to prevent crime; patrolling the streets to deter crime; identifying, arresting and cooperating in the prosecution of criminal offenders; recovering lost or stolen property to its lawful owner; enforcing traffic laws; and advising the public in emergency situations.

The commanding officer, Operations Headquarters Bureau, under the director, Office of Operations, exercises command over operations of Operations Headquarters, coordinating matters concerning uniformed and investigative services. The commanding officer, Air Support Division, under the commanding officer, Headquarters Uniformed Services Group, exercises command over the operation of the Air Support Division.

Office of Special Services

The Office of Special Services (OSS) is under the direction of the director, Office of Special Services, which further falls under the direction of the chief of police, and exercises line command over the OSS. The OSS is composed of (1) the Internal Affairs Division; (2) Organized Crime Intelligence Division; (3) Bureau of Special Investigations; (4) Narcotics Division; and (5) Administrative Vice Division. Responsibilities include: recording and investigating complaints against department employees and processing disciplinary cases; collecting and disseminating intelligence information relative to organized crime; monitoring narcotic and vice enforcement efforts and investigating major occurrences involving narcotics and dangerous drugs, including drugs illegally manufactured, supplied or distributed; monitoring labor disputes and investigating selected related crimes; maintaining the Undesirable Informant File; issuing consular identification cards; maintaining records of aggravated incidents involving consular officers and members of their families.

Organization of the LAPD Office of Operations

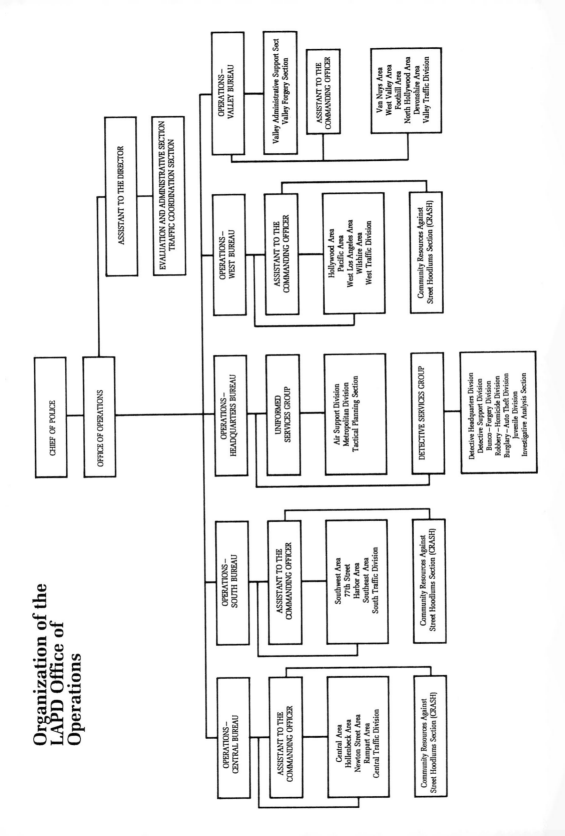

CHIEF OF POLICE

OFFICE OF OPERATIONS

ASSISTANT TO THE DIRECTOR

EVALUATION AND ADMINISTRATIVE SECTION
TRAFFIC COORDINATION SECTION

OPERATIONS–CENTRAL BUREAU

ASSISTANT TO THE COMMANDING OFFICER

Central Area
Hollenbeck Area
Newton Street Area
Rampart Area
Central Traffic Division

Community Resources Against
Street Hoodlums Section (CRASH)

OPERATIONS–SOUTH BUREAU

ASSISTANT TO THE COMMANDING OFFICER

Southwest Area
77th Street
Harbor Area
Southeast Area
South Traffic Division

Community Resources Against
Street Hoodlums Section (CRASH)

OPERATIONS–HEADQUARTERS BUREAU

UNIFORMED SERVICES GROUP

Air Support Division
Metropolitan Division
Tactical Planning Section

DETECTIVE SERVICES GROUP

Detective Headquarters Division
Detective Support Division
Bunco–Forgery Division
Robbery–Homicide Division
Burglary–Auto Theft Division
Juvenile Division
Investigative Analysis Section

OPERATIONS–WEST BUREAU

ASSISTANT TO THE COMMANDING OFFICER

Hollywood Area
Pacific Area
West Los Angeles Area
Wilshire Area
West Traffic Division

Community Resources Against
Street Hoodlums Section (CRASH)

OPERATIONS–VALLEY BUREAU

Valley Administrative Support Sect
Valley Forgery Section

ASSISTANT TO THE COMMANDING OFFICER

Van Nuys Area
West Valley Area
Foothill Area
North Hollywood Area
Devonshire Area
Valley Traffic Division

The Administrative Office — Special Duties prepares correspondence; conducts research and surveys; makes required recommendations; reviews information or material on official positions of the department that will disclose procedures, case events or other confidential matters. It conducts background investigations of persons applying for employment with the city and maintains and monitors a master file of all narcotics reports.

The Internal Affairs Division is responsible for investigating personnel complaints involving staff and command officers except as directed by the chief of police. It records and investigates selected complaints against other department personnel. In serious disciplinary matters, it reports findings and makes recommendations to concerned commanding officers, the chief of police and the director, Special Services. It represents the department in disciplinary cases.

The Organized Crime Intelligence Division is responsible for gathering, recording and investigating information concerning individuals and organizations whose backgrounds, activities or associates identify them with or are characteristic of organized crime. The division also provides information concerning organized crime to concerned units of the department and to other law enforcement agencies. It maintains a detail at the airport to observe and report arrivals and departures of persons known to be associated with organized crime. It also maintains a master index file containing data and information concerning persons investigated by the division; press clippings concerning racketeers and criminals indexed to the master file; a file of telephone numbers checked by the division in connection with investigations; a record of telephone toll bill search-and-warrant information; and a file of arson involving organized crime.

Bureau of Special Investigations

The responsibilities of the Bureau of Special Investigations include monitoring narcotic and vice enforcement; investigating major occurrences involving narcotics and dangerous drugs that are illegally manufactured, supplied or distributed; and monitoring labor disputes and related crimes, as well as those duties that fall

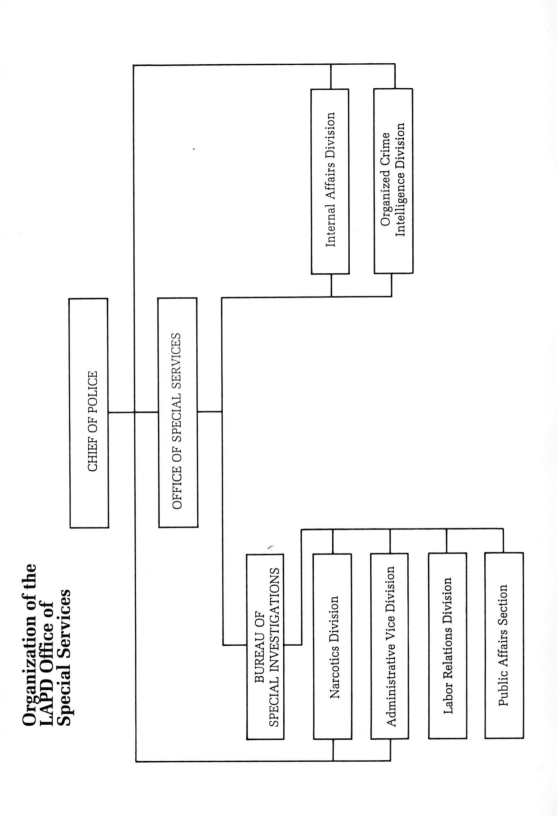

Organization of the LAPD Office of Special Services

CHIEF OF POLICE

OFFICE OF SPECIAL SERVICES

Internal Affairs Division

Organized Crime Intelligence Division

BUREAU OF SPECIAL INVESTIGATIONS

Narcotics Division

Administrative Vice Division

Labor Relations Division

Public Affairs Section

under the responsibility of the Public Affairs Section. The bureau is composed of (1) the Narcotics Division; (2) the Administrative Vice Division; (3) the Labor Relations Division; (4) the Public Affairs Section; and (5) the Drug Abuse Resistance Education (DARE) Division.

The Narcotics Division is responsible for the enforcement of narcotics laws when the violations are committed by adults. It obtains, exchanges and coordinates information concerning narcotics suspects and drug traffic. It develops narcotics statistics, including department enforcement efforts and the availability of drugs. It investigates major suppliers and distributors of narcotics and dangerous drugs who engaged in illegal activities on an organized commercial basis. This includes evaluating the circumstances of each case to determine the advisability of seizing a conveyance and initiating formal forfeiture proceedings, and providing advice on geographic location of storage and maintenance of vehicles, boats and airplanes seized. They also direct and prepare necessary documents for presentation to the district attorney for completion of a petition for forfeiture.

It disposes of any seized asset related to controlled substance trafficking, and when appropriate, conducts investigations on a state university campus. It exchanges and coordinates information concerning narcotics suspects and drug traffic with Narcotics Information Network (N.I.N.) and other agencies concerned with control of drug abuse. It obtains, records and coordinates use of information concerning suspects and drug traffic. It administers the activities of the department's Undercover Buy Program. It reviews and coordinates all requests for pretrial destruction of excessive quantities of controlled substances and maintains the following files: narcotics information inquiries; N.I.N. investigations; department undercover buy locations; narcotic expertise certification card files; narcotics arrest and seizure statistics; narcotics resource materials; narcotics arrests and dispositions; narcotics suspects moniker information; and border crossings of suspects. It maintains liaison with the state's tax board for possible state tax violations by narcotics suspects and administers the undercover and narcotics sting operations.

The Administrative Vice Division is composed of (1) an Administrative Section; (2) Gaming Section; (3) Pornography Section; and (4) Prostitution Section. The responsibilities of this division include monitoring and auditing geographic vice units' enforcement efforts to ensure uniformity and effectiveness; investigating vice activities of an organized nature; assisting geographic vice units, on request, with operations exceeding their own resources or geographic jurisdictions; correlating and maintaining intelligence information related to organized vice activities; and coordinating, procuring, returning and maintaining a file of undercover driver's licenses on a department-wide basis.

This division's Administrative Vice Section is specifically responsible for securing complaints from the District Attorney's Office on all felony vice arrests and crime reports made in the metropolitan area; researching proposed and new legislation and developing procedures to assist in maintaining effective vice control; storing, maintaining and disseminating the division's electronic equipment; maintaining intelligence information related to organized vice activities; conducting electronic investigations and ensuring that standard procedures and policies are adhered to; identifying problem establishments suitable for abatement proceedings, and providing assistance and functional supervision to vice/narcotic personnel in abatement proceedings; and maintaining files on bookmaking arrestees, mugs of all vice arrestees suspected of being connected with organized crime, and pimping arrestees.

The Gaming Section is responsible for investigating violations of gambling and bookmaking laws when violations are of an organized nature; maintaining liaison with Department of Animal Regulations regarding dog and cock fighting; maintaining liaison with Bingo Division of Social Services Department for investigation of licenses, and with the State Lottery for lottery-related crimes within the city.

The Prostitution Section investigates violations of pimping, pandering, prostitution and prostitution-related laws; violations of alcoholic beverage control laws when violations are of an organized nature; and monitors live stage acts when performance is generally of a sexually related nature.

The Pornography Section is responsible for investigating violations of pornography and obscenity.

The Labor Relations Division is responsible for maintaining liaisons with labor and management groups and monitoring labor disputes; and investigating crimes arising from labor disputes except homicides, bombings, kidnappings and bomb threats.

The Public Affairs Section is responsible for providing news releases and public service announcements to the news media; establishing guidelines for public relations material by the department; preparing the department's magazine and annual report; answering requests for information; preparing department commendations and arranging for the formal presentation of all department awards to employees; preparing police commission citations for private citizens, and certificates of appreciation and recognition; handling arrangements for visiting VIPs and law enforcement personnel; maintaining the department's archives; conducting tours; and processing requests for speaking engagements.

The Anti-Terrorist Division operates solely under the direction of the chief of police. It is responsible for gathering intelligence, as well as investigating and maintaining records and information on terrorists and terrorist organizations known to be in the city while maintaining liaison with other local, state and federal agencies involved in antiterrorist activities.

The Special Weapons Assault Team (SWAT) is a trained tactical unit specializing in security for visiting dignitaries, high vantage and sniper fire, the rescue of officers pinned down under fire and terrorist or barricade situations. The SWAT organization consists of approximately one hundred officers, and is broken down into teams of six to eight members in addition to a sergeant and a lieutenant. When summoned, teams wearing dark or black pants, shirts, jackets and hats usually respond to a crime scene in patrol cars or unmarked police vehicles. Their weapons, flack jackets and other equipment are usually stored in the trunk of the vehicle they arrive in.

Crisis/negotiating teams work out of the Metro Division and are specially trained in the psychology of crisis situations at the police academy. Crisis/negotiating teams usually consist of two officers and a sergeant, and whenever possible, are accompanied by a trained police psychologist schooled in the behavioral sciences. These teams are used primarily in suicide attempts, hostage taking and terrorist and barricaded-suspects situations.

The Canine Section teams dogs with uniformed officers who receive their training together. Most police departments utilizing dogs for patrol work use Rottweilers or German Shepherds, although other dogs can be trained for the job. Dogs are used primarily to reach a barricaded suspect, chase a fleeing suspect, search buildings and outdoor areas and search for missing persons. Dogs used for drug sniffing are not part of the canine corps. They are trained and used by Narcotics.

Mounted police from the Metro Division are used for patrol and riot and crowd control. In addition to the psychological factor, officers perched high atop their mounts can get a more unobstructed view than officers in patrol cars or on foot.

Bicycle patrols are fairly new to most U.S. police departments, although the British and many other foreign law enforcement agencies have used them for years. LAPD's bicycle patrols are used primarily in beach areas and other areas of the city for crime prevention and greater mobility in chase situations.

LOS ANGELES COUNTY SHERIFF'S DEPARTMENT

The following was provided by the Los Angeles County Sheriff's Department:

The sheriff is the chief law enforcement officer of the county. As such, the sheriff is responsible for general law enforcement in all unincorporated areas of the county and in those cities that contract for the services of the Sheriff's Department to avoid the cost of outfitting their own departments, equipment, personnel and investigative expertise.

Duties and Responsibilities

The California Government Code and the California Penal Code authorize the sheriff of a county to perform certain duties and assign the responsibility for certain actions within the sheriff's county. Duties and responsibilities include: preserve the peace;

arrest all persons attempting or committing public offenses; prevent and suppress affrays and investigate public offenses; attend superior courts and obey all lawful orders and directions of all courts within the county; take charge of and keep the county jail and the prisoners in it; release attachments or garnishments of property; endorse receipts of process and issue certificates of delivery; serve all processes and notices; and act in attendance upon court as the crier thereof.

The sheriff may supply ambulance service; enforce the vehicle code; search for and rescue persons who are lost or are in danger of their lives within the county; command the aid of all adult male inhabitants in the county to accomplish sheriff's duties; carry out the duties of the Office of County Director of Emergency Services; transport and deliver prisoners committed to state prisons; and transport prisoners to hospitals or to the custody of an officer of another jurisdiction.

Upon request of the court, the sheriff may have responsibility for care and custody of minors charged with or convicted of felonies; execute writs and transport persons who are narcotics addicts and sexual psychopaths to places of confinement; execute search warrants and arrest warrants; sit as a member of the Board of Parole Commissioners; and take possession of, appraise and keep safely found or wrecked property.

The sheriff may be directed to remove intruders from waste or ungranted lands of the state, and may serve all writs, notices or other processes issued by superior, municipal or justice courts, and lawful orders of the state government.

The sheriff may be required to serve processes or warrants issued by any court-martial officer, labor commissioner or insurance commissioner to a person within the county.

Administrative Organization

The sheriff of Los Angeles County is elected to a four-year term of office and is responsible to the electorate. The sheriff is subject to fiscal control by the Los Angeles County Board of Supervisors.

The sheriff's department is a quasi-military organization. All sworn personnel are deputy sheriffs, regardless of rank, and are subordinate in order of rank to the sheriff. The rank structure is as follows:

Sheriff
Undersheriff
Assistant Sheriff
Chief
Commander
Captain
Lieutenant
Sergeant
Deputy

The undersheriff, an appointed position, is second in command and subordinate only to the sheriff. This person commands the department in the sheriff's absence and otherwise conducts the affairs of the department as directed by the sheriff.

The third level of command is the assistant sheriff. This department has two assistant sheriffs, each with separate areas of responsibility. In the absence of the sheriff and the undersheriff, the designated assistant sheriff assumes full command of the department.

Other major staff executives are the eight division chiefs, who command the activities of their respective divisions in accordance with the policies of the sheriff.

Departmental Organization

The sheriff's department is composed of eight divisions, each commanded by a chief. These divisions operate on a twenty-four-hour schedule to provide full services whenever needed. The divisions are:

Administrative
Court Services
Custody
Detective
Field Operations Region I
Field Operations Region II
Field Operations Region III
Technical Services

Los Angeles County Sheriff's Department

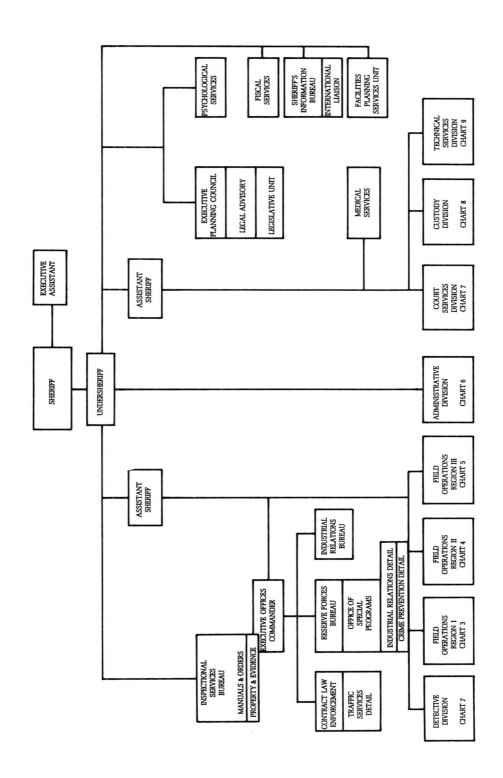

Administrative Division

This division functions as the major coordinating unit for the department's overall operations. It is responsible for providing administrative staff services to the entire department. These services include recruiting, training, coordinating retirements, maintaining personnel and payroll records, conducting pre-employment background investigations, researching problem areas and analyzing legislation. Through its Internal Investigations Bureau, this division investigates citizen complaints and other cases involving departmental personnel.

Court Services Division

This division is responsible for carrying out part of the mandated duties of the sheriff as set forth in the government code, including the primary requirement to act as the chief ministerial officer of the Los Angeles County Superior Court. The Court Services Division serves and enforces civil and criminal processes submitted by the court, attorneys and litigants, and provides bailiffs to the superior and justice courts. This division is also responsible for transporting prisoners to and from court and between custodial facilities.

Custody Division

This division is responsible for the operation of the sheriff's custody system, which includes incarceration of all sentenced and pretrial inmates detained in sheriff's facilities. Medical services are also provided for the approximately 17,500 inmates housed in custody facilities.

Detective Division

This division has the responsibility for investigating, among others, the major crimes of arson, forgery, fraud, robbery, flight from prosecution and homicide. Specialized bureaus within this division have responsibility for the investigation of narcotics and vice operations. The Hazardous Materials Team is also part of the Detective Division.

Los Angeles County Sheriff's Department Administrative Division

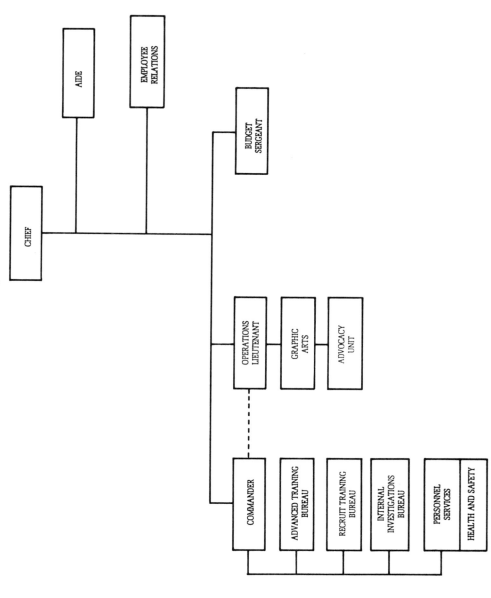

Los Angeles County Sheriff's Department Court Services Division

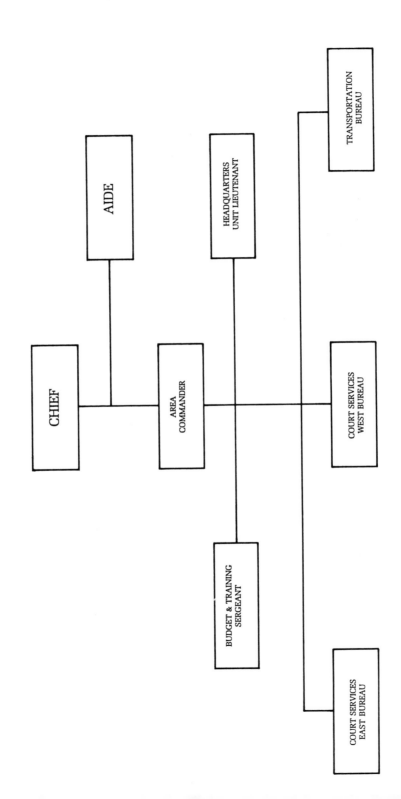

CHIEF

AIDE

AREA COMMANDER

HEADQUARTERS UNIT LIEUTENANT

BUDGET & TRAINING SERGEANT

COURT SERVICES WEST BUREAU

TRANSPORTATION BUREAU

COURT SERVICES EAST BUREAU

Los Angeles County Sheriff's Department Custody Division

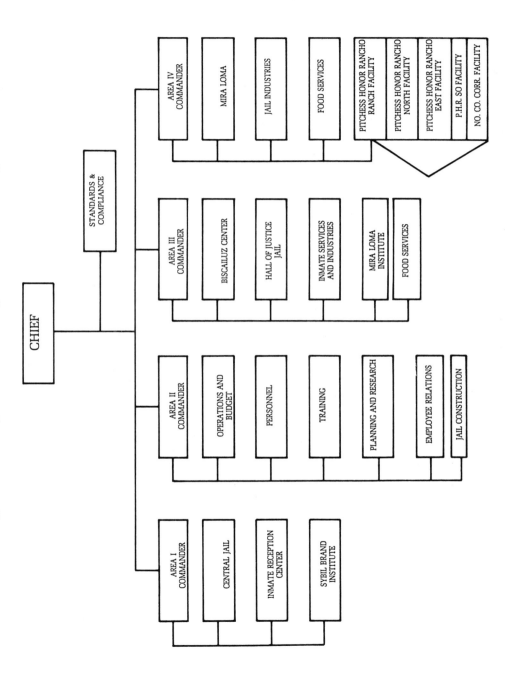

CHIEF

STANDARDS & COMPLIANCE

AREA I COMMANDER
- CENTRAL JAIL
- INMATE RECEPTION CENTER
- SYBIL BRAND INSTITUTE

AREA II COMMANDER
- OPERATIONS AND BUDGET
- PERSONNEL
- TRAINING
- PLANNING AND RESEARCH
- EMPLOYEE RELATIONS
- JAIL CONSTRUCTION

AREA III COMMANDER
- BISCAILUZ CENTER
- HALL OF JUSTICE JAIL
- INMATE SERVICES AND INDUSTRIES
- MIRA LOMA INSTITUTE
- FOOD SERVICES

AREA IV COMMANDER
- MIRA LOMA
- JAIL INDUSTRIES
- FOOD SERVICES
- PITCHESS HONOR RANCHO RANCH FACILITY
- PITCHESS HONOR RANCHO NORTH FACILITY
- PITCHESS HONOR RANCHO EAST FACILITY
- P.H.R. SO FACILITY
- NO. CO. CORR. FACILITY

Field Operations Regions

Three Field Operations Regions provide general law enforcement, patrol and investigative services to unincorporated areas of the county. In addition to these services, contract cities are also provided with traffic law enforcement. When major or specialized crimes occur, follow-up investigations are conducted by the Detective Division. The department's jurisdiction extends to inland waters.

To supplement and improve the effectiveness of field operations, specialized units have been established as separate bureaus within the Field Operations Regions. These include Aero, Emergency Operations, Special Enforcement and Juvenile Operations Bureaus.

Technical Services Division

This division is responsible for providing the specialized technical services necessary for the efficient operation of the department's line units and for maintaining the official activity records of the department. Other services include maintaining the department's vehicles, operating the telecommunications system, operating the criminalistics and photographic laboratories and preparing the department's statistical reports on jail population and criminal activity.

This division is also responsible for operating the department's communications center and coordinating the Justice Data System (JDS).

Specialized Investigations

Two highly specialized bureaus, Special Investigations and Inspectional Services, operating from the office of the undersheriff, conduct sensitive staff support functions. The Inspectional Services Bureau was established in 1975. This bureau conducts specialized inspections on a department-wide basis to ensure uniformity of procedures, maximize efficiency, project future problems and recommend solutions to identified problems.

The Special Investigations Bureau was organized to investigate

Los Angeles County Sheriff's Department Detective Division

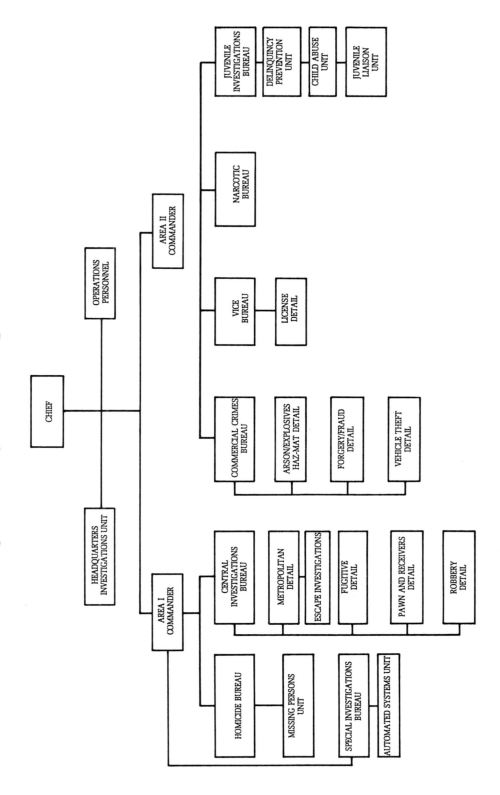

Los Angeles County Sheriff's Department Field Operations Region I

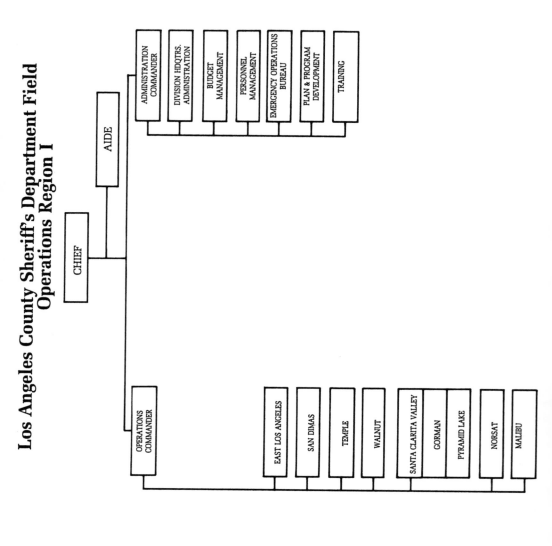

CHIEF

AIDE

ADMINISTRATION COMMANDER
- DIVISION HDQTRS. ADMINISTRATION
- BUDGET MANAGEMENT
- PERSONNEL MANAGEMENT
- EMERGENCY OPERATIONS BUREAU
- PLAN & PROGRAM DEVELOPMENT
- TRAINING

OPERATIONS COMMANDER
- EAST LOS ANGELES
- SAN DIMAS
- TEMPLE
- WALNUT
- SANTA CLARITA VALLEY
- GORMAN
- PYRAMID LAKE
- NORSAT
- MALIBU

Los Angeles County Sheriff's Department Field Operations Region II

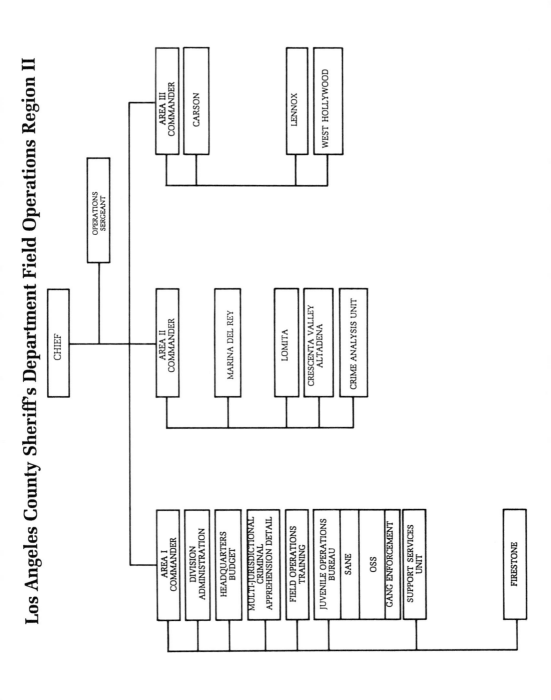

Los Angeles County Sheriff's Department Field Operations Region III

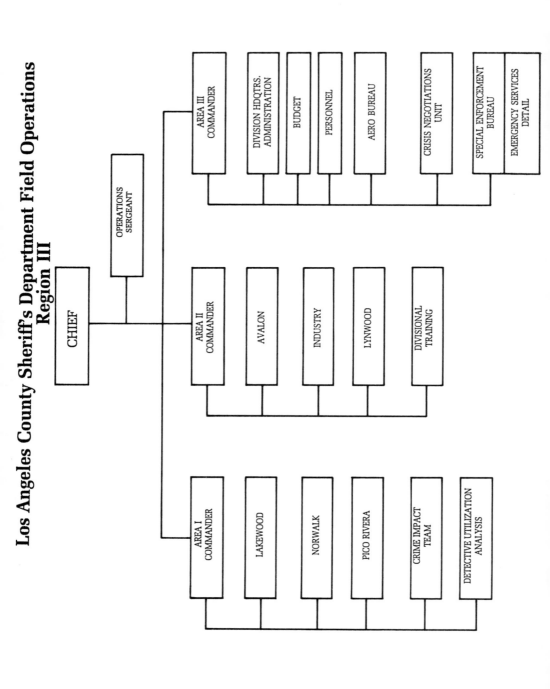

Los Angeles County Sheriff's Department Technical Services Division

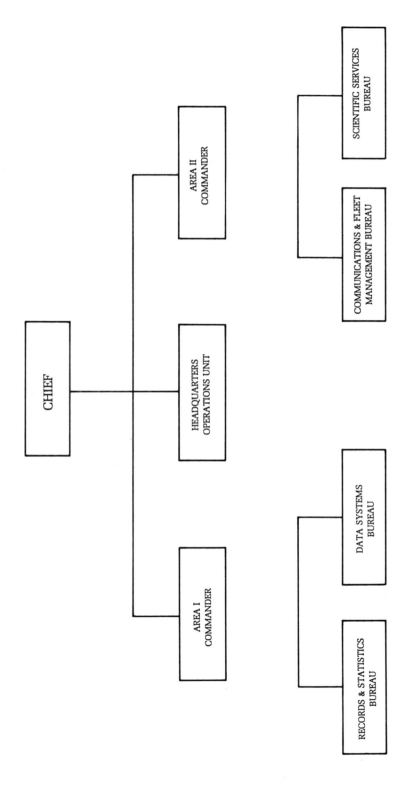

known or suspected organized crime, prison gang activity and individuals or groups involved in terrorist-type conduct.

Emergency Services Detail

The Emergency Services Detail is recognized as one of the finest emergency services groups in the nation.

Deputies from this detail were the first law officers in the country to earn the paramedic title. To achieve this distinction, deputies completed a rigorous one thousand-hour training course at the University of Southern California Medical Center. Once certified, and acting under the supervision of a licensed medical doctor, these deputy-paramedics are able to provide immediate medical aid in the field. This extra care for the injured has saved many lives.

In addition to paramedic training, these deputies are trained extensively in search-and-rescue techniques, mountain rescue, helicopter evacuation of the injured and underwater search and recovery.

Technological Advances

To adequately serve an area the size of Los Angeles County, the sheriff's department must have a fast, accurate and dependable communications system. This system uses decentralized command and control with centralized dispatching. There are twenty patrol stations located throughout the vast 4,083-square-mile county, and each station operates as a self-contained law enforcement unit. The key element in the communications system is the centralized radio center, which coordinates all two-way radio communications with mobile units. These include patrol and investigative vehicles, helicopters, airplanes, buses, trucks, jeeps, boats and assorted mobile support equipment.

To provide countywide coverage, the communications system utilizes transmission and reception sites on fourteen mountaintop and nineteen local sites. They are connected to the centralized dispatching center by a county-owned microwave system — one of the largest private microwave systems in the world. The system uses fifty-five frequencies operating through one or more of the

116 base transmitters, 344 receivers and more than one thousand mobiles. Over 61 million transmissions are generated within a single year.

In 1975, the Sheriff's Radio Communications Center computerized its capabilities. This highly flexible communications computer maintains a bookkeeping operation of the workload and distributes incoming traffic equally among all the radio-dispatching positions.

The computer senses an incoming digital message from a station, assigns a console within fifty milliseconds, and activates a bank of relays that provides the dispatching console with all of the transmitters, receivers, telephone lines and status signals necessary to handle the transmission. The relays, located in a central equipment room, can be accessed by all consoles; thus, every console in the facility can be considered a master console, able to handle any frequency at any transmitter/receiver location.

The computer also monitors and records the status of on-duty units, the calls assigned to them and whether or not the call has been handled within a preset time. When the mobile unit finishes an assignment, clearance for the call is manually entered into the computer, which is programmed to print out a complete log of each original call and its clearance, as well as various other reports.

A primary part of the communication system is the Justice Data System (JDS), which was developed to handle the booking and court information on all persons who enter the criminal justice system. Pertinent information on identification, charges and court appearances on adults and juveniles detained in police custody for more than one hour is entered into this system. JDS now includes sixteen other police agencies, including the Los Angeles Police Department. Future plans are to include all law enforcement agencies in Los Angeles County and to become the data base for information on persons going through the criminal justice system.

Justice Data System also serves as a central information source for all criminal justice agencies within the county area. Information is organized into two groups of information in the Automated Index—the Personal History Index and the Event Index. The Personal History Index provides data to attain a positive identification of individuals as well as their arrest and conviction recap. The

Event Index provides information relevant to a particular criminal offense. The two indexes retain enough information to satisfy approximately 90 percent of all inquiries from the various justice agencies.

One of the many advantages of JDS is the ability of each sheriff's station to immediately obtain complete criminal information. In cases where there is limited information regarding an individual under investigation, the Event Index enables the recall of information contained in reports by a number of criteria, such as victim's/witness's name, vehicle license and other identifiers.

In addition, the department will be able to perform special searches on partial fingerprint classifications. These searches will fulfill information needs on types of arrest, names under investigation, name of officer, date of occurrence and report status.

Using computerized systems pioneered and developed by this department, they have achieved a truly innovative, efficient and reliable communications network. An important phase of this network is the Justice Data Interface Controller (JDIC). This system replaced the Fully Automatic Switching Teletype (FAST) system formerly used by most law enforcement agencies in the county to gain access to law enforcement agencies and criminal-justice-system data banks.

Aero Bureau

The use of aircraft, with its unprecedented degree of flexibility and mobility, has added an entirely new dimension to law enforcement patrol.

Originally started in 1929 by volunteers, it was not until 1966 that modern airborne law enforcement came into its own, with the establishment of the Sky Knight program.

The department's Aero Bureau fleet has been increased with the most modern and varied equipment available. Currently, the rotary fleet consists of five Hughes 300s, five Hughes 500s, three Bell 47G3Bs, one Bell 20 GL, one Sikorsky S-58 and three Sikorsky CH38 helicopters. Fixed wing aircraft include two Cessna 210s.

Based at Long Beach Airport, Aero Bureau provides services for over thirty-one hundred square miles of Los Angeles County, including many of the incorporated cities that contract with the sheriff's department for police services. Within this jurisdiction, there is a great variety of terrain: high mountains, rugged wild canyons, vast desert areas, large ocean stretches and offshore islands. Because of this, Aero Bureau also maintains helicopters at strategic locations throughout the county to minimize response times and increase efficiency. The Aero Bureau flies numerous medical evacuation missions, surveillance missions, prisoner transfers, hazardous materials investigations, photo flights and investigator transportation flights.

Search and rescue is another facet of the Aero Bureau. There were 718 rescue missions flown during fiscal year 1984-85. Search-and-rescue teams from various sheriff's stations are frequently assisted by paramedic-equipped helicopters able to reach areas inaccessible by ground crews. In addition to the paramedic crews, who are available twenty-four hours a day, doctors from the Sheriff's Department's Reserve Forces volunteer their services to the citizens of Los Angeles County. Aero Bureau assigns rescue helicopters staffed with these doctors and paramedics primarily on weekends in strategic areas, where their lifesaving services are frequently needed.

Aero Bureau employs one Hughes 500, chiefly to locate illegal hazardous materials disposal sites, as well as to conduct surveillances of suspected unlawful disposals. Aero Bureau also investigates aircraft accidents and thefts of aircraft parts, and performs any mission requiring the use of aircraft as directed and approved by the sheriff.

Harbor Patrol

Since its construction in 1962, Marina del Rey has become the world's largest small-craft harbor. Anticipated population growth in the Marina del Rey community, as well as plans to increase the number of channels and slips, led to the establishment of the twentieth station facility there in 1984. That same year, the Los Angeles County Harbor Patrol merged with the sheriff's department, resulting in more streamlined law enforcement service to the citizens in the marina.

The Sheriff's Harbor Patrol enforces both California State Statutes and Los Angeles County Codes, placing an emphasis on boating and marine laws. It also performs search-and-rescue missions, and provides services to boaters in the marina.

The many years of nautical experience accumulated by former harbor patrolmen still benefit the citizens of Los Angeles County, as each of them are now deputy sheriffs. Each deputy sheriff assigned to the Sheriff's Harbor Patrol has received 895 hours of specialized training in addition to the standard Sheriff's Academy curriculum. This training includes instruction in marine firefighting, navigation, diving and search and rescue. All Harbor Patrol Deputies have also received 120 hours of emergency medical technician training.

The Sheriff's Harbor Patrol maintains a fleet of six specialized boats. Facilities include several hundred feet of dock, a boat maintenance center and a haul-out yard.

The sheriff's department also has a contingent of harbor patrol deputies. Their mission is the same as that of deputies — to enforce boating laws and to ensure the safety of the water-faring public.

OFFICE OF THE DISTRICT ATTORNEY OF LOS ANGELES

The size of the staff and the extent of the responsibilities of the district attorney may vary depending on the location. The Los Angeles District Attorney's Office, which has nearly two thousand support personnel, is the largest such office in the United States and has been chosen to best illustrate the full capacity of such an office.

The Los Angeles District Attorney's Office is primarily responsible for prosecuting felonies under state law, although it also prosecutes misdemeanors in Los Angeles County and for cities in the county that do not wish to retain their own city attorney.

The administration of the district attorney's office is composed of the district attorney, the chief deputy and the assistant district attorney. Reporting directly to the Administrative Section are two deputy DAs, one in charge of organized crime and the second in charge of special investigations, primarily dealing with public officials.

Reporting to the administrative command is the director of Central Operations, who oversees career criminals, special trials and central trials; the director of Special Operations, who oversees major frauds, hard-core gangs, consumer protection, environment, and COPOS (crimes against police officers), the Special Crimes Division, Special Legal and the Juvenile Division; the director of Branch and Area, who supervises the large number of deputy district attorneys in the district attorney's office.

A Family Support Section has its own deputy, called the deputy in charge, along with its own director and support staff. Its mission is investigation and prosecution with regard to family violence, child abuse and related situations.

The Bureau of Investigation is the investigative arm of the District Attorney's Office, and its personnel are assigned to the various sections and divisions as required.

OFFICE OF THE CITY ATTORNEY OF LOS ANGELES

The Los Angeles City Attorney's Office, the largest municipal law office in the nation, is divided among the Civil Branch, the Criminal Branch and the Special Operations Branch. The city attorney is the legal advisor to all city departments and agencies, including the office of the mayor, city council, police and fire departments, city commissions and other city departments.

Under the direction of the city attorney, attorneys from this office appear in all courts of the state, federal courts and the U.S. Supreme Court, as well as before a large number of state and federal regulatory and administrative agencies.

The Special Operations Branch of the City Attorney's Office deals with the Consumer Protection Section, Environmental Protection Section and Housing Enforcement Section.

The Criminal Branch, headed by the senior assistant attorney, handles all infraction and misdemeanor cases within the city, including consumer fraud, labor law violations, battery, theft, burglary, assault with a deadly weapon, vice, drunk driving, election compliance and air pollution violations. A special section of the Criminal Branch is the gangs unit (COPE), dealing with youth-gang problems.

The Civil Branch is headed by a senior counsel and handles everything from land use, contracts, personal injury and zoning, to the harbor and airports departments and the Department of Water and Power.

CINCINNATI POLICE DIVISION

The following was provided by the Cincinnati Police Division:

The Cincinnati, Ohio, Police Division consists of four bureaus: Operations Bureau, Investigative Bureau, Technical Services Bureau and Personnel Resources Bureau.

The Operations Bureau consists of five police districts and the Operational Support Section. These five districts are charged with the responsibility of patrol covering general criminal activities, along with community relations. The Operational Support Section, as part of the Operations Bureau, is responsible for the SWAT Coordination Unit, the Crime Prevention Unit, the Traffic Unit, Youth Aid and a new unit called the Alarm Enforcement Unit, which is charged with reducing the number of false alarms requiring police response.

The Investigations Bureau (I.B.) is charged with the responsibility for drug, vice and criminal investigation and enforcement. It comprises the Criminal Investigation Section (C.I.S.), Central Vice Control Section, Intelligence Section and Narcotics Liaison. Under the C.I.S., the Youth Squad is assigned the function of investigating child abuse, child neglect, custody and missing persons. The Homicide Squad is responsible for investigating all homicides, questionable deaths, aggravated assaults where death may occur, rape and sex-motivated offenses where the victim is eighteen or older, all police interventions in shootings or death, kidnapping and abductions and patient-abuse offenses.

Also under the I.B. are the Robbery Unit; the Major Offender Project, which coordinates cases involving serious and repeat career criminal offenders; and the Criminalistics Squad, which re-

Cincinnati Police Division

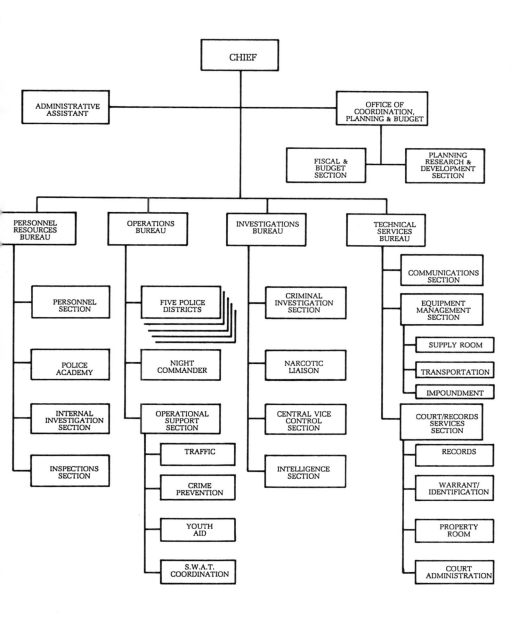

sponds to the crime scene. There, they assist the district investigators in handling the identification of suspects through fingerprint comparison, photography and video recording, and in handling the collection of crime scene material and evidence. This material is then routed by the squad to various laboratories, such as the Hamilton County Coroner's Office, the Ohio Bureau of Identification and the Federal Bureau of Investigation for processing. Also operating under the Investigations Bureau are Burglary and Auto Theft, the Pawn Shop Unit, the Polygraph Unit and the Fraud Unit.

The Central Vice Control Section is charged with enforcing laws and controlling criminal conduct in the areas of drugs, prostitution, gambling, liquor law enforcement and pornography.

The Intelligence Section develops information and initiates investigations into cults, gangs and terrorists, and conducts in-service training for division personnel.

The Narcotics Liaison Section provides investigative and supervisory personnel to the Regional Enforcement Narcotics Unit (RENU). In 1988, personnel in this unit were assigned to the newly formed DEA Cincinnati Task Force, a multiagency drug enforcement unit composed of Cincinnati police, DEA agents and Hamilton County sheriff's officers.

The Technical Services Bureau comprises three sections: the Police Communications Section; the Equipment Management Section, which includes the Impoundment Unit, responsible for all vehicles in custody; the Transportation Unit, which oversees the division's motor fleet; the Supply Unit, which fields all supplies and equipment requests; and the Court/Records Services Section, the last of which operates four units: Court Administration, County Property, Warrant/Identification and Records.

Personnel Resources Bureau comprises the Personnel Section, the Police Academy, the Inspection Section and the Internal Investigations Section. These sections provide recruit training, maintenance of personnel records, investigation of citizens' complaints, processing of employment records and liaison with organizations represented in the Police Division.

The Office of Coordination, Planning and Budget provides administrative assistance and staff to the police chief by reviewing and expediting official business, budgeting, planning, conducting research and generally developing the department.

DEPARTMENT OF JUSTICE

Headed by the attorney general of the United States, the Department of Justice exists to provide legal advice to the president, representation of the executive branch in court, investigation of federal crimes, enforcement of federal laws, operation of federal prisons and provision of law enforcement assistance to states and local communities.

Organization of the Department of Justice

Antitrust Division
Bureau of Prisons
Civil Division
Civil Rights Division
Community Relations Service
Criminal Division
Drug Enforcement Administration
Executive Office for Immigration Review
Executive Office for U.S. Attorneys
Federal Bureau of Investigation
Federal Prison Industries
Foreign Claims Settlement Commission
Immigration and Naturalization Service
International Criminal Police Organization—United States
    National Central Bureau
Justice Management Division
Land and Natural Resources Division
Office of the Associate Attorney General
Office of the Attorney General
Office of the Deputy Attorney General
Office of Intelligence Policy and Review
Office of Justice Programs
Office of Legal Counsel
Office of Legal Policy

Department of Justice

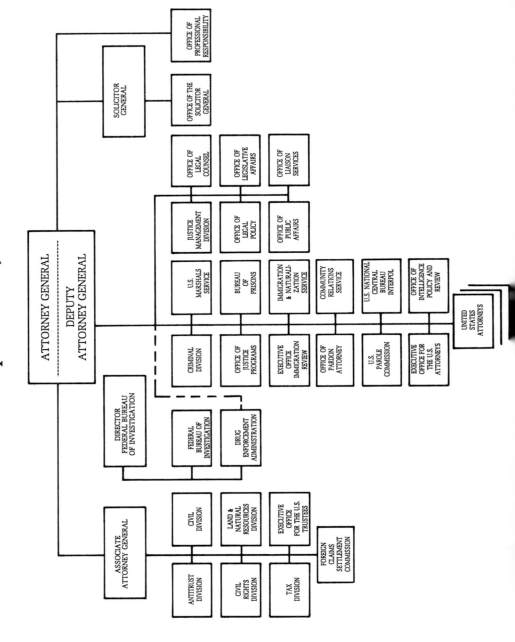

Office of Legislative Affairs
Office of Liaison Services
Office of Pardon Attorney
Office of Professional Responsibility
Office of Public Affairs
Office of the Solicitor General
Tax Division
U.S. Attorney's Office
U.S. Marshal's Service
U.S. Parole Commission
U.S. Trustee's Offices

The attorney general supervises and directs the administration and operations of the boards, divisions and bureaus of the Department of Justice. The deputy attorney general advises and assists the attorney general. The associate attorney general advises and assists the attorney general and the assistant attorney general. The solicitor general is responsible for conducting and supervising all aspects of government litigation in the U.S. Supreme Court. The Office of Legal Counsel assists the attorney general.

The Office of Legislative Affairs helps formulate and coordinate legislative policy among organizations within the department and maintains the department's liaison with Congress. The Office of Liaison Services is an outreach service to governors, state legislators and the law enforcement community. The Office of Legal Policy is a strategic legal "think tank" serving the attorney general's policy development staff.

The Office of Professional Responsibility reviews, and where appropriate, investigates allegations of misconduct against the department's employees.

The Justice Management Division controls and oversees department management issues and the department's liaison on budgetary matters. It includes such staffs as procurement, audit, security, equal opportunity, general counsel, policy and planning, comptroller, budget, information technology, computer technology and telecommunications, information systems, library, litigation systems, personnel and administration and general services.

The Office of Intelligence Policy and Review helps ensure that the national security-related activities of the United States are consistent with relevant law.

The U.S. Parole Commission is an independent agency in the department whose primary function is to administer a parole system for federal prisoners. It is responsible for developing a federal parole policy and is authorized to grant or deny parole to eligible federal prisoners.

Although the president exercises the pardon power, the Office of Pardon Attorney receives and reviews all petitions for executive clemency, initiates investigations and prepares recommendations to the attorney general.

The Criminal Division establishes federal criminal law enforcement policies and facilitates their implementation. It is responsible for the general supervision of all federal criminal laws except for those assigned specifically to Antitrust, Civil Rights, Land and Natural Resources or Tax Division. Operating as part of the Criminal Division is the Organized Crime and Racketeering Section, which develops and coordinates nationwide enforcement programs to reduce the influence of organized crime groups in the United States, working primarily through twenty-six strike forces and field offices throughout the nation.

The Public Integrity Section is responsible for independent counsel matters, investigations and prosecution of federal judges, major federal corruption and misconduct investigations, election and campaign financing crimes and significant state and local corruption cases.

The Office of Policy Management Analysis studies and recommends positions on policy and management issues of concern to both the division and the department.

The Fraud Section deals primarily with economic crime, especially in the areas of waste, fraud and abuse in government programs and contracts.

The General Litigation and Legal Advice Section develops and implements enforcement programs in key statutory areas, including terrorism, pornography, intellectual property and nuclear safety.

The Appellate Section handles cases and renders advice to the

U.S. Attorney's offices, especially with regard to the Comprehensive Crime Control Act of 1984.

The Internal Security Section is responsible for enforcing criminal statutes affecting national security and foreign relations. It also administers and enforces the Foreign Agents Registration Act, supervising investigations and prosecution of offenses involving espionage, sabotage, treason, violations of the Atomic Energy Act, neutrality statutes, Trading With the Enemy Act, Arms Export Control Act and Export Administration.

The Office of Internal Affairs is responsible for formulating, supervising and executing international, criminal justice enforcement policies and procedures, including the following: negotiating international agreements and treaties related to criminal law enforcement (extradition and prisoner transfers); preparing and litigating requests for international extradition; obtaining evidence for foreign jurisdictions; and coordinating requests to and from foreign countries to obtain evidence in connection with investigations and prosecutions in the United States and abroad.

The mission of the Office of Special Investigations is to investigate and take legal action against anyone in the United States who incites, participates or assists in the persecution of persons based on race, religion or political beliefs.

The Narcotics and Dangerous Drugs Section's activities are primarily to prosecute and convict major drug traffickers involved in the importation, manufacturing, shipment and distribution of illicit drugs and narcotics.

The Office of Legislation is responsible for developing and supporting the Criminal Division's legislative program. The Office of Administration provides the division's administrative services through its Personnel Unit; Fiscal Unit; Mail, File and Records Unit; Procurement, Security, Safety and Space Unit; and the Information Systems Unit.

The Office of Enforcement Operations uses the most sensitive investigative tools at the department's disposal: electronic surveillance, hypnosis in the interrogation of witnesses, etc. It is also responsible for the authorization of witness immunity and witness relocation. This office supervises all aspects of the Witness Security Program for the Criminal Division and oversees all electronic and consensual monitoring efforts pursued within the federal justice system.

The Asset Forfeiture Office reduces criminal activity by depriving criminals of the profits obtained from their illegal acts.

The Executive Office for U.S. Attorneys provides general executive assistance and nonlitigative oversight to the ninety-four offices of the U.S. Attorneys. Under this office function the Office of Administration and Review, the Office of Legal Education, the Office of Legal Services, the Office of Management Information Systems and Support, the Law Enforcement Coordinating Committee Staff and the U.S. Attorneys, who are the chief law enforcement representatives of the attorney general.

The Executive Office for U.S. Trustees supervises the administration of all cases filed under chapters 7, 11 and 13 of Title I of the Bankruptcy Reform Act.

The Bureau of Prisons has forty-seven institutions and is responsible for the operation of federal correctional facilities and their inmates.

The Office of Justice Programs works to improve the treatment of victims of crime and family violence and administers the Crime Victims Fund.

The Bureau of Justice Assistance administers state and local justice assistance programs to improve justice system operations.

The Bureau of Justice Statistics collects, analyzes, publishes and disseminates statistical information on crime, victims and criminal offenders as well as on the operations of justice systems at all levels of government.

The National Institute of Justice is the primary federal sponsor of research on crime and justice.

The Office of Juvenile Justice and Delinquency Prevention develops and implements programs to respond to the mandate of the 1984 Missing Children's Assistance Act.

The Executive Office for Immigration Review is responsible for the ongoing improvement of the immigration adjudication process. It is independent of the Immigration and Naturalization Service, which is responsible for the enforcement of immigration laws. This office contains the Board of Immigration Appeals and the Office of the Chief Immigration Judge.

The Antitrust Division investigates, detects and prosecutes price fixing and related restraints of trade.

The Civil Division has four basic missions: to defend or assert programs and initiatives of the federal government, including the president's foreign and domestic policies; to bring suit and collect monies owed the United States by delinquent debtors and to recover sums lost to government by waste, fraud and corruption; to defend government, officers and employees seeking damages from the U.S. Treasury or from its employees, personally; and to enforce federal consumer protection laws, the nation's immigration laws and other program initiatives.

The Civil Rights Division enforces eight major civil rights sections prohibiting discrimination in education, employment, credit, housing, public accommodations and facilities, voting and certain federally funded and conducted programs, along with identifying and eliminating sexual discrimination.

The Tax Division is responsible for representing the United States and its officers in all litigation arising under the internal revenue laws other than proceedings in the U.S. Tax Court. This division is involved in both civil and criminal proceedings at the trial and appellate levels. Its principal client is the Internal Revenue Service, but it also represents other federal departments and agencies in matters involving immunity from state and local taxes.

The Land and Natural Resources Division represents the United States, its agencies and its officers in matters relating to environmental quality, natural resources, public lands, Indian lands and native claims, and wildlife and fishery resources. Its clients include the departments of agriculture, commerce, defense, energy, interior and transportation, and the Environmental Protection Agency.

The Immigration and Naturalization Service carries out federal laws, regulations and policies governing immigration, naturalization, refugees and asylum. It is responsible for all activities related to the temporary or permanent admission of people into the United States and the exclusion of illegal entries and residents. Its Enforcement Division is primarily its Border Patrol, whose agents patrol U.S. borders and detain and deport illegal aliens. This office also is heavily involved in marriage frauds, smuggling, narcotics and black-market-baby operations from foreign countries. The INS also maintains an Intelligence Office, which is heavily involved in U.S. and Asian organized crime and Mexico's illegal migration; a data base on potential and alien terrorists; a data base on smugglers, perpetrators of fraud and other immigration violators. In addition, it cooperates with other agencies that are also involved in national antidrug efforts.

INTERPOL, U.S. NATIONAL CENTRAL BUREAU

USNCB is the U.S. liaison to 142 nation members and to the General Secretariat of the International Criminal Police Organization, headquartered in Paris, France. The goal of USNCB and INTERPOL is to provide mutual assistance between international law enforcement authorities in the prevention and suppression of international crime. INTERPOL's constitution prohibits intervention and investigation by its members of matters concerning any military, religious, racial or political character.

FEDERAL BUREAU OF INVESTIGATION

The primary function of the FBI is to investigate violations of certain federal statutes and to collect evidence in cases in which the United States may be an interested party. The FBI also performs other duties specifically imposed by law or presidential directive and conducts a number of service activities for other law enforcement agencies. In the field of organized crime, the FBI seeks to eradicate large-scale intrastate gambling, loansharking, gangland infiltration of legitimate business and interstate travel in aid of racketeering. Other statutes often applied are those dealing with pornography, arson-for-hire, extortion, thefts from interstate shipments and labor racketeering.

It costs approximately $1 billion to operate the FBI and its fifty-eight field offices throughout the United States and Puerto Rico in a given year. The office employs more than twenty-one thousand employees, nine thousand of whom are special agents. Although the FBI has authority to operate only in the United States and its possessions, certain grants of Congress occasionally give the bureau jurisdiction on the high seas. The FBI also has foreign counterintelligence responsibilities inside the United States and its possessions. In addition to working with other local and federal law enforcement agencies, the FBI maintains a master fingerprint identification center and the Criminalistics Laboratory Information System (CLIS). CLIS is a communications network for local, state and federal agencies, which allows them to access scientific reference information contained on the CLIS data base. The CLIS is currently composed of a general rifling characteristics file, which is used to identify the manufacturer and type of weapon that may have been used to fire a bullet or cartridge.

The FBI has jurisdiction in crimes against U.S. citizens in foreign countries. For example, if a terrorist murders a U.S. citizen elsewhere, the FBI may investigate and bring the defendant to trial in the United States.

At its headquarters in Washington, D.C., the FBI also maintains the following types of files, primarily of a technical nature, which are helpful in criminal investigations by city, state and federal agencies:

Anonymous Letters File
Bank Robbery Note File
Hair and Fiber Reference File
National Automotive Altered Number File
National Automotive Paint File
National Fraudulent Check File
National Stolen Property File

These files contain copies of or records about evidence as well as reference samples for comparison purposes.

Fingerprint and Index Files

The subject matter and names of individuals and organizations are indexed at FBI headquarters in alphabetical order. At the end of 1986 there were more than 178 million fingerprints on file. Ninety-two million contain criminal history data, and 84 million civil print identifications cover federal employees, alien registration, military personnel and individuals requesting their prints be on file for identification purposes.

The fingerprint section is broken down into three divisions: identification of arrests and applications, posting of wanted and parole/probation notices and examination of physical evidence of latent prints for court testimony.

The FBI maintains records of missing persons and handles identification of amnesia victims and deceased persons.

In addition to the FBI's automated data processing system for accounting, statistical, administrative and investigative control operations, in 1967 it instituted the Automated Identification Division System (AIDS). Today the advanced phase three of that system, which can process the required information within twenty-four hours, is in full operation. Although computer data systems do most of the work, the final identification is made by an analyst within the FBI.

FBI Case Classifications

Admiralty Matters
Alien Property Custodian Matters
Antiracketeering
Antitrust
Applications for Executive Clemency and Pardon
Assaulting a Federal Officer
Assaulting the President of the United States
Automobile Information Disclosure Act
Bank Robbery, Burglary and Larceny
Bills of Lading Act
Bond Default
Bribery and Conflict of Interest
Civil Rights Act of 1964
Contempt of Court
Contract Settlement Act
Copyright Matters
Court of Claims
Crime Aboard Aircraft
Crimes on the High Seas

Desertion, Harboring Deserter, Enticing to Desert
Destruction of Aircraft
Election Laws
Escaped Federal Prisoners, Parole, Probation and Conditional
  Release Violations
Extortion
False Entries in the Records of Interstate Carriers
Falsely Claiming Citizenship
Federal Firearms Act
Federal Housing Administration Matters
Federal Lending and Insurance Agencies
Federal Tort Claims Act
Federal Train Wreck Statute
Foreign Police Cooperation
Fraud Against the Government
Government and Indian Reservation Matters
Harboring Fugitives
Illegal Use of Railroad Pass
Illegal Wearing of Uniforms
Impersonation
Interstate Transmission of Wagering Information in Aid of
  Racketeering, Fireworks, Gambling Devices, Lottery Tickets,
  Obscene Matter, Stolen Cattle, Stolen Motor Vehicles and
  Aircraft, Stolen Property, Strikebreakers, Wagering Para-
  phernalia
Irregularities in Federal Penal Institutions
Kickback Racket Act
Kidnapping
Labor-Management Relations Act
Labor-Management Reporting and Disclosure Act of 1959
Mail Fraud
Migratory Bird Act
Motor Vehicle Seat Belt Act
Narcotics
National Bank and Federal Reserve Acts—Banks, Federal
  Credit Unions and Savings and Loans
National Bankruptcy Act
Obstruction of Justice

Passports and Visas
Perjury
Railway Labor Act
Red Cross Act
Renegotiation Act
Selective Service Act of 1948
Sports Bribery
Switchblade Knife Act
Theft From Interstate Shipment
Theft or Embezzlement of Government Property
Unauthorized Publication or Use of Communications
Unlawful Flight to Avoid Prosecution, Confinement or the Giving of Testimony
Veterans Administration Matters
Welfare and Pension Plans Disclosure Act

U.S. MARSHAL'S SERVICE

The USMS is the nation's oldest federal law enforcement agency. The U.S. Marshal is a presidentially appointed agent of the Department of Justice whose activities are supervised and coordinated by the director of the U.S. Marshal's Service under the authority of the attorney general. Almost every federal law enforcement initiative involves the USMS, including the custody, care and transportation of federal offenders, and the tracking and apprehension of federal criminals who jump bail, violate parole and escape prison.

USMS is also responsible for the protection of the courts, judges, attorneys and witnesses, through the Federal Witness Protection and Relocation Program; enforcement of court orders; and management of assets seized or forfeited as a result of their acquisition from profits of certain criminal activities. Also included in the USMS's duties are the receipt and processing of federal prisoners, the custody of unsentenced federal prisoners and the apprehension of fugitives wanted by foreign nations, who are believed to be in the United States. This service accepts custody and escorts extradited or expulsed prisoners from foreign nations to the United States.

USMS provides security assistance to the Department of Defense and the air force during the movement of missiles between military facilities. The Missile Escort program is part of USMS's Special Operations Group (SOG), which also includes the USMS Air Operations Branch. This branch responds to emergency situations, such as civil disturbances, terrorist incidents or hostage situations where there is a violation of federal law or where federal property is endangered.

IMMIGRATION AND NATURALIZATION SERVICE

Special Agents of the INS plan and conduct investigations of persons and events subject to the administrative and criminal provisions of the Immigration and Nationality Act and other statutes under the U.S. code. These officers carry firearms, make arrests, prepare investigative reports, present cases to the U.S. Attorney for prosecution and give testimony in judicial and administrative proceedings. Special Agents' missions are diverse, ranging from background studies to determine an alien's eligibility for benefits under the Immigration and Nationality Act to investigations of large-scale, international organizations that smuggle aliens or perpetrate other fraudulent or criminal actions against the United States.

The INS, located in Washington, D.C., is under the supervision of the commissioner of the Immigration and Naturalization Service, its chief executive officer. The commissioner is assisted by a deputy commissioner; an executive assistant; general counsel; associate commissioners for enforcement, examinations, management and operations support; the assistant commissioners; and other staff members.

Field Service

The Field Service comprises four regions. Within each region are district offices headed by district directors. Border Patrol functions are administered by border patrol sectors within each region, supervised by chief patrol agents. Each district is divided into sections to facilitate operations. The Investigations Section investigates aliens and citizens whose actions fall within the jurisdiction of the INS and make arrests in the enforcement of the act and other laws related to the immigration and naturalization of aliens.

The Examinations Section adjudicates various petitions submitted for alien benefits and inspects aliens seeking entry into the United States. The Detention and Deportation section controls the movements of aliens after they have been placed under service proceedings.

Border Patrol

The Border Patrol is a mobile, uniformed enforcement arm of the Immigration and Naturalization Service. It has thirty-seven hundred agents nationwide patrolling the northern and southern borders to detect and prevent the unlawful entry of aliens into the United States.

Over three thousand agents are assigned to the southern U.S. border with Mexico, and 150 agents are assigned to New Orleans, Miami and Puerto Rico. Three hundred agents are stationed along the Canadian border. San Diego is geographically the smallest sector, but it is the most active of all Border Patrol operations and has approximately eight hundred personnel.

U.S. Border Patrol agents perform their duties along roughly eight thousand miles of international boundaries by automobile, boat, aircraft and on foot. In some areas the Border Patrol employs horses, all-terrain motorcycles, mountain bikes and snowmobiles. Assignments are often in isolated communities and along borders often barely discernible in uninhabited deserts, canyons and mountains.

An important activity of the Border Patrol is Linewatch. This program involves the detection and apprehension of smugglers and illegal aliens at or near the land border by surveillance; following up leads; responding to electronic sensor alarms and aircraft sightings; interpreting tracks, marks and other physical evidence, and through traffic checks, intelligence and antismuggling investigations.

The Border Patrol also protects the U.S. border against narcotics and other contraband. In 1991, the Office of National Drug Control Policy designated the Border Patrol as the primary agency for narcotics interdiction between ports of entry.

For further information regarding the U.S. Border Patrol, contact the U.S. Border Patrol, U.S. Department of Justice, Immigration and Naturalization Service, 425 I Street, N.W., Washington, D.C. 20536, telephone (202) 514-3073.

Investigations Program

Under the direction of the deputy commissioner and the associate commissioner, the assistant commissioner for Investigations is responsible for the guidance, management and direction of the Investigations Program. Service investigative activities not under the assistant commissioner for Investigations are the Anti-Smuggling Unit and the Employer and Labor Relations Unit. The Anti-Smuggling Unit is under the direction of the associate commissioner for Enforcement implemented by Border Patrol Sectors. The assistant commissioner for Employer and Labor Relations is charged with education of employer sanctions provisions of the Immigration Reform and Control Act of 1986 and the administration of the Systematic Alien Verification Entitlement Program. Special agents of the INS are trained at the Federal Law Enforcement Training Center (FLETC) and at the Immigration Officer Academy for basic training, both at Glynco, Georgia.

DRUG ENFORCEMENT AGENCY

The primary mission of the DEA is to enforce the drug laws and regulations of the United States. It is charged with investigating those organizations involved in the illegal growing, manufacturing and distribution of controlled substances in the United States, along with regulating those individuals and companies who are legitimate handlers or manufacturers of controlled substances. The DEA is divided into enforcement and regulatory operations. Criminal investigations are handled by special agents empowered to make arrests, perform search-and-seizures and carry firearms. Regulatory matters are handled by division investigators.

DEA special agents conduct criminal investigations and criminal surveillance, and infiltrate, identify, confiscate and arrest violators in criminal drug activities. They prepare evidence, write reports, testify and cooperate with municipal, state and federal law enforcement organizations. The DEA maintains its own training academy, sharing facilities on the FBI's training grounds in Quantico, Virginia.

BUREAU OF ALCOHOL, TOBACCO AND FIREARMS

The Bureau of Alcohol, Tobacco and Firearms (ATF) is headquartered in Washington, D.C. The ATF has a multimission responsibility to enforce federal laws on firearms, explosives, arson, alcohol and cigarette smuggling. With the alarming rise in criminal activities, terrorism and international conflicts, arms smuggling has become an ATF priority. In addition to these responsibilities, the ATF is charged with regulating the alcohol, tobacco, firearms and explosives industries. Special agents of the ATF undergo eight weeks of training in general law enforcement and investigative techniques at the Criminal Investigative School, Federal Law Enforcement Training Center in Glynco, Georgia.

Investigative ATF agents are involved in surveillance, participate in raids, interview suspects and witnesses, obtain search warrants seeking physical evidence and make arrests. Team composition and support in criminal bombings or arson incidents call for four teams, each composed of ten special agents, a forensic chemist and an explosives expert from ATF's explosives technology branch. Supported by technical, scientific, legal and intelligence sources, they conduct the investigation, seek explosive tracings, perform lab analysis and case link analysis, provide legal counsel and work in device reconstruction and classification.

CUSTOMS SERVICE SPECIAL INVESTIGATIVE DIVISION

Of the many missions it is responsible for, the U.S. Customs Service is empowered to prevent frauds and smuggling, to intercept illegal high technology exports, to cooperate with other federal agencies in suppressing illegal narcotics and pornography and to enforce some four hundred provisions of the law on behalf of forty federal agencies. This division is the principal border enforcement agency of the United States. Among its many units, the U.S. Customs maintains: an Organized Crime Strike Force; a National Patrimony Unit to protect national antiquities; a Steroid Investigative Unit; a Child Pornography and Protection Unit; currency investigations primarily with respect to the laundering of currency; Operation Exodus, which tightens controls on illegal exports; Technology Investigations; and an Extraterritorial Investigative Group.

The U.S. Customs Service also conducts tactical operations involved in the smuggling of narcotics and maintains the customs office of Aviation Operations, an airborne detection unit. Its Enforcement Support section includes communications security, a research and development division for electronic surveillance and detection equipment, boat detection systems and border surveillance systems. The U.S. Customs Service Intelligence Program supports all major operational, inspection and enforcement priorities for collection, analysis and dissemination.

INTERNAL REVENUE SERVICE CRIMINAL INVESTIGATIONS

The IRS maintains an Office of Criminal Investigations and the Automated Criminal Investigations Project Office under an assistant commissioner, who serves as head of Criminal Investigations. The mission of Criminal Investigations is to encourage the highest possible voluntary compliance with IRS laws by conducting quality investigations and recommending criminal prosecution when warranted. Criminal Investigation special agents target their efforts against organized crime, narcotics traffickers, money laundering, questionable refund schemes, tax shelters and other domestic and international violations.

The Automated Criminal Investigations System is an extensive automation effort whose primary purpose is to improve the efficiency and effectiveness of all Criminal Investigation employees.

The IRS works closely with other federal agencies in combating organized crime through the Department of Justice Strike Force. The IRS is also a significant participant in the Organized Crime Drug Enforcement Task Force. In addition, the IRS investigates cases not connected to any special emphasis of organized crime, narcotics trafficking, etc., such as "skimming" and abusive tax shelters.

COAST GUARD

The U.S. Coast Guard is assigned the task of enforcing all applicable federal laws on the high seas and waters subject to U.S. jurisdiction. This includes the interdiction of illegal drugs and migrants, and the enforcement of U.S. Economic Zone laws and regulations extending two hundred miles off the United States and territorial waters, as well as of a myriad of laws and regulations on safety issues. At times, Coast Guard Law Enforcement Detachments (LEDETS) serve aboard navy vessels and perform the actual boarding and arrest.

POSTAL INSPECTION SERVICE

The Postal Inspection Service, the law enforcement arm of the U.S. Postal Service, is headed by the chief postal inspector, who oversees three divisions: Mail Investigations, Financial Investigations and Administrative Investigations. Postal inspectors are responsible for protecting the mail, postal facilities and employees from criminal attack and for protecting the American public from mail fraud, pornography and other postal-related crimes.

Investigations are conducted into internal crimes such as mail theft, mistreatment, financial, compensation abuses and various miscellaneous internal crimes. In the area of external postal crimes, investigations are conducted into mail theft, burglaries, robberies, mail fraud and prohibited mailings such as pornography, narcotics and bomb and explosive materials sent through the mail. The Postal Inspection Service maintains its own fully equipped, state-of-the-art crime laboratories, which investigate questioned and known documents, fingerprints, audiotapes, firearms, tools and tool marks, forensic photography, suspected controlled substances, poisons and biological and unknown substances.

In the 1970s, the Postal Inspection Service established the Office of Security, a uniformed security force designed to patrol major postal facilities, escort shipments of valuable mail and provide security for postal employees. The U.S. Postal Inspector's Office is our country's oldest law enforcement agency. Inspectors and investigative agents possess statutory power of arrest, apprehend violators and work closely with U.S. Attorneys in prosecuting cases in court.

There are approximately nineteen hundred postal inspectors in the United States and Puerto Rico who also participate with Department of Justice national strike force teams. Postal inspector trainees undergo an eleven-week basic training course in firearms, legal matters, search-and-seizure, arrest, court procedures and postal operations, as well as a detailed study of federal laws pertaining to their jurisdiction.

FEDERAL AIR MARSHALS

Working under the Federal Aviation Administration, Federal Air Marshals (FAMs), also known as sky marshals, are assigned to U.S. air carriers on selected flights operating in sensitive or threatened areas around the world. The enactment of Public Law 99-83 established a basis for the FAM program. Authorized by the secretary of transportation and with the approval of the attorney general and the secretary of state, Federal Air Marshals are empowered to carry firearms and to make arrests without warrants if they have reasonable grounds to believe the person to be arrested has committed a felony.

FAMs are recruited as civilian aviation security specialists (special agents) and when not on FAM missions they perform a variety of aviation security functions. As FAMs, they receive high intensity, specialized law enforcement training at the Federal Law Enforcement Training Center.

BUREAU OF LAND MANAGEMENT

The Bureau of Land Management (BLM) is the caretaker of more than three hundred million square miles of public land. It is charged by law to manage and protect these vast resources, including timber, minerals, livestock, forage, historic artifacts and wild horses. BLM has highly trained special agents and uniformed rangers to enforce applicable laws on federal land and to work closely with federal and state agencies and sheriff's departments.

BLM special agents are responsible for enforcing federal laws and regulations relating to public lands and resources, and they conduct criminal investigations and arrest violators. BLM special agents investigate numerous cases of archaeological thefts of cultural artifacts, pottery, ornaments and human remains. Treating free-roaming or adopted wild horses and burros in an inhumane manner, selling them to slaughterhouses or other misuse is a federal violation investigated by BLM special agents, as are destruction, vandalism or pollution of streams and lakes, starting fires and growing marijuana.

Rangers who drive marked patrol vehicles are a law enforcement arm of BLM. Rangers enforce the laws, conduct search-and-rescue operations, eliminate hazards and investigate accidents.

DEFENSE CRIMINAL INVESTIGATIVE SERVICE

The Defense Criminal Investigative Service (DCIS) is responsible for criminal investigations. Working in conjunction with the military's Criminal Investigation Division, Office of Special Investigations and Naval Investigative Service, this organization is involved in combating and prosecuting fraudulent acts perpetrated against the U.S. Department of Defense, i.e., product substitution, overcharging, false charges, etc. Investigators working for DCIS are called special agents and are under the supervision of the director of DCIS, who is also the assistant inspector general for investigations.

DEFENSE INVESTIGATIVE SERVICE

Headquartered in Washington, D.C., and supervised by the director of DIS, this organization and its special agents are responsible for investigating personnel for security clearances, investigating the unauthorized disclosure of classified government information and administering industrial security programs for the Department of Defense and eighteen other government agencies.

ARMY CRIMINAL INVESTIGATIVE COMMAND

Often referred to as the Criminal Investigation Division (CID), this section of the army is an investigative, fact-finding agency. Although CID has arrest powers, it does not prosecute. Instead it turns its suspects and investigation reports over to the proper branch of service for prosecution.

Trained by the army at the FBI Academy in Quantico, Virginia, and often at Great Britain's Scotland Yard, the CID and its agents conduct criminal investigations involving both military and civilian personnel on military bases. Additional responsibilities include crime prevention surveys and protective services to the secretary of defense; chairman of the Joint Chiefs of Staff; secretary of the army; and army chief of staff. CID also plays an important role in terrorism counteraction, hostage negotiations, supplying protective services, security vulnerability assessments, criminal information collection, hostage negotiation and narcotics investigations.

CID operates three crime laboratories and the Army Crime Records Center and maintains liaison with other police and investigative agencies. CID agents, who normally work in civilian clothes, are noncommissioned officers.

NAVAL INVESTIGATIVE SERVICE

NIS special agents conduct criminal, narcotics and fraud investigations; counterintelligence and undercover operations; and hostage negotiations. They also provide protective services and investigate infractions of military law governing naval personnel and civilians contracted or employed by the navy or the marine corps. NIS is part of the Naval Security and Investigative Command (NSIC), headquartered in Washington, D.C., and commanded by a rear admiral who reports to the secretary of the navy and the chief of Naval Operations.

AIR FORCE OFFICE OF SPECIAL INVESTIGATIONS

The OSI operates very much like the NIS in that it, unlike the CID, conducts counterintelligence operations. OSI special agents are trained at the OSI's academy at Bolling Field Air Force Base, Washington, D.C. Like its sister agencies, OSI conducts criminal investigations and serves as a fact-finding agency. Like CID, OSI maintains its own forensic laboratories and criminal records center.

MILITARY POLICE

The army military police corps is responsible for the army's law enforcement in both war and peace. In combat operations, the military police are the tactical commander's primary response force against terrorists and saboteurs. Military police provide security operations, oversee and evacuate enemy prisoners of war and provide security for armament. In peace and in war, military police officers advise and assist army commanders in establishing discipline, enforcing laws and preventing crime.

MP officers plan for the security of VIPs, military banks and hospitals, storage areas, airfields, ports, harbors, inland waterways, railroads and petroleum pipelines. When normal processes of government are disrupted, military police may be called on to help restore order. Military police conduct criminal investigations and are responsible for the humane treatment of prisoners, including POWs. The major training site for MP officers is Fort McClellan, Alabama.

OTHER FEDERAL INVESTIGATIVE AGENCIES

Central Intelligence Agency
Defense Logistics Agency
Federal Reserve Board
Fish and Game Commission
General Accounting Office
Maritime Commission
National Parks Service
Office of the Inspector General
Office of the Special Prosecutor
Securities and Exchange Commission

INTERPOL

INTERPOL is the International Criminal Police Organization. Through its 136-member nations' police forces, INTERPOL gathers and processes information and helps solve international criminal cases.

Although not based on treaty, the United Nations Economic and Social Council has granted the association status as an inter-governmental agency. It can assist in locating and interviewing witnesses, tracing weapons and vehicles, drug trafficking, money laundering, electronic funds transfer fraud and stolen art.

Organization of INTERPOL

INTERPOL has a two-tiered structure: a world headquarters establishment called the General Secretariat and a network of National Central Bureaus (NCBs), with one in each member country. The organization operates under a constitution that designates a general assembly as its governing authority. Each member nation has one vote in the general assembly. Its annual budget is around $6 million, the dues of the United States being a little over 5 percent of the total. The General Secretariat is located in a suburb of Paris but is expected to move to Lyons for expansion.

INTERPOL has three divisions. The Police Coordination Division is the central core of the organization, managing liaison with

and among the NCBs and channeling requests for assistance between countries. It manages a criminal records system with more
than 3.3 million names of criminals, case files, fingerprints, mug
shots and indexes that cover boats, ships, aircraft and other objects
used in criminal enterprises. It issues approximately one thousand
wanted notices annually, supplies over twenty thousand reports to
NCBs and transmits about eight hundred thousand radio messages.

The remaining two divisions handle administrative services
and research. The Administrative Division operates the organization's communications systems, including its police radio network,
teletype and fax systems and postal services.

The Research Division assembles and analyzes crime data of
value to member nations and the general assembly and publishes
confidential studies regarding hostage-taking, drug trafficking, car
theft, international fraud, computer crimes, counterfeiting and
forgery.

PRIVATE INVESTIGATORS

Private investigators (PIs) seldom work on murder cases. Most
PIs are employed by industry and in family and marital disputes.
However, the fictional image of the private eye has been successful
in crime and murder stories.

If writers only wrote about the actual work done by private
investigators, they would vanish from literature. However, writers
must bring some semblance of honesty and logic to their writing.

In writing about fictional private investigators, be aware of the
attitude taken by cops. Remember that PIs must have permits to
carry concealed weapons, and they are vulnerable to arrest for driving at excessive speeds, breaking and entering, assault, harassment, firing a weapon unlawfully and trespassing. When a PI investigates a case and apprehends the guilty party, the normal rules
of evidence apply.

Most private investigators work domestic cases, insurance
frauds and corporate theft. True, some ex-cops go into private investigation and have police contacts to help them out, but most
don't. Have a good reason for a PI to take the case. That's why *The*

Rockford Files worked so well. Jim Rockford was always reluctant to take on something he wasn't adept at handling. Give some validity to your story and the PI character and it won't sound like something that's been — pardon the pun — done to death. For example:

The police are sure it's an open and shut case. The PI's client claims to be innocent and has nowhere else to turn.

The police think it's a suicide but the client is sure it's murder.

There's insurance involved, and the insurance company is not satisfied with the police report.

A company suspects computer fraud but doesn't have enough evidence to go to the police.

The murder is the result of industrial sabotage and the police ask for more evidence.

The PI is personally involved.

The PI's license is threatened if he or she doesn't solve the case.

That's just a sampling of plot notions. There are hundreds more. Just try to give the PI some validity.

WHERE TO GO FROM HERE

Most of the material in this chapter came directly from the agencies mentioned. If you are writing about an agency, one way to start learning about it is to contact the agency's public affairs or public information office. Ask for general information about the agency, and try to make a personal contact, that is, get the name of the person you're talking to. That will make it easier to follow up with more specific questions later.

The following books are the stories of cops working in most of the agencies described in this chapter. Many are autobiographical, a few are historical.

Eddy, Paul, and Sara Walden. *Hunting Marco Polo: The Pursuit of the Drug Smuggler Who Couldn't Be Caught, by the Agent Who Wouldn't Quit.* Boston: Little, Brown, 1991. The dual story of a sophisticated British drug smuggler and the street cop turned DEA agent who finally caught him.

Emsley, Clive. *The English Police: A Political and Social History.*

New York: St. Martin's Press, 1991. Covers the development of police institutions in England from their beginnings to 1990.

Fletcher, Connie. *Pure Cop: Cop Talk for the Street to the Specialized Units*. New York: Villard Books, 1991. The author's sister is a cop, which is how the author got access to other cops in special units of the Chicago Police Department. Covered are the bomb squad, arson, prostitution, crime scene investigation, major accidents and hostage and barricade incidents.

Goddard, Donald. *The Insider: The FBI's Undercover "Wiseguy" Goes Public*. New York: Pocket Books, 1992. The story of one of the most dedicated undercover cops ever, including his seven years in prison to protect his cover.

Hicks, Robert. *In Pursuit of Satan: The Police and the Occult*. Buffalo, New York: Prometheus Books, 1991. Hicks, a criminologist with a master's in anthropology, takes a very skeptical look at claims of widespread Satanism. This could be a good source for a story line in which someone is unjustly accused of involvement in a cult crime.

Kirkpatrick, Sidney. *Turning the Tide: One Man Against the Meddellin Cartel*. New York: Dutton, 1991. The story of a college professor who became involved with drug dealers while on vacation in the Bahamas.

Manca, John, and Vincent Cosgrove. *Tin for Sale: My Career in Organized Crime and the NYPD*. New York: William Morrow and Co., 1991. This is the story of a (wise) guy whose family had mob connections. He became a cop but eventually got fired and ran scams for a living. It's a good look at street-level organized crime.

McDonald, Cherokee Paul. *Blue Truth: Walking the Thin Blue Line—One Cop's Story of Life in the Streets*. New York: Donald I. Fine, 1991. A former cop gives a well-written account of his ten years with the Fort Lauderdale Police Department.

McDonald, Cherokee Paul, and Allen Smith. *Under Contract: The True Account of a Cop Hired to Kill*. New York: Donald I. Fine, 1992. The story of a cop who was assigned to intercept solicitations to murder for hire and then pose as a hitman to arrest his would-be employers.

O'Neill, Hugh, Hy Hammer, and E.P. Steinberg. *Police Officer.* New York: Arco Publishing, 1989. This is a set of sample civil service tests with explanatory answer keys. The questions are mostly about what a cop should do in very plausible situations, so it gives some idea of police procedure.

Reaves, James. *Black Cops.* Philadelphia: Quantum Leap, 1991. The autobiography of a black cop who joined the Philadelphia police force in 1940 and retired in 1980, it also has profiles of other leading black cops.

Ressler, Robert, and Tom Shachtman. *Whoever Fights Monsters: My Twenty Years Hunting Serial Killers for the FBI.* New York: St. Martin's Press, 1992. The stories of a number of famous investigations by an FBI veteran.

Robins, Natalie. *Alien Ink: The FBI's War on Freedom of Expression.* A history of the agency's surveillance of writers from the Russian Revolution and World War I to the Library Awareness Program of the late 1980s.

Sabbag, Robert. *Too Tough to Die: Down and Dangerous With the U.S. Marshals.* New York: Simon & Schuster, 1992. The stories of arrests of some pretty unsavory characters. It also gives a view of the inner workings of the U.S. Marshals and some of the politics of law enforcement.

Stutman, Robert, and Richard Esposito. *Dead on Delivery: Inside the Drug Wars, Straight From the Street.* New York: Warner Books, 1992. The first author is the former head of the New York DEA office. Strong narrative.

Ulasewicz, Tony, and Stuart McKeever. *The President's Private Eye: The Journey of Detective Tony U. From N.Y.P.D. to the Nixon White House.* Westport, Connecticut: MACSAM Publishing, 1990. Chronicles the first author's years with an intelligence unit of the NYPD and his work as a private investigator, including his role in Watergate.

4

Investigations

WRITING ABOUT INVESTIGATIONS

Police work is often oversimplified in fiction. You may justify a superficial presentation by claiming you have just so much time to set the stage, begin the investigation, develop enough clues to put the investigator on the trail, get into a hot chase and catch the perpetrator. Unfortunately, writers seldom give a true insight into the criminal investigator's problems.

All cops must use the law to gain a conviction, and that means they must apprehend the criminal, and then prove the case. They must adhere to the letter of the law to protect the suspect's constitutional rights. One mistake can force the court to declare a mistrial or dismiss the accused altogether. It is essential to be aware of what the cops must contend with.

Many times the drama can be heightened by making these problems work for you. Use your creativity and ingenuity to help the investigator use the law rather than going around or above it.

You must decide what jurisdiction the crime will be committed in and whether the perpetrator will leave the scene and enter another jurisdiction. If the criminal moves from one state to another, the crime may become federal. Most agencies cooperate with one another whenever possible.

Law enforcement agencies employ a variety of equipment and technologies. Each law enforcement agency has its own table of organization, jurisdiction and operating procedures. You should check out the law enforcement agency you intend to employ.

When writing about an investigation, it is imperative to be as authentic as possible about the law enforcement agency, the officers involved in the investigation and the methods, equipment, weapons and technologies they use. If you want a cop to "not go by the book" or to go "above the law" in an investigation, you must know what "the book" and "the law" are.

Remember that cops are human beings. There are good ones and bad ones, they have personal problems, they may become frustrated and disillusioned, and much of their lives are spent with other cops and their families. They have a different outlook on life than those not involved in law enforcement.

Almost every law enforcement agency has a public affairs or public relations section, and you will find them cooperative in answering questions. Many times they will put you in touch with an officer in the area of law enforcement that you're interested in. Develop a list of contacts for further use, and send a letter of appreciation to the officer who assisted you. It will be remembered the next time you ask for help.

FUNDAMENTALS OF INVESTIGATION

In addition to solving the crime, investigators must satisfy the requirements of the prosecutor and the court. Catching the crook is not enough to achieve a conviction. The investigator must provide the prosecutor with evidence. The three objectives of any investigation are to identify the criminal, arrest the criminal and prove the criminal's guilt in court.

Identifying the Criminal

Before investigators can trace, locate and prove a criminal's guilt in court, they must first identify the criminal. This can be accomplished by a confession, although it is often necessary to support the confession with corroborative evidence. Otherwise, the confession may be denied in court, with the defense counsel charging the prosecution with obtaining the admission or confession by duress or coercion.

If no one confesses to the crime, investigators must then try to find a suspect. Identification of a suspect involves assessing circumstantial evidence, motive, opportunity, physical clues, witnesses and a pattern, or modus operandi (M.O.).

Good investigators can often determine if the crime was committed by a professional or a novice. If investigators believe a professional committed the crime, they will look for records of similar M.O.s. Criminals with similar M.O.s will be brought in for questioning.

If investigators conclude that the perpetrator is an amateur, sudden flight could betray guilt. They will look for a suspect with a motive such as anger, profit or revenge. Tipoffs, paid informers and associates of a suspect can help investigators.

Arrest

Arrest is the taking of a person into custody in a manner provided by law and holding or detaining that individual to answer a criminal or civil charge. It may be made with a warrant issued by a competent authority, or, under some circumstances, without a warrant. The following are some key concepts concerning arrest:

Admissions: In cases where conspiracy is charged, the admission of one of the accused may become, by reason of the other proof in the case, admissible against the other. By themselves and without other proof, however, admissions are not admissible against the other. But if the proof shows the existence of the conspiracy, statements made by one of the parties as to details of the charged crime become admissible against the other. There is no distinction between civil and criminal cases in respect to the use of admissions.

Authorized arrest in unauthorized manner: The fact that an authorized arrest is made in an unauthorized manner may render the officer or arresting person liable, but it will not affect the state's right to detain the accused if lawful cause exists.

Complaint: A charge proffered before a magistrate stating that a person (known or unknown) has committed a specific offense, so that a prosecution may begin. It is necessary that a proper complaint under oath be brought before the magistrate, who determines if a crime has been committed and whether there is probable cause to suspect the accused.

Confession: When a confession is used against an accused person, the whole confession must be introduced. A confession, like an admission, is always open to explanation by the person against whom it is used.

Confession while intoxicated: Confessions made by the accused when under the influence of any intoxicating substance are inadmissible. Any condition that renders a person temporarily incompetent renders that individual's statements valueless.

Duty after arrest: After making an arrest, the officer must take the prisoner before a magistrate for examination without unnecessary delay. A private person has the option of delivering the prisoner to an officer instead of the magistrate.

Issuance of a warrant: In order to authorize the issuance of a warrant before indictment, a complaint must be made before a magistrate showing that a crime has been committed and there is good cause to suspect the accused. After indictment, the usual practice is to issue a bench warrant. An arrest under an insufficient warrant, or without any warrant if one is necessary, is illegal.

Lawful arrest by private person: Private persons may make an arrest when the person to be arrested has committed a breach of the peace or a felony in their presence, or when a felony has been committed and there are reasonable grounds to believe that the person to be arrested has committed it. A private person, when making an arrest, shall inform the person to be arrested of the intent to arrest and the cause of the arrest, unless the person to be arrested is then committing the offense; is pursued after its commission or after an escape; or forcibly resists before the person making the arrest has opportunity to so inform.

Lawful arrest by officer without warrant: A peace officer may, without a warrant, arrest a person when the person to be arrested has committed a felony or misdemeanor in the officer's presence. A warrantless arrest may also be made if a felony has been committed and the officer has reasonable grounds to believe that the person to be arrested has committed it. When making an arrest without a warrant, the officer informs the person arrested of the officer's authority and the cause of the arrest, unless the person to be arrested is then committing the offense; is pursued after its commission or after an escape; or forcibly resists before the officer has opportunity to so inform.

Lawful arrest by officer with a warrant: When making an arrest with a warrant, officers shall inform the persons to be arrested of the cause of the arrest and that a warrant has been issued for their arrest, except when the subjects to be arrested flee or forcibly resist before the officers have opportunity to so inform. The officers need not have the warrant in their possession at the time of the arrest, but after the arrest the warrant shall be produced as soon as possible.

Reasonable cause, probable cause: Reasonable cause or probable cause exist when: (1) the persons to be arrested resemble those accused and fail to identify themselves as persons who did not commit the felony; (2) the persons' movements or actions are similar to those of the suspects; (3) it becomes known that the persons to be arrested committed a felony or were in the company of the perpetrator before or after commission of same; or (4) the persons to be arrested have proceeds of the felony in their possession or have been seen leaving the place where the felony was committed.

Rights and liabilities of parties to a lawful arrest: If an arrest is authorized and is attempted or made in a proper manner, the officer or private person making it merely performs a duty, and that person incurs no liability. If the persons to be arrested resist, they are criminally liable for the resistance. If the resistance involves force, the persons are civilly and criminally liable for assault and battery. If the individuals, or someone assisting them in resisting, kill the person making the arrest, the charge is murder. If persons unlawfully depart from custody after having been legally arrested, they are guilty of a misdemeanor known as escape. If the persons break from or forcibly escape from the place of imprisonment, they are guilty of prison breach, which is either a misdemeanor or a felony, depending on circumstances. If third persons interfere in aid of the persons to be arrested, the interference is a misdemeanor or a felony, and if they use force, they are also guilty of assault and battery. If the force used results in the killing of the person attempting to make the arrest, they are guilty of murder. If they procure the escape of the persons after their arrest, they are guilty of rescue, which can be either a misdemeanor or a felony.

Rights and liabilities of parties to an unlawful arrest: If an arrest or attempt to arrest is illegal, either because there is no authority to arrest or because the arrest is made in an unlawful manner (for instance, by the use of unnecessary violence), the officer or private person arresting, with or without a warrant, is guilty of false imprisonment or of assault and battery or both, and is civilly and criminally liable. An unlawful attempt to arrest or a false imprisonment may be lawfully resisted by any necessary force short of taking life or inflicting grievous bodily harm. Even when life is taken in resisting an unlawful arrest, the attempt to arrest or the false imprisonment is generally deemed sufficient provocation to reduce the charge to manslaughter. Within certain limits, third persons, particularly relatives, may interfere to prevent an unlawful arrest or imprisonment.

Warrant: A warrant is a writ issued by an authorized magistrate to an officer, requiring the officer to arrest the offenders or suspects therein named, and bring them before a proper magistrate to be dealt with according to law.

Proving Guilt in Court

Once an investigator has a suspect, the investigator must determine what means are available to seek more evidence, such as stakeouts and electronic surveillance equipment.

The suspect's connection to the crime must be firmly established. The investigator must be able to prove motive, opportunity, the elements of the offense and intent. In violent crimes, malice must be proved, showing intent to do injury. Legal malice doesn't necessarily imply animosity or hate.

The First Twenty-Four Hours

The first twenty-four hours following a crime are the most important. During this period clues and evidence are less likely to be disturbed and witnesses' recollections are fresh. If a description or clues implicate a suspect, the trail will be easier to follow. Roadblocks can be set and airports, train stations and bus depots can be watched. The sooner a suspect has been identified, the sooner associates, family or friends can be contacted.

THE SCENE OF THE CRIME

The crime scene is where the investigator has the best chance to determine how the crime was committed and to find evidence that can point to a suspect.

The first officer on the scene should note the time and as many elements of the crime scene as possible without touching anything. These may include sounds, odors, the amount of light present, whether doors and windows are open or shut and witnesses present. Above all, the first officer should make sure nothing is disturbed.

The area should be cordoned off to keep family, friends and curiosity seekers away from the scene. The first officer on the scene should make immediate radio contact with the appropriate section of the department (burglary or homicide, for example). For a homicide, the coroner or the medical examiner should also be called.

If a suspect is discovered by the first officer on the scene, the officer should attempt to apprehend the suspect. While awaiting superiors or the investigator who will take charge of the case, the first officer on the scene must also get the names of witnesses, keep witnesses separated until they are questioned and protect the crime scene from disturbance.

The six most important questions the officer in charge of the investigation must try to answer are: who, what, where, when, why and how. The primary reasons for visiting a crime scene are to:

Attempt to reconstruct exactly what happened.

Establish a motive for the crime.

Attempt to discover a suspect.
Discover clues that can lead to the identification of both the
    victim and the suspect.
Find evidence to be used in a court.

To accomplish these goals, the investigator must always be
concerned that the crime scene remain as it was discovered. Once
something has been moved or touched, it can never again be as it
was. The investigator should enter the crime scene with caution,
bearing in mind that there can be trace or impression evidence all
around the scene. If the victim has been shot, knifed or beaten to
death, the investigator needs to pay particular attention to any
blood spatterings.

Weapons and other evidence generally should not be bagged
in plastic bags; moisture gathering in the bag could affect the evidence. Paper bags are better.

Nothing at the scene should be overlooked, no matter how mi-
nute it is, and the investigator should always take copious notes. In
a homicide scene, no one should move the body until the medical
examiner gives permission.

Criminalists are responsible for collecting and transporting
trace and imprint evidence to the police lab for testing. Crime scene
photographs should be taken, and sketches should be made of the
victim and the scene.

Witnesses must be questioned separately. Reporters must not
be given all information to avoid informing the perpetrator about
every discovery at the crime scene. Those individuals important
to the on-scene investigation, depending on the crime committed,
might include any of the following:

Arson investigators
Crime scene artist
Crime scene still photographer
Criminalist
District attorney
Forensic psychologist
Forensic technician
Homicide investigator
Medical examiner

Print specialist
Videotaping specialist

Measurements, still photos and videotaping are essential in the processing of a crime-scene. Outdoor crime scenes require special care because impression prints could easily be destroyed. Brush and twigs might contain blood samples, hair and fibers. In a homicide, it is essential to determine whether the remains have been touched by animals or insects. Investigators should look carefully for marks, scratches, traces, stains and weapons. When the crime scene is a vehicle, both the inside and the outside of the vehicle must be carefully scrutinized, along with the surrounding area.

Determining the time of death is very important because it can affect a suspect's alibi. The medical examiner can determine time of death by taking the victim's liver temperature.

Scene of the Crime Checklist

Age of victim
Background on victim
Blood spatterings
Condition of crime scene
Condition of victim's clothing
Contents of closets, drawers, furniture
Description of assailant(s)
Documents
Employment
Family and friends of victim
Interrogation of witnesses
Letters, notebooks, etc.
Location of offense
Marital status
Medical examination of victim
Motive
Persons seen prior to offense
Photographs, mementos
Physical, trace and impression evidence
Places victim visited prior to crime
Position of victim

Previous assaults on victim, if any
Reading material, news clips
Resistance offered by victim
Signs of a fight
Suspects
Time of day
Weapon
Wills, insurance policies
Wounds on victim

For a more complete discussion of investigation at the scene of the crime, see Anne Wingate's book, listed in the last section of this chapter.

SOURCES TO INVESTIGATE

In writing a detective novel, screenplay or teleplay, investigators can't have clues just dropping into their laps. Some clues or leads are usually discovered at the scene of the crime, but the writer must make the investigator work for more clues. How does your investigator go about it? Here are some of the people your investigator might talk to and some possible places and things that can be checked out:

People
Attorney
Auto mechanic
Banker
Bartender
Bookie
Cabdriver
Coworker
Doorman
Family members
Former schoolmate
Former spouse or lover
Friends of victim or suspect

Gardener
Maid
Poolman
Religious leader
Secretary
Stockbroker
Street informants
Switchboard operator
Teacher or college professor
Travel agent
Waiter or waitress

Places and Things

Airlines
Appointment pad
Article missing from normal place
Awards, plaques
Bank accounts
Bills
Business cards
Checkbook
Cigarette and cigar butts
Clothing labels, cleaning marks
Country club
Diary
Files and records
Garage
Home
Home safe
Hotels
I.O.U.s
Key ring
Legal papers
Lockers
Luggage stickers, tags
Mail
Medallions, religious medals

Medications
Membership cards
Memoirs
Mismatches
Newspaper morgue
Office
Old letters
Old shopping lists
Papers in wastebasket
Parking tickets
Passport
Personal effects
Photographs
Police records
Possible hiding places
Receipts
School class book
Signet ring
Signs of a visitor
Stock certificates, bonds
Storage
Strange markings, symbols
Telephone and address book
Telephone answering service or recorder
Telephone bill
Threatening letters
Unfinished correspondence
Unopened packages
Vehicle
Yacht club

MISSING PERSONS

A missing person is not the same as a wanted person. A wanted person is sought by the police in connection with a crime. A missing person is someone:

Missing for more than twenty-four hours.

Missing less than twenty-four hours who is under the age of
   eighteen.
Who has disappeared without any apparent reason.
Who is handicapped or impaired.

Although the police department's Missing Persons Bureau will
attempt to locate a juvenile runaway, their primary concern is
whether or not the subject has involuntarily disappeared. The same
applies to adults, except those who are reported missing and are
not in full possession of their faculties. Determining the identity of
a Jane Doe or a John Doe, the names given to unidentified female
and male corpses, is also a responsibility of the Missing Persons
Bureau.
Crimes usually associated with missing persons are kidnap-
ping and homicide. Suicide must also be considered.
Those attempting to locate a missing person should learn all
they can about:
Access to funds
Addictions
Business and professional skills
Educational background
Family history
Hobbies and interests
Medical history
Personal relationships
Physical description
Romantic involvements
Sexual habits

STEPS IN IDENTIFYING A BODY

Check Missing Persons records.
Check fingerprints locally and send to state identification bu-
   reau and FBI.
Distribute photographs to TV and newspapers.
Identify clothing markings, labels, etc.
Examine remains for birthmarks, tattoos, scars.
Make impressions of teeth for possible dental identification.

Take X rays to determine any illness, broken bones or surgery. Determine whether drugs or poisons are present, and the last food ingested.

Identification Sources

Albums
Auto licenses
Bank books
Bills and invoices
Biographies
Birth certificates
Birthmarks
Books
Business cards
Charge accounts
Checks
Church membership
Clothing tags
Club membership
College records
Court records
Credit cards
Criminal records
Dental records
Eyeglasses and case
Family Bible
Fingerprint records
Hearing aid
I.D. bracelets
Inscriptions
Laundry and dry cleaning marks
Matchbooks
Medical records
Military records
Mortuary records
Office records
Passport records

Real estate records
Repair receipts
Sales slips
School records
Social Security records
Voting records
Welfare records

SURVEILLANCE

One of the most important elements of police work is surveillance: shadowing, tailing, photographing or listening in on a suspect. Police officers and investigators conduct surveillance to detect criminal activity, prevent crime and discover information about accomplices, witnesses and the location of evidence.

Tailing

Sometimes tailing is used to learn the habits, contacts and associates of the suspect. Other uses are when the suspect must be followed despite being aware of the tail, or when a witness is being protected.

Tailing might be done by one individual or by teams alternating at various points. Tailing is done on foot, in a vehicle or vehicles, by airplane or helicopter and through various forms of electronic surveillance.

Telephone Taps

Telephone tapping is probably the easiest form of electronic eavesdropping because it takes no special skill and can be done with common sense and a dime-store screwdriver. A court order is required to authorize a tap.

Tapping can be done with a pickup device that is not connected to the telephone, a direct tap that is installed inside the instrument itself or a tap between the instrument and the telephone exchange. A wireless FM or VHF radio receiver can also be used. Bugs vary in size, some being as small as a microchip.

All of these means can be fed into a simple tape recorder. The range of a tap wired into the instrument is naturally limited to the length of the connecting wires and can usually be detected by a physical search of the premises. A bug wired in the room is also limited to the length of the wire because its microphone is connected to the recorder by wire. This method requires a bit more skill to put in place; however, the sound that is reproduced is of much better quality.

A wireless tap has a range, depending on the transmitter, of one hundred yards to three miles. It is a simple device to install, but it can be detected.

A combined telephone tap and room bug is unique because it can pick up the conversation on the phone and in the room as well. Only a physical search can reveal it.

Electronic Surveillance Equipment

Bumper beepers
Decoder
Electronic stethoscope
Jammer
Monitor
Parabolic microphone
Phone tap
Pocket bug
Receivers
Recorder
Rifle microphone
Room bug
Scrambler
Snake electronic keyhole listener
Tap detectors
Transmitter
Wall listeners

Other Surveillance Techniques

Nightscope
Photographic

Telescopic
Undercover
Videotaping

FORENSIC SCIENCES

Over the last century the deductive processes of Sherlock Holmes have been replaced with highly skilled technicians and criminalists. Modern forensic labs in major cities cover all areas of crime. Forensic sciences include the following:

Firearms deals with bullet comparisons, tool mark examinations, gun makes and serial numbers restoration.

Questioned Documents deals with the analysis of written documents or those from a dubious source, including bad checks, forgeries, typewriter and computer analysis and indented writings.

Identification is involved in fingerprint comparison and field work, including the collection of latent prints on various surfaces using chemical and mechanical means.

Physical Evidence works on comparison of hair and fiber evidence, shoe prints, tire prints, physical matches, arson and explosives and gunshot residue analysis.

Serology deals with identification and subsequent grouping of blood and other body fluids.

Narcotics analyzes bulk narcotics evidence.

Toxicology analyzes drugs and their metabolites in blood and urine.

Polygraph handles administration and interpretation of the polygraph test.

Photographic produces crime scene photography, microphotography, infrared and ultraviolet photography.

New Equipment and Technology

The following equipment and technology are among the latest available to law enforcement:

Lasers are used to better visualize fingerprints, fibers, semen evidence and other trace material in the field and in the lab.

Electrostatic Detection Apparatus (ESDA) is an instrument that allows sensitive analysis of indented writing, sometimes as deep as fifteen to twenty sheets in a pad of paper.

CAL ID is a computer system that has all criminal fingerprints on file from the state of California. This system enables a possible match of a single latent print of an individual from a data base of all convicted criminals. The generic term for CAL ID is Automated Fingerprint Identification System (AFIS), which is operational in many states. Check with the police department you are writing about to determine if a similar computer system exists in that state.

High Pressure Liquid Chromatography (HPLC) is a separation technique that can positively identify drugs and other organic compounds for toxicology or narcotic examinations.

Gas Chromatography-Mass Spectroscopy (GCMS) is a separation technique that can positively identify a substance (narcotic, poison, etc.) and compare the spectrum against a computer library of standard spectra.

DNA identification is based on the fact that deoxyribonucleic acid (DNA) from body fluids (blood, semen) and hair can be compared to samples from a suspect or victim to make a positive identification. This genetically based form of identification was at first thought to be 100 percent accurate because no two individuals have exactly the same genetic makeup, with the possible exception of identical twins. However, there may be more overlap and common factors than originally thought, and experts differ on the reliability of DNA identification. As with all rapidly changing technologies, check on the current status of this procedure before making it a crucial element in a story.

Behavioral Science Section is usually separate from the crime laboratory. Most agencies, except the FBI, don't have a formal behavioral science unit. More often, police officers assigned to detective functions have specialized training in this area.

INTERROGATION

Interrogation is part of any investigation. Although many suspects are questioned away from a police station, they are usually suspects whose guilt is uncertain. Suspects whose guilt is virtually certain are interrogated in an interrogation room at a police station or police headquarters.

Interrogation rooms are private and are usually located on the second floor or higher so there is no inference that the suspect was questioned in a basement dungeon. The room is windowless or barred, contains normal overhead lighting, has one door, and is usually bare except for a table and chairs for the suspect and officers involved in the interrogation.

Rights of Suspects

Everyone has certain basic rights. These include the right to be free of unreasonable search and seizure; the right to counsel of one's choosing or to an appointed counsel if indigent; to bail; to phone calls; to be arraigned within seventy-two hours; to have a preliminary hearing within ten days; to receive a transcript of the trial proceedings; and to receive a speedy trial within sixty days.

Other rights of the accused vary from state to state. Questions related to the rights of the accused should be researched in the penal code and the evidence code for the jurisdiction in question.

Miranda Rights

When suspects are arrested, they are supposed to be read the Miranda Rights:

"You have the right to remain silent. If you give up the right to remain silent, anything you say can and will be used against you in a court of law. You have the right to speak with an attorney and to have the attorney present during questioning. If you so desire and cannot afford one, an attorney will be appointed for you without charge before the questioning begins.

"Do you understand your rights as I have read them to you?

"Do you waive and give up those rights?"

If the accused waives (gives up) these rights, questioning of that person may begin. If the accused refuses to give up those rights or is uncertain, equivocates or does not understand, the accused may not be questioned. The accused should not be tricked into giving up these rights with statements such as, "It's only a formality that we must read this to you before we talk to you," or "Nothing you tell us will be used against you," or "It will go easier on you if you talk to us."

Defendants are often quick to inform their attorneys or the judge that they were not read their rights, but no Miranda warning is required if no statement was made and they were not questioned at the time of the arrest. A suspect who refuses to be questioned, having refused to waive Miranda rights, can be held for further investigation, including questioning, warrant check, fingerprints check, I.D. lineup and other procedures.

In California, the person may be held for seventy-two hours excluding Saturday, Sunday and court holidays. Check the jurisdiction you are writing about as to the number of hours a suspect can be held. The period must be reasonable or it violates the defendant's constitutional rights.

Under constitutional guarantee, no individual needs to answer to a capital crime unless the accused has been indicted by a grand jury. However, the court interpretation of the due process requirement is met when a state law authorizes a criminal proceeding to be instituted by sworn statement made by the person or agency bringing the charge. In such case, a warrant may be issued, resulting in a hearing by a magistrate who then determines if the accused should stand trial. At this hearing, the accused is entitled to be represented by counsel and to cross-examine witnesses. Any officer who willfully delays taking an arrested person before a magistrate is guilty of a misdemeanor.

After being booked and, except where physically impossible, no later than three hours after arrest, the accused has the right to make three complete phone calls to an attorney, bondsman, relative or other persons. The calls are at no expense to the accused if within the local calling area, or if outside the local calling area, at the expense of the accused.

Preparation for Interrogation

Officers involved in interrogation of a suspect should be prepared for the interview, knowing the suspect's personal and criminal history, including any alibis, and the facts of the case.

Two officers usually conduct the interview, one doing most of the questioning, the other taking notes. If the suspect is a woman, at least one of the interrogating officers should be a woman. If the suspect is handcuffed, the cuffs should be removed. A dominant role must be established by the officers, but threats or physical abuse are prohibited.

Interrogating officers should take the position that they are only seeking the truth, although their questioning should show their confidence in the suspect's guilt and indicate that they've been through this routine hundreds of times. Although interrogators should never reveal all that they know, small pieces of information connecting the suspect to the crime should be fed to the suspect a little at a time.

Interrogators should know gestures, nonverbal signs and tones of voice that indicate lies or deception on the suspect's part. These include:

Change in voice
Checking wristwatch or moving jewelry around
Clenched teeth
Crossing and uncrossing of feet
Difficulty in maintaining eye contact
Dry mouth
Hesitancy in answering questions
Inability to remain seated
Need for a cigarette or water
Playing with hands
Reddening of face
Repetition of questions by the suspect
Tapping of fingers

If a suspect is confined to a cell for a long time before questioning, the suspect's attorney may argue that imprisonment contributed to statements or confessions made by the client. Sweating a suspect over a protracted period could also be used to invalidate any statement or confession signed by the suspect.

Also remember that the suspect may often watch the interrogating officers for nonverbal signs. Skilled interrogators who are aware of this may from time to time use some nonverbal signs to purposely lead the suspect in a desired direction.

It is essential that interrogators tell the suspect they will not accept lies or evasions and will continue to search for the truth. If the suspect is caught in a lie, the interrogator should hammer away at it. When a suspect fabricates a story, it is hard to remember what was said earlier, and sooner or later a slight alteration can confuse the suspect.

Good guy/bad guy is a technique in which one officer is more sympathetic and shows more respect for the suspect than the other officer. Although trickery by interrogators can be argued in court by defense counsel, the law considers that such devices are often necessary to solve a crime.

If the suspect had an accomplice, it might be possible to play one against the other.

Written Statements

Statements and confessions should be typed from the notes taken by one of the interrogating officers and given to the suspect to read before signing. However, statements and confessions can be argued in court even though the suspect read the statement or confession before signing.

POLICE CODES

Police communications has never been more essential than today, when radio and television are being used so effectively in crime prevention and detection. To facilitate communication, codes have been devised in which one or two words can tell the whole story. Codes are used principally for saving air time and not for security reasons.

Two basic codes, usually called the Nine and Ten Codes, are used with many variations. In recent years, the Ten Code has been gaining favor. The Association of Police Communications Officers has urged the universal adoption of the Ten Code to standardize code systems. Consult the police department of the locale where your story is set to determine the equivalents of these LAPD codes.

Ten Code

Code 1: Your convenience
Code 2: Urgent, no red light and siren
Code 3: Emergency, use red light and siren
Code 4: No further assistance needed
Code 5: Stakeout
Code 6AD: Felony wanted, armed and dangerous
Code 6F: Felony wanted
Code 6M: Misdemeanor wanted
Code 7: Mealtime
Code 8: Box alarm
Code 10: Bomb threat
Code 20: Assist officer, urgent
Code 30: Officer needs help, emergency
Code 33: Emergency in progress, do not transmit
187: Murder
207: Kidnapping
211: Robbery
245: ADW (assault with deadly weapon)
261: Rape
288: L & L conduct (lewd & lascivious)
311: Indecent exposure
415: Disturbance
415F: Family disturbance
460: Burglary
480: Felony hit-and-run
481: Misdemeanor hit-and-run
487: Grand theft
488: Petty theft
502: Drunk driver
503: Stolen vehicle
505: Reckless driving
510: Vehicle speeding
647: Vagrant
647A: Child molestation
10-1: Receiving poorly
10-2: Receiving O.K.

10-4: Message received O.K.

10-5: Relay to

10-7: Out of service at

10-7B: Out of service, personal

10-70D: Off duty

10-8: In service

10-8X: In service with female

10-9: Repeat

10-10: Out of service at home

10-12: Visitors or officials present

10-13: Weather and road conditions

10-14: Escort

10-14F: Funeral detail

10-15: Have prisoner in custody

10-16: Pick up

10-19: Return to station

10-20: Location

10-21: Phone your office, or:

10-21A: Phone home, my ETA is:

10-21B: Phone your home

10-21R: Phone radio

10-22: Cancel

10-23: Standby

10-25: Do you have contact with

10-28: Registration

10-29: Check for wanted

10-32: Drowning

10-33: Alarm sounding

10-34: Open door

10-35: Open window

10-39: Status of

10-40: Is available for phone call

10-45: Ambulance, injured

10-46: Ambulance, sick

10-49: Proceed to

10-50: Obtain a report

10-51: Drunk

10-52: Resuscitator

10-53: Man down
10-54: Possible dead body
10-55: Coroner's case
10-56: Suicide
10-56A: Attempted suicide
10-57: Firearms discharged
10-58: Garbage complaint
10-59: Malicious mischief
10-62: Meet the citizen
10-65: Missing person
10-66: Suspicious person
10-67: Person calling for help
10-70: Prowler
10-71: Shooting
10-72: Knifing
10-73: How do you receive
10-80: Explosion
10-86: Any traffic for
10-87: Meet officer
10-91: Stray animal
10-91A: Vicious animal
10-91B: Noisy animal
10-91C: Injured animal
10-91D: Dead animal
10-91F: Animal bite
10-91H: Stray horse
10-97: Arrived at the scene
10-98: Finished with last assignment
11-24: Abandoned vehicle
11-26: Abandoned bicycle
11-54: Suspicious vehicle
11-79: Accident, ambulance en route
11-80: Accident, major injury
11-81: Accident, minor injury
11-82: Accident, property damage
11-83: Accident, no detail
11-84: Traffic control

11-96: Leaving the vehicle to investigate an auto. If not heard from in ten minutes, dispatch cover.

Traffic Violation Codes

001: Operating after permit refused, canceled or suspended
002: Driving under the influence of liquor or drugs
003: Minor law
004: Failure to stop; accident resulting in death or injury
005: Perjury, false affidavit or statement under oath
006: Turning off lights to avoid identification
007: Manslaughter or negligent homicide
008: Any felony in which a vehicle is used
009: Legally adjudicated insane
010: Minor
012: Violation while transporting explosives
201: Loaning or altering a permit
202: Operating after permit revoked
203: Displaying canceled, revoked, suspended or fraudulent license
204: Smoke screen
301: Leaving after colliding, no personal injury
302: Failure to give information and render aid, personal injury
401: Failure to report an accident
501: Permitting unlicensed operator to drive
601: Reckless driving
602: Speeding (ten MPH or more)
603: Violation contributing to an accident
604: Failure to grant right of way
605: Failure to grant pedestrians right of way
606: Failure to grant blind pedestrian right of way
701: Speeding
702: Improper passing
703: Automatic signal
704: Stop sign
705: Failure to keep right of center
706: Crossing center line
707: School bus

708: Following too closely
709: Operating without a license
710: Operating on expired license
711: Failure to dim headlights
712: Improper license
713: Driving too slowly
714: Racing or speed contest
715: Wrong way, one-way street
716: Improper turn
717: Failure to give hand signal
718: Failure to stop for emergency vehicle
719: Operating unregistered motor vehicle
720: Failure to obtain special chauffeur's license
721: License restriction
722: Operating on instruction license unaccompanied
723: Inadequate brakes
724: Failing to obey officer's signal
725: Operating emergency vehicle unsafely
726: Failing to obey traffic control device
727: Failing to obey flashing signal lights
728: Failure to make required stop
729: Failure to leave car tracks
730: Coasting down grade
731: Operating motorcycle or motor bicycle contrary to law
732: Driver of emergency vehicle failing to exercise care
733: Failure to stop at railroad crossing
734: Driver's view obstructed
735: Following fire apparatus too closely
736: Operating unfit vehicle
737: Displaying license of another
738: Failing to stop at through highway
739: Unlawful taking of motor vehicle
740: No headlights
741: Crossing over fire hose
742: Improper truck loading
743: Improper lights
744: Restricted use of television
745: Improper equipment

746: Motor vehicle height, weight, width and length requirements
747: Improper loading
748: Failure to obtain chauffeur's license
801: No license in possession
802: No registration card in possession
803: Failing to change address
804: Inadequate muffler
805: False evidence of title or registration
806: Improper registration
807: Failing to obtain license tags within thirty days
808: Tampering with motor vehicle
809: Damage to highways
810: Unlawful use of license
811: Failure to display warning device on disabled vehicle
812: Failure to deliver certificate of title
813: Unnecessary use of horn

WHERE TO GO FROM HERE

The best source of information about the investigative techniques used by a particular police department is the department
itself. Before you start asking them questions, though, think your
story through so that you know what questions to ask, and read
enough about standard procedures to know the right terms. These
books cover a variety of technical topics, and several are fascinat-
ing stories of actual investigations:

Blye, Irwin. *Secrets of a Private Eye: How to Be Your Own Private
Investigator.* New York: Henry Holt, 1987. How to do simple
investigations and how to decide when you need profes-
sional help.
Greene, Marilyn, and Gary Provost. *Finder: The True Story of a
Private Investigator.* New York: Crown, 1988. Ms. Greene is
one of the most expert finders-of-lost-persons in the world.
Joyce, Christopher, and Eric Stover. *Witnesses From the Grave:
The Stories Bones Tell.* Boston: Little, Brown, 1991. The story

of Clyde Snow, the forensic anthropologist who has investigated famous cases around the world.

Lampton, Christopher. *DNA Fingerprinting*. New York: Franklin Watts, 1991. Somewhat technical presentation of an identification method that is becoming more widely accepted and its social and legal consequences.

Livingstone, Neil. *The Complete Security Guide for Executives*. Lexington, Massachusetts: Lexington Books, 1989. The emphasis is on terrorism, but it also has useful information on less exotic crimes.

Reisner, Marc. *Game Wars: The Undercover Pursuit of Wildlife Poachers*. New York: Viking, 1991. A look at the illegal trade in wildlife through the eyes of perhaps the most inventive and daring undercover investigator.

Sparrow, Malcolm, Mark Moore, and David Kennedy, *Beyond 911: A New Era for Policing*. New York: Basic Books, 1990. Describes the efforts of a number of cities to find new solutions to the problem of crime.

Thompson, Josiah. *Gumshoe: Reflections in a Private Eye*. Boston: Little, Brown, 1988. A former philosophy professor, Thompson writes about why he left academia and what it's like to be an investigator.

Wilson, Keith. *Cause of Death: A Writer's Guide to Death, Murder and Forensic Medicine*. Cincinnati: Writer's Digest Books, 1992. How to write convincingly about death and forensic medicine. The author is a physician and novelist.

Wingate, Anne. *Scene of the Crime: A Writer's Guide to Crime-Scene Investigations*. Cincinnati: Writer's Digest Books, 1992. A former cop and current novelist and teacher tells how crime scenes are processed.

Zonderman, Jon. *Beyond the Crime Lab*. New York: Wiley, 1990. A thorough discussion of recently developed detection techniques including genetic fingerprinting.

5
The Courts

THE GRAND JURY

A grand jury is a panel of citizens brought together to hear cases for possible indictment. The population and size of the county determine whether the grand jury works all year or is convened only when a hearing or investigation is to take place. The Los Angeles County Grand Jury consists of twenty-three citizens and requires a quorum of fourteen or more to vote for an indictment. Each jurisdiction has a manual of procedures to be followed in bringing a case to the grand jury and the laws pertaining to grand jury indictments. Because laws differ from state to state, contact the county you are writing about for a copy of their grand jury manual.

Cases suitable for presentation to a grand jury include:

Filed complaints, regardless of the charge, in which the preliminary hearing has been unreasonably delayed.

Cases involving complicated factual issues, multiple counts or multiple defendants.

Cases involving official misconduct or corruption.

Cases involving crimes committed by members of organized criminal groups.

Cases in which there is a need to temporarily protect the identity of a victim or witness.

Cases in which either the victim or witnesses needs protection at the early stages of the proceedings.

Cases that could potentially generate publicity prejudicial to a fair trial.

Cases in which an indictment may be needed to prevent flight of a defendant from the jurisdiction, or assist in the extradition of an accused from another jurisdiction.

Many murder cases pending preliminary hearings remain in municipal court longer than other criminal cases and in excess of legal necessity. If a hearing cannot be conducted within the time required by the penal code (sixty days in Los Angeles County), the deputy DA consults with a superior on whether to refer the case to the grand jury.

The district attorney's office can appear before the grand jury to present witnesses and give information or advice, and a deputy district attorney is assigned as a full-time legal advisor.

The grand jury holds hearings at the request of the district attorney's office to inquire into public offenses committed or triable within the county and to return indictments. An indictment hearing is conducted to initiate a prosecution.

Investigative Hearings

The grand jury can function in an investigative capacity in which its power of subpoena may help in finding the truth. This investigative power may be used any time before a preliminary hearing. A matter that begins as an investigatory hearing may conclude with a request for an indictment. The subject matter of an investigatory hearing may include any of the categories listed previously.

The grand jury is charged with both civil and criminal functions. In investigating county matters of civil concern, such as investigating county government departments, the grand jury can engage an auditing firm to assist in the investigation.

Prior to a Grand Jury Hearing

A deputy DA wishing to present a case to the grand jury prepares a Request for a Grand Jury Hearing Memorandum.

After a hearing date is set, the deputy DA provides the jury's secretary with the information necessary to prepare subpoenas for witnesses and records. It is also the deputy's responsibility to present to the legal advisor, at least two days prior to the hearing, the following information: a foreperson's statement, tentative witness list, exhibit list and copies of substantive jury instructions applicable to the charges sought.

Grand jury sessions are secret. Neither the deputies nor the grand jurors are permitted to disclose the evidence presented or the fact that an indictment has been returned until the defendant has been arrested. Only the deputy, legal advisor, grand jurors, court reporter, witness and an interpreter, if necessary, are present during the hearing. Neither the defendant nor the defendant's attorney is present. The deputy presenting the case determines whether to invite or subpoena the subject.

The legal standard for an indictment is whether the evidence presented warrants the strong suspicion of the guilt of the accused. Usually more evidence is presented at a grand jury hearing than at a preliminary hearing.

Procedures

Each daily session begins with roll call to ensure a quorum. The foreperson reads a statement describing the case and admonishes jurors who are biased regarding the case to excuse themselves.

The deputy DA then makes an opening statement and presents the witnesses and exhibits pertaining to the case. Jurors may submit written questions at the conclusion of each witness' testimony, and the legal advisor and deputy review these questions and, when possible, ask them of the witness.

If aware of exculpatory information, the deputy DA must tell the grand jury about it. The deputy then asks the foreperson to receive all evidence and makes a brief closing statement. The legal advisor gives the grand jurors instructions germane to the case.

The grand jurors then deliberate in secret, voting whether to return an indictment. If an indictment is returned, the deputy and foreperson sign the indictment and the grand jury and the deputy present the indictment to the court. The deputy must be prepared to recommend appropriate bail, request bail deviation, request the issuance of a bench warrant or indicate the defendant's date of surrender.

A transcript of the hearing is prepared and filed within ten days of the indictment. The transcript becomes public ten days after it has been delivered to the defendant unless it is sealed by the court.

Federal Grand Juries

Federal grand juries are selected in each district. They consist of twenty-three members. Whereas county grand juries require a quorum of fourteen, the federal grand jury calls for a quorum of sixteen. While county grand juries hold hearings at the request of the District Attorney's Office, federal grand juries hold their hearings at the request of the U.S. Attorney General's Office.

County grand jury procedures vary from county to county and state to state. Check the location you are using in your story.

For further information regarding federal grand juries, contact the Office of the Attorney General, Department of Justice, 10th Street and Constitutional Avenue, N.W., Washington, D.C. 20530, telephone (202) 514-2000.

RIGHTS OF DEFENDANTS

The accused is entitled to a speedy public trial, consistent with the necessity for the prosecution to prepare for trial and to have witnesses available to testify.

Another right of the accused is to be present in court during the trial. Also, the accused may not be prosecuted twice for the same offense. The plea of former jeopardy, however, is only entertained if the current prosecution is for the same offense as the prior offense.

All persons have an obligation to testify in court on matters within their knowledge pertaining to the case in question. Defendants have a constitutional right to use the subpoena power to compel witnesses to testify. However, in some circumstances, testifying might create more harm. For example, spouses normally cannot be compelled to testify against each other because the preservation of the marriage is held to be the greater good.

Also, the government cannot compel the testimony of the following individuals:

Physician or psychologist against patient
Lawyer or accountant against client
Minister against parishioner

Without privilege, citizens would be deprived of the services of these professions. There are exceptions to these cases, however. For example, if the patient is no longer alive, the privilege does not normally apply. Also, therapists have a positive duty to warn anyone who has been threatened by a patient.

Under the Fifth Amendment, the accused is not bound to testify on matters that would be self-incriminating.

Right to Appeal

Everyone convicted of a crime has a right to appeal the conviction, and the judge must advise the convicted felon of that right at the time of sentencing. If the defendant cannot afford an attorney one will be appointed.

Appeals may be made because:

Evidence was illegally obtained.
Inadmissible evidence was presented to the jury.
The evidence against the accused was insufficient.
Counsel was incompetent.
The prosecutor engaged in misconduct.
An error of law was committed during the trial.

If it can be shown that there was a violation of due process or equal protection under the law, the defendant may raise the matter for reconsideration. If new evidence is discovered, it can be presented to the original trial judge, who may void the verdict.

THE COURTROOM

Many crime dramas wind up in courtrooms, and much of a crime story can be played out there. One famous television series with substantial courtroom scenes was Erle Stanley Gardner's *Perry Mason*.

Writers should be familiar with courtroom procedures. This book contains information on courts and judges, but it is advisable to consult a legal expert when writing about legal issues and procedures.

Courts

Bankruptcy Court
Chancery Court
County Court
Court of Claims
Court of Inquiry
Court of Record
Court of Special Sessions
Courts of Common Plea
District Court
Domestic Relations Court
Felony Court
Garrison Court-Martial
General Court-Martial
Juvenile Court
Magistrate's Court
Maritime Court
Night Court
Police Court
Probate Court
Regimental Court-Martial
Small Claims Court
Special Court-Martial
State Appellate Courts
State Supreme Court
Summary Court-Martial
Superior Court

Surrogate's Court
Tax Court
Traffic Court
U.S. Supreme Court

Courtroom Characters

The jury box can be on either side of the courtroom between the bench and the attorneys' tables. A railing marks off that part of the courtroom where the case is heard and tried. Behind the railing are rows of spectators' benches; the number of benches is determined by the size of the courtroom. Witnesses are usually seated in the viewers' section or just outside the courtroom. The people normally present in court include:

Attorney for the Plaintiff
Attorney for the Respondent
Bailiff
Court Stenographer
Defense Attorney
Family of Participants
Judge
Jury
Prosecuting Attorney
Spectators
Witnesses

Legal Specialties

Bankruptcy
Civil
Corporate
Criminal
Divorce
Forensic
Insurance
International
Legal Aid
Marine
Patent

Probate
Public Defender
Real Estate
Tax
Trial

Officials Who May Appear in Court
Chief of Detectives
Chief of Police
Coroner
Deputy Marshal
Deputy Sheriff
Detective
Marshal
Medical Examiner
Sheriff
State Attorney General
State Police Officer
Transit Police Officer

MILITARY JUSTICE SYSTEM

The following is excerpted from the United States Army Command and General Staff College Student Text 27-1:

1.1 Introduction.

We often think of the law as being fixed and eternal, but in reality, the law is man-made, fallible and ever-changing. Today's rules may become of historical interest only by tomorrow's court decision. Today's commanders and staff officers cannot rely on past knowledge of the military justice system. Today's officers must be aware of the current system and use it fairly and intelligently. Recent changes to the Uniform Code of Military Justice and the *Manual for Courts-Martial* have greatly improved the ability of commanders to effectively use disciplinary measures. This book will assist you to understand the current system and use it effectively.

This book is not intended to make you an expert in military justice. Rather, it is to provide an awareness of the major requirements of military justice. This book is not intended to replace the basic sources of military law. It is, however, an aid to effective decision making in the military justice arena. The most important thing to take away from this material is the ability to recognize a military justice problem so as to know when to contact your "expert" in the legal area—the staff judge advocate.

1.2 Background and Development.

An understanding of the legal basis for the military justice system must rest on an understanding of the history and tradition which shaped its development. Among the concepts that emerged from the American Revolution were the fear of excessive military power and the desire to keep the military strictly subservient to civilian control. These notions were embodied in the Constitution. That document is the basic source for the military justice system.

Our system of military justice had its inception in the American Revolution. The Uniform Code of Military Justice that we currently use can be traced back through the Articles of War used during the American Revolution to the British Articles of War. The first Articles of War were adopted by the Second Continental Congress on June 30, 1775, just three days before George Washington, who was on the committee appointed to prepare the rules and regulations for the newly created Continental Army, took command of it.

Our separate system of military justice differs from that of many other countries. A servicemember can be tried by court-martial for what is essentially a civilian offense as well as for uniquely military misbehavior before the enemy. In many countries, civil courts handle all offenses committed by servicemembers which are not uniquely military. The reason for this expansive jurisdictional reach is the need to maintain discipline in order to have an effective fighting force. Because of the force deployment, the military requires a justice system which is literally worldwide in its criminal prohibitions and its jurisdictional reach—unlike civilian criminal processes which are usually localized. Finally, it is doubtful that the civilian justice system could appreciate and meet all the varied concerns of military discipline.

1.3 The Purpose of Military Law.

The 1984 *Manual for Courts-Martial* probably states the purpose of Military Law best:

> The purpose of military law is to promote justice, to assist in maintaining good order and discipline in the armed forces, to promote efficiency and effectiveness in the military establishment, and thereby to strengthen the national security of the United States.
> Preamble, *MCM*, 1984, 3.

1.4 The Ever-Changing Military Law.

As is the case with most of our laws, military law has been reconsidered and revised in the light of new knowledge and experience. Among the major revisions were:

The Uniform Code of Military Justice, 1950. This Act of Congress combined the separate laws formerly governing the army, navy and air force into one uniform code which governs all of the armed forces of the United States.

The Military Justice Act of 1968. A major revision of the Uniform Code occurred with this act. This act first gave servicemembers the right to a qualified lawyer at special courts-martial and established the military judiciary.

Since the 1968 Act, Congress has amended the Uniform Code several times in order to increase the efficiency of our military criminal law system:

In November 1979, Public Law 96-197 amended Articles 2, UCMJ, to authorize court-martial jurisdiction over servicemembers entering the armed forces as a result of recruiter misconduct.

The Military Justice Amendments of 1981 eliminated the right of the accused to be represented by more than one military lawyer and permitted a commander or convening authority to direct excess leave for servicemembers who have been convicted by court-martial and are awaiting appellate review. Previously the accused could only be placed on excess leave upon the approval of his or her request.

The Military Justice Act of 1983. On December 6, 1983, the President signed this act, Public Law No. 98-209, 97 Stat. 1393. The effective date is August 1, 1984. A new Manual for Courts-Martial has also been written. It includes provisions to implement the legislation. Its effective date is also August 1, 1984. This revision is intended to streamline the military justice system and make it more responsive to commanders while retaining the fundamental rights of servicemembers. Among its provisions are a lessening of the commander's responsibilities to review courts-martial for legal sufficiency; streamlining procedures for detailing and excusing courts-martial personnel; and permitting appeal of final courts-martial to the U.S. Supreme Court.

1.5 Sources of Military Law.

Article I, section 8, of our Constitution provides that "The Congress shall have Power . . . To make Rules for the Government and Regulation of the land and naval Forces, . . ." This language is what gives the Congress the authority to enact the federal law called the Uniform Code of Military Justice.

Article II, section 2, explains that "The President shall be Commander in Chief of the Army and Navy of the United States, . . ."

In Article 36 of the Uniform Code of Military Justice, the Congress authorized the President, as Commander in Chief, to issue procedural rules to implement the military justice system. This is the authority the President has used to issue the Presidential Proclamation called the Manual for Courts-Martial. It contains a detailed set of regulations supplementing and explaining the Uniform Code. It also contains maximum punishments. Article 36 of the UCMJ gave the President the power to establish punishments. This power was recently used to change the maximum sentences for drug offenses by Executive Order on December 23, 1982. These Executive Orders have the force of law, although in the case of a conflict, the Constitution, then the UCMJ, have precedence.

The services can publish regulations to further implement the provisions of the [aforementioned] sources of military law. One example is Army Regulation 27-10, Military Justice. This regulation contains procedures that must be followed for such matters as administering nonjudicial punishment, reviewing the legality of pretrial confinement, etc.

Court decisions from military and civilian appellate courts must also be considered as sources of military law. For example, the United States Supreme Court's decision that counsel were not required at summary courts-martial is an example of court-made, as opposed to statutory or regulatory, law.

All of the foregoing, the Constitution, the UCMJ, the MCM, regulations, and the decisions of the appellate courts, are sources of military law. [Note: If your story turns on a precise point of military law or military judicial procedure, consult the appropriate regulation(s), as then amended, in the reference section of any large public library. The public information divisions of the various armed services may also be able to provide helpful materials for further research.]

1.6 Military Justice Personnel.

The staff judge advocate is the legal adviser to the command. He will normally be a senior lieutenant colonel when assigned to a division, and a colonel for higher commanders and major installations. The UCMJ authorizes the SJA direct access to the convening authority. Besides supervising military justice, the SJA has functions in the administrative law, claims and legal assistance areas.

Trial court personnel include military judges, trial counsel (prosecutor) and defense counsel.

Military judges belong to the U.S. Army Trial Judiciary. They are appointed by the judge advocate general from JAGC officers who have extensive trial experience and satisfactorily complete the judge's course. Special court-martial judges are usually majors. General court-martial judges are lieutenant colonels or colonels. Judges are assigned to the Trial Judiciary, which is independent of any local command, so they are rated by other judges, not commanders. This helps to preserve their independence and avoid command influence.

Defense counsel belong to a similar organization, the Trial Defense Service. It comes under the same parent organization as the trial judiciary, the U.S. Army Legal Services Agency. Thus, defense counsel are not assigned to local commands and owe their undivided loyalty to their clients. Defense counsel are rated by senior defense attorneys. A regional defense counsel supervises the defense counsel within a geographical region, and is who the commander can go to if he has a problem involving a defense counsel. The canons of ethics of the American Bar Association are applicable to all military lawyers. The canon that requires counsel to represent their clients zealously within the bounds of the law is especially important to defense counsel.

The trial counsel works for the command, and presents the case for the government (prosecution). His ethical duty is to see justice done. The trial counsel works for the chief of criminal law (sometimes called chief of justice), under the staff judge advocate.

1.7 Commander's Role.

One of the major differences between the military and the civilian justice systems is that the latter has no counterpart to the commander. Both systems have judges, prosecutors and defense attorneys. The commander in our system has powers substantially equivalent to those of civilian judges and prosecutors. For example, a commander can issue a search authorization which is the military counterpart to the search warrants issued by civilian judges. Also, in the military, the commander decides who is to be prosecuted, a decision made by district attorneys or prosecutors in the civilian sector.

It should be noted that it is the commander in our system who makes many of these decisions — whether to prosecute or not, whether to approve a pretrial agreement (plea bargain) — not the military lawyers. Of course, the commander should seek the advice of his staff judge advocate before making these decisions.

Because the commander has so much power — unlike that of any civilians except judges — he or she must exercise that power wisely and fairly. The civilian sector has always watched carefully for abuses of the military justice system. In order that the people, acting through Congress, continue to permit commanders to exercise these broad powers, commanders' military justice actions must not only be fair, but be perceived to be fair.

It should also be remembered that the military justice system is a "tool" of discipline — and not the only one — not a substitute for good leadership. This is the reason that the commander has the ultimate decision-making power in the military justice system. The commander is in the best position to evaluate the effect of an offense on good order and discipline and to choose a "tool" to correct the situation. Many times military justice procedures will not be the best way to dispose of a disciplinary problem; courts-martial and nonjudicial punishment are often too severe, slow or cumbersome, unsuited to the incident, the accused or the commander's purpose. Often an administrative action such as counseling will suffice.

The complexity of the system and of the myriad of factors that impact on good order and discipline requires that the commander exercise a Solomon-like judgment. As long as he or she obtains the facts and the advice of the staff judge advocate and dispassionately assesses them to make a reasoned, fair and impartial decision, the military justice system will remain in the capable hands that have used it effectively for over two hundred years — the hands of commanders.

STATUS OF FORCES

The Status of Forces Agreement (SOFA) is the agreement between the United States and foreign countries where U.S. forces are stationed. This agreement determines who retains jurisdiction when a U.S. servicemember commits a crime off the military base.

In most instances, U.S. personnel serving overseas who commit major crimes off the military base are arrested and tried by a civilian criminal court of that nation. They may be represented by either military or civilian counsel. If convicted, they may be imprisoned in the foreign country. In some cases, a person may be charged and tried by both the host country and a U.S. military court.

COURTROOM CONCEPTS

A crime is an act contrary to law and punishable by fine, imprisonment or both. The laws of the state you're writing about must be examined to determine the criminal character of any act.

A defendant has the right to plead not guilty or guilty. If the plea is guilty, the defendant will come before the court for sentencing. If the defendant pleads not guilty, a trial is ordered. The defendant is represented by private counsel, or if the defendant cannot afford counsel, one is appointed by the court.

At the trial, both the defense and the prosecution present their cases. If the jury finds against the defendant, the defendant is then sentenced and committed to prison or given a term of probation. The judge may grant a reduction of the sentence or the possibility of parole.

The following are some of the more important concepts and rules used in trials:

Accessory after the fact: One who receives, comforts or assists another, knowing that the other person has committed a felony. Three things are necessary: (1) the felony must have been completed; (2) the person charged as accessory must have assisted the felon personally; and (3) the person must have known when giving assistance that the person had committed a felony.

Accessory before the fact: One who was absent when the act was committed, but who procured, counseled, ordered or abetted the principal or actual perpetrator of the criminal act.

Accident or misfortune: A person cannot be held criminally liable for an accident happening in the performance of a lawful act with due care.

Accusation: Accusations of guilty conduct may be made by complaints or affidavits, and sworn to by injured persons or by police officers. This is true especially in the case of minor offenses. Accusations of felonies are made by indictments found by grand juries or by information filed by prosecuting attorneys, generally following preliminary examinations in magistrates' courts.

Act and intent must coexist: The criminal intent or negligence must unite with the overt act, and they must occur in the same point of time.

Acts of state legislatures: Unlike the Congress, state legislatures have inherent power to declare acts criminal and to impose penalties for their violation. State power in these respects, however, is not absolute. Enactments of the state legislatures must not conflict with any provision of the U.S. Constitution, the state constitution or with any valid act of Congress.

Acts that may be both a crime and a tort: In some cases, the wrongdoer faces both criminal action by the state and civil action by the injured party. These two actions are separate and distinct. The object of the former is to punish as an example; the object of the latter is to compensate the injured party. Either action may precede the other, depending on the laws of the state.

Administration of criminal justice: Includes criminal procedure, police organization and administration, prosecution, accusation, the defense of accused persons, the organization of courts, pleadings, arraignment and trial, evidence, judgment and sentence, appeals, probation, parole, pardon, penology and prison administration, juvenile courts, special procedures for crime prevention and laws designed to change social and industrial conditions in order to prevent crime.

Agent's liability for own acts: Agents are criminally liable for their own acts, though they are ordered by a principal and in the course of the principal's business.

Aider and abettor or accomplice: The term *aider and abettor* applies to principals in the second degree. The term *accomplice* applies to all who take part in the commission of a crime, whether they are principals or accessories.

American common law: Similar in most respects to the English common law, insofar as the U.S. Supreme Court has decided that English statutes that were in force at the time of the American Revolution, and that are applicable to our conditions and surroundings, constitute a part of our common law.

Attempts: An act done with intent to commit that crime but failing in the commission of the act. (1) The act must be connected with the completed crime. (2) There must be a possibility to commit the crime in the manner proposed. (3) There must be specific intent to commit the crime at the time of the act. (4) The crime was not actually committed. Attempts to commit either a felony or a misdemeanor, whether at common law or by statute, are usually classified as misdemeanors, although some attempts are felonies by statute. Attempts to commit certain classes of statutory misdemeanors are not indictable.

Change of venue: Changing the place of trial from one county to another in the same state, or from one local jurisdiction to another similar jurisdiction within the same county. In exceptional cases, the place of trial may be changed from one state to another if the nature of the crime being charged, or reportage of the circumstances surrounding the offense, are so inflammatory as to provoke intense public sentiment across the state, thus rendering a fair trial within that state improbable.

Classification of crimes: Crimes at common law are divided into treason, felonies and misdemeanors. Some jurisdictions have a fourth classification, minor or petty offenses.

Commutation of sentence: A change from the original punishment to which a person has been condemned to a less severe one.

Concurrence of act and intent: To constitute a crime, act and intent must concur. Not only must there be both an act and an intent to constitute a crime, but the act and intent must concur in point of time. An intent to do a prohibited act, abandoned before the act is done, is not punishable.

Conditions of criminality: To render a person criminally responsible for the commission of a common law crime, four conditions of criminality must exist. The person must: (1) be of sufficient age; (2) have sufficient mental capacity; (3) act voluntarily; and (4) have criminal intent.

Construction of statutes: Penal statutes are to be construed strictly against the state and in favor of the accused. Words must be given their full meaning. The courts will not look for a meaning that may essentially declare the statute of no effect. In construing statutes, the intention of the legislature is to be sought, and for this purpose the court will consider not only the act itself but its preamble, and will also look into similar statutes on the same subject. All statutes are to be construed with reference to the provisions of the common law.

Constructive intent: Where a person commits an act that could be reasonably expected to cause harm, and harm in fact results.

Credibility and weight of the testimony of police officers, private detectives and experts: Even though it may be in the interests of certain witnesses to convict the accused, there is no rule of law that their testimony is to be weighed by any other method than that employed with other witnesses. It has been held improper for the court to instruct the jury that the testimony of police officers should be received with caution or distrust, although the jury may consider the fact of the interest of such witnesses in securing a conviction. Similarly, the fact that a witness was paid for gathering evidence or for testifying as an expert against the accused does not necessarily invalidate that person's testimony.

Crime versus tort: A crime is a wrong that affects the community in its aggregate capacity. A tort is a wrong apart from contract, which affects persons in their individual capacity. One is a public wrong, whereas the other is a private wrong. In the case of a crime, the wrongdoer is liable to criminal prosecution, whereas in the case of a tort, the offender is liable only to a civil action by the person injured.

Criminal capacity: There can be no guilt for a crime unless a person has a certain degree of mental capacity. Mental incapacity, which criminal law recognizes, exists to a greater or lesser extent in four classes of persons: infants, the disabled, drunken persons and corporations.

Criminal procedure: Consists of the rules according to which the substantive law is administered. It includes pleading, evidence and practice, and means those rules that direct the course of proceedings to bring defendants into court, and the proceedings followed in court after they are brought in.

Cruel and unusual punishment: Such punishment as would amount to torture or barbarity, and any cruel and degrading punishment not known to the common law.

Defense of accused person: In the United States, a person accused of a crime is entitled to the advice of a lawyer and to be represented by that lawyer at trial. In felony cases, this principle is carried further, and in many states, counsel is provided without cost for a defendant who is too poor to employ a lawyer. In most states, such counsel is appointed by the judge in the court where the defendant is standing trial. Some jurisdictions have an officer, known as a public defender, who represents defendants unable to provide counsel for themselves.

Deputy sheriff: One appointed to act in the place and stead of the sheriff in the official business of the latter's office. An under-sheriff, by virtue of appointment, has the authority to execute all the ordinary duties of the office of sheriff. A special deputy, who is an officer appointed for one particular occasion or a special service (such as to serve a writ or assist in keeping the peace when a riot is expected or in progress), acts under a specific authority.

Drunkenness: Voluntary drunkenness furnishes no ground of exemption from criminal responsibility, except (1) where the act is committed by one permanently disabled from intoxication; (2) where a specific intent is essential to constitute the crime, the fact of intoxication may negate its existence; (3) the fact of intoxication may be material, where provocation for the act is shown; (4) no criminal responsibility attaches for acts committed while in a state of involuntary drunkenness.

Effect of joining in criminal purpose: When one or more persons join in the execution of a common criminal purpose, each is criminally liable for every act that is done in the execution of that criminal act.

English common law: The basis of the English common law, sometimes called the unwritten law, is immemorial usage and custom, and not legislative enactment. The generic term *common law* has been defined as "those maxims, principles and forms of judicial proceedings which have no written law to prescribe or warrant them, but which, founded on the laws of nature and the dictates of reason have, by usage and custom, become interwoven with the written laws; and, by such incorporation, form a part of the municipal code of each state or nation."

Federal administration of criminal justice: The U.S. District Courts, which have one or more divisions in each state, the District of Columbia and the territories, are the courts of general trial jurisdiction in criminal cases; they hold power also to grant probation. The U.S. Circuit Court of Appeals, organized in ten circuits and in the District of Columbia, have appellate jurisdiction in criminal cases. The U.S. Supreme Court is the final court of appeals, both for cases arising in federal trial courts and in criminal cases arising in state courts that involve federal constitutional questions. Rules of procedure and evidence and forms of pleadings used in the federal courts are similar to those in the state courts, and probation, parole and pardon are similarly used.

Five sources of law: (1) The U.S. Constitution, (2) acts of Congress, (3) state constitutions, (4) acts of state legislatures (known as statutes) and (5) the common law. If a provision of the U.S. Constitution conflicts with an act of Congress, the latter is void. If a valid act of Congress conflicts with a provision of a state constitution, the latter is void. If a provision of a state constitution conflicts with a statute of the same state, the latter is void. And if an act of a state or territorial legislature conflicts with a provision of the common law, the latter is void.

General intent: Where an act is prohibited on pain or punishment, intention on the part of one capable of intent and acting without justification or excuse constitutes criminal intent. In such a case, the existence of the intent is presumed from commission of the act, on the grounds that a person is presumed to intend the voluntary act and its probable consequences. Criminal intent exists when a person intends to do that which the law says is a crime.

Ignorance of law: Ignorance on the part of the wrongdoer of the law that makes an act criminal is no excuse. If a specific intent is essential to a crime, and ignorance of the law negates such intent, such ignorance prevents the crime from being consummated.

Infancy: At common law, a child under the age of seven years is presumed incapable of entertaining criminal intent and cannot commit a crime. Between the ages of seven and fourteen, a child is presumed to be incapable, but the presumption may be rebutted. After the age of fourteen, a child is presumed to have sufficient capacity. In some states, the age of incapacity has been raised by statute, and in others, the age at which presumption of capacity begins has been lowered.

Insanity: In its legal sense, insanity is any defect or disease of the mind that renders a person incapable of entertaining a criminal intent. Criminal intent is an essential element of every crime. Consequently, if a person is insane enough so that there is no understanding of the crime, that person cannot be held criminally responsible. How this basic concept is applied varies from state to state.

Intent in cases of negligence: In crimes that consist of neglect to observe proper care in performing an act, or in culpable failure to perform a duty, criminal intent consists in the state of mind that necessarily accompanies the negligent act or culpable omission.

Jurisdiction: Jurisdiction is the authority by which the court acts, and the territory over which its authority extends. Unless extended by statute, a state has jurisdiction over only those crimes committed within its territorial limits and crimes committed by its own citizens abroad. A crime must be prosecuted in the county where it was committed (unless a change of venue is ordered by the court by virtue of evidence to show that a fair trial cannot be obtained within the venue in which it was committed).

Where a blow is struck in one county and death ensues in another, the offense is generally held to have been committed in the latter. When a person in one county commits a crime in another by means of an innocent agent, such as the U.S. Postal Service, the latter county has jurisdiction. Several states have special statutes governing the subject of jurisdiction, such as provisions for prosecuting homicides in the county where the body is found (even though the homicide took place in another county); giving jurisdiction to either county when the crime is committed partly in one county and partly in another, or to either state when the crime is committed partly in one state and partly in another.

Justification: The law, on the ground of public policy, imposes the duty or allows the doing of certain acts, under certain circumstances, although individuals are injured thereby. In such cases, the acts are justifiable, such as certain acts done: (1) under public authority; (2) under parental authority; (3) in prevention of a crime; (4) in suppressing a riot; or (5) in making an arrest or preventing an escape.

Justification — duress: When forced to do an act against a person's will, that person is, in general, not responsible for it. Therefore, on prosecution for any crime except murder, if the accused committed the act only because compelled to do so by threats of immediate death or serious bodily harm, that person is excused.

Juvenile courts: In the juvenile court, the usual rules of procedure, pleading and evidence are dispensed with and an informal administrative procedure is used instead. Under some circumstances, a child may be tried as an adult.

Locality of crime against the United States: The Constitution and the acts of Congress provide the right to be tried where the offense was committed. A trial shall be held in the state where the crime was committed. Should the crime not be committed within any state, the trial shall be at such place or places as Congress may, by law, have directed. Those accused of a crime shall have the right to trial by a jury of the state and district wherein the crime was committed. There are various provisions by act of Congress for crimes committed on the high seas, or elsewhere out of the jurisdiction of any particular state or district, to be tried in the district where the offender is first found, or into which the offender is first brought.

Marshals: Officers belonging to the executive department of the federal government, who with their deputies are empowered to execute the laws of the United States.

Merger of offenses: As a rule, where a person commits two crimes by the same act, one a felony and the other a misdemeanor, the misdemeanor merges into the felony; but if the crimes are of the same degree, both felonies or both misdemeanors, there is no merger. In some states, this doctrine has not been recognized, and in most states, it has been abolished by statutes allowing conviction of a lesser offense than is charged in the indictment if it is included in the offense charged.

Motive versus intent: Motive is not an essential element of crime. A bad motive will not make an act a crime, nor will a good motive prevent an act from being a crime. Motive may, however, tend to show that an act was willful and done with criminal intent.

Necessity for overt act: The law does not punish mere intention but requires some overt act in an attempt to carry the intention into execution. There is an exception to this rule in the case of conspiracy, unless the conspiring may be regarded as an overt act.

Negligence and recklessness: Neglect in the discharge of a duty, or indifference to consequences, is in many cases equivalent to a criminal intent. On the ground that people are presumed to contemplate the natural consequences of their acts, neglect and reckless conduct may be evidence of malicious intent. And negligent performance of a duty imposed by law or assumed by contract or by wrongful act may render a person guilty of such negligence criminally liable, except in cases in which a specific intent is essential to constitute the crime charged.

Overt act: An open act; a physical act, as distinguished from an act of the mind; an act done pursuant to a formed intent. To constitute assault, there must be an overt act or an attempt. In homicide cases, an overt act is an open act, indicating a present purpose to do immediate, great bodily harm.

Pardon: The power to pardon generally belongs to the governors of the states. Pardon differs in theory from both probation and parole in that it assumes the innocence of the defendant, or circumstances mitigating responsibility for the crime, and returns the defendant to society, free of ignominy and acquitted of all penalties related to the offense for which the pardon was granted.

Parole: After a portion of the term of imprisonment determined by the sentence has been served, the prisoner may be released on parole, on conditions similar to those imposed in the case of probation. The power to grant parole, however, is vested in a state parole board or officer.

Penal codes: Many of the states have adopted penal or criminal codes that define what acts shall be punished as crimes. The code is intended to cover the whole law, and no act is a crime unless it is expressly declared so. Even in states that have penal codes and do not recognize common law crimes, the common law is in force to the extent that it may be resorted to for the definition of crimes that are not defined in the statutes prohibiting them.

Pleadings: Pleadings in criminal cases are comparatively simple. The pleadings used by the state in felony and some misdemeanor cases are the indictment and the information; affidavits and complaints in misdemeanor cases; and by the defendant, usually an oral plea of "guilty" or "not guilty." Other pleas, such as "former jeopardy," "insanity," or "alibi" are available or required in some states. Pleas in abatement, demurrers, motions to quash the indictment and arrest of judgment are also available under some circumstances.

Preliminary examination: An investigation by a magistrate of a person who has been charged with a crime and arrested, or of the facts and circumstances alleged to have attended the crime.

Principal and accessories: Those involved in the commission of felonies are either principals or accessories, depending on whether they are present or absent when the crime is committed. Principals are either principals in the first degree, or principals in the second degree. Accessories are either before the fact, or after the fact.

Principal in the first degree: Individuals who actually perpetrate the deed, either by their own hand or through an innocent agent.

Principal in the second degree: Individual who is actually present, aiding and abetting another in the commission of the deed. Accordingly, the person must be present, actually or constructively; the person must aid or abet the commission of the act; there must be community of unlawful purpose at the time the act is committed; and such purpose must be real on the part of the principal in the first degree.

Principal's liability for acts of agents: As a rule, no person is criminally liable for the act of another unless that person has previously authorized or agreed to it; and consequently a principal is not liable for acts of agents or servants that the principal did not authorize or agree to, even if the crime is committed in the course of the employment. Exceptions: (1) In libel, the principal is liable, under certain circumstances, for the acts of agents upon the ground of negligence in failing to exercise proper control of them. (2) Under some statutes, the principal is liable for prohibited acts, regardless that they are committed by agents without authority or instructions.

Probation: Following a plea or verdict of guilty, the defendant may be placed on probation by the trial judge, on such conditions as this judge may impose. In some states, the conditions of probation may be reimbursement to the injured person and payment of costs. In most states, conditions of probation include: keeping employed, avoiding bad companions, refraining from committing other crimes and reporting to a probation officer. Violation of the conditions of probation makes the defendant liable to sentence as provided by law.

Probation officer: An officer who investigates and reports to the court upon an application for probation and supervises persons placed on probation by a court.

Provocation: Provocation is no ground for absolute exemption from criminal responsibility for a person's acts. However, grounds for mitigating circumstances may reduce the degree of the crime and the punishment.

Provost marshal: An army officer whose duties correspond to those of a chief of police.

Purposes of punishment: One of the prime objectives is the protection of society. The object is to prevent the offender from committing future wrongs while providing opportunity to reform the offender, to make public punishment an example to others and to bring about retribution for the wrong committed.

Rights guaranteed under the Constitution: (1) Right of the writ of habeas corpus. (2) Protection against the passage of bills of attainder or ex post facto laws. (3) Equality before the law by prohibiting the federal government from granting titles of nobility. (4) Right to a speedy trial in the case of accusation of a crime before an impartial jury at the place of the commission of the crime. (5) Freedom of religion, press, speech, assembly and petition. (6) Right to keep and bear arms for national defense. (7) Protection against the unlawful quartering of troops. (8) Right to a grand jury indictment before trial for a crime, to be confronted by witnesses, and to have the compulsory process to obtain witnesses and the assistance of counsel to establish innocence. (9) Protection against unreasonable search and seizure. (10) Protection against self-incrimination in any trial or in the giving of testimony. (11) Protection against being twice placed in jeopardy of life or limb for a crime. (12) Protection against cruel and unusual punishment and excessive bail. (13) Right to just compensation for any property taken for public use. (14) Right to a trial by jury in civil cases. (15) Protection against being deprived of life, liberty or property without due process of law. (16) Protection against the impairment of the obligations of contracts by the states. (17) Equal protection of the law. (18) Guarantee of a republican form of government in the state in which the citizen resides. (19) Protection from abridgment by the states of the privileges and immunities of citizens of the United States. (20) Protection from slavery and involuntary servitude except as punishment for a crime. (21) Right to hold public office in the United States if the citizen meets the statutory and constitutional qualifications. (22) Rights to freedom of ingress and egress from a state. (23) Protection from domestic violence and foreign invasion. (24) Protection from the abridgment of the right to vote by a state on account of race or sex.

Sheriff: The chief law enforcement officer of a county, chosen by popular election. The sheriff's principal duties involve aiding the criminal courts and civil courts of record, such as serving process, summoning juries, executing judgments, holding judicial sales and the like. Also serves as the chief conservator of the peace within a territorial jurisdiction.

Specific intent: When a crime consists not merely of commission but of an act accompanied by a specific intent, the existence of that intent is an essential element. In such cases the existence of criminal intent is not presumed from the commission of the act, but the specific intent must be proved.

State constitutions: Each differs materially from the U.S. Constitution. The former constitutes the restrictions or limitations of powers, whereas the latter constitutes, for the most part, grants of power.

State courts: The courts in the various states are created, and their jurisdiction is conferred and defined, by statutes. In some states, crimes committed on public conveyances may be prosecuted in any county through which the conveyance passed on the trip when the crime was committed.

Statutes: A statute provides that the state legislatures can punish any act unless restricted by the state or federal Constitution. Congress has no power to declare and punish crimes except those derived from the federal Constitution.

Substantive criminal law: Generally relates to the definition and classification of crimes, the criminal act, the criminal intent, the capacity to commit crime and exemptions from criminal liability, the parties to crime and a consideration of the important elements or characteristics of particular offenses.

U.S. Constitution: Together with the treaties made in pursuance thereof, the U.S. Constitution constitutes the supreme law of the land.

EVIDENCE

Evidence is any type of proof presented by the parties at trial through testimony of witnesses and the presentation of documents and other objects to induce belief in the court or jury. Evidence is either judicial or extrajudicial. Judicial evidence is the lawful means to ascertain the truth about a question of fact. Extrajudicial evidence is used to satisfy persons about facts requiring proof.

The following are some key concepts concerning evidence:

Acts and declarations of conspirators: When two or more persons conspire to commit a crime, everything they do to further their common purpose is admissible against each of them.

Adminicular evidence: Auxiliary or supplementary evidence presented to explain and complete other evidence.

Admissions and declarations by defendant: Declarations by the defendant or by the defendant's authority, if relevant, are admissible against the defendant.

Against whom confessions are admissible: A confession is admissible only against the person who made it. A confession by one defendant is not competent evidence against a codefendant.

Character evidence: Evidence of the character of a person is admissible in the following cases: (1) The fact that the defendant has a good character may be shown, but the state cannot show that the defendant has a bad character unless the individual's character is at issue, or unless evidence has been given that the defendant has a good character. (2) In prosecutions for homicide, the character of the victim as a violent and dangerous person may be shown when addressing the question of whether the defendant acted in self-defense. (3) A witness may be impeached by proof of bad character for truth and veracity.

Circumstantial evidence: Evidence directed to the attending circumstances; evidence that is inferential by establishing a condition of surrounding and limited circumstances, a premise from which the existence of the principal fact may be concluded by reasoning. When the existence of the principal fact is only inferred from one or more circumstances, the evidence is circumstantial. All presumptive evidence is circumstantial because it is derived from or made up of circumstances. All circumstantial evidence, however, is not presumptive, as it leads to necessary, instead of probable, conclusions.

Competency of witnesses: There is little difference between civil and criminal cases as regards the competency of witnesses and the mode of examining them. All persons are deemed competent to testify except those types described here. If, in the opinion of the judge, the witnesses are prevented by extreme youth, mental disability or any other cause of the same kind — including: (1) recollecting the matter on which they are to testify; (2) understanding the questions put to them; (3) giving rational answers to those questions; or (4) knowing that they ought to speak the truth — the individuals are deemed incompetent to testify. A witness unable to speak or hear is not incompetent, but may give evidence by writing or by signs, or in any other manner in which that witness can make it intelligible. Generally a husband or a wife cannot be a witness against a spouse, except for a crime committed against one spouse by the other spouse; the laws on this subject vary. In most states by statute, accused persons are allowed to testify in their own behalf, but they cannot be compelled to testify.

Competent evidence: That evidence which the law considers admissible.

Conclusive evidence: That evidence which is so strong and convincing that the law considers it beyond contradiction; that which establishes beyond any doubt.

Confessions: A confession is a statement made by a person charged with a crime, and is admissible against that person if voluntary. No confession is deemed voluntary if it was caused by any inducement, threat or promise from a person in authority.

Corroborative evidence: Strengthening or confirming evidence. Additional evidence of a different type that supports the same fact or proposition.

Declarations by persons other than defendant: Declarations by persons other than the defendant cannot be proved unless: (1) they are part of the *res gestae*, that is, statements made during the crime by the participants; (2) they are dying declarations; (3) they are declarations by authority of the defendant; or (4) they are evidence given in a former proceeding.

Direct evidence: Proof that shows a fact without needing to establish any other fact, as opposed to circumstantial or indirect evidence.

Documentary evidence: That which is supplied by writings and documents of every kind.

Dying declarations: An exception to the hearsay rule. In prosecutions for homicide, a statement made on behalf of the deceased as to the cause of death, and as to the circumstances that resulted in death, is admissible if it appears to the judge that when the statement was made, the person had given up all hope of recovery. The deceased must have been competent as a witness, and the facts stated must be such that the deceased could have testified to them. To be competent to testify to dying declarations, a witness must be able to state the substance as it was made, though the witness need not state it verbatim.

Evidence aliunde: Evidence "from another source." In some cases, a document can be explained by a witness to conversations or negotiations, that is, a source other than the document itself.

Evidence given in a former proceeding: Any evidence given in a former proceeding is admissible to prove the matter stated in a later stage of the same proceeding, under the following circumstances: (1) When the witness is dead. (2) When the witness is insane. (3) When the witness is out of the jurisdiction. (4) When the witness cannot be found within the jurisdiction. (5) When the person against whom the evidence is to be given had the right and the opportunity to cross-examine the witness during the former proceeding.

Evidence wrongfully obtained: If no objection is made at trial to illegally obtained evidence, an error cannot be claimed for the first time on appeal. If the record is unclear about whether the officers had a valid warrant, the seizure is presumed lawful.

Evident: Conclusive; plain; obvious.

Examination, cross-examination: Witnesses examined in open court must be first examined in chief. They may then be cross-examined and subsequently reexamined. The examination and cross-examination must relate to facts in issue. In most states, the cross-examination must be confined to the facts the witness testified about during the examination in chief. Reexamination must be directed to the explanation of matters referred to in the cross-examination. If a new issue is raised in reexamination, the adverse party may cross-examine about it.

Ex facie: "From the face"; apparent or evident.

Expert testimony: Testimony with respect to science or art may be given by persons specially skilled in any such matter. The words "science" and "art" include subjects on which a course of special study or experience is necessary. Where a witness possesses knowledge, not of the facts of the case but of a trade, science or art beyond that of the average person, that witness may give an opinion based on such special knowledge so that the jury may have this knowledge in arriving at a verdict.

Extraneous evidence: Refers to a contract, deed or other document. Extraneous evidence comes not from the document but rather from outside sources, as in evidence aliunde.

Extrinsic evidence: External evidence, or that which is not contained in the body of an agreement, contract or the like.

Facts in issue: Facts in issue include all facts that are in dispute or that tend to establish the guilt or innocence of the accused, or tend to support or disprove any special defense, such as former jeopardy or legal capacity of the accused to commit the crime charged.

Facts necessary to explain or introduce relevant facts: Facts are admissible: (1) If necessary to explain or introduce a fact in issue, or relevant to the issue. (2) If they support or rebut an inference suggested by any such fact. (3) If they tend to establish or disprove the identity of any thing or person whose identity is an issue or is relevant to the issue. (4) If they fix the time or place at which a fact occurred. (5) If they show the relation of the parties by whom any such fact was transacted. (6) If they afforded an opportunity for its occurrence or transaction. (7) If they are necessary to show the relevancy of other facts.

Facts relevant to the facts in issue: Evidence of any fact that, though not itself in issue, has a bearing on any fact in issue, is admissible.

Hearsay: Testimony of a witness who states what others have said rather than what the witness knows directly; it is admissible only in exceptional cases.

Impeaching the credit of a witness: A witness may be questioned on cross-examination as to bias, motive and interest in the case. The witness' credit may be impeached by the adverse party by the evidence of persons who are able to swear that they know the general reputation of the witness for truth and veracity. In some states, the inquiry may be made to the witness's general moral character, but in all states, the inquiry is open to general reputation. Specific acts by the witness sought to be impeached cannot be shown.

Incompetent evidence: Evidence inadmissible because of some defect in the witness or the evidence.

Indirect evidence: Evidence that supports a claim by consistency of presumptions and inferences.

Leading questions: Questions put or framed in such a form as to suggest the answers that are sought to be obtained by the person interrogating. Questions are leading that suggest to the witness a desired answer, or that embody a material fact and may be answered by a mere negative or affirmative, or that involve an answer bearing immediately upon the merits of the cause.

Legal evidence: All admissible evidence, both oral and documentary, that can prove the point at issue rather than raise more questions.

Material evidence: That which is relevant to the substantial matters in dispute. Evidence that has a direct bearing on the decision of the case.

Mathematical evidence: Evidence that establishes a necessary conclusion with certainty.

Moral evidence: As opposed to mathematical evidence, that type of evidence that results in a feeling of probability, based on induction, analogy, experience or testimony.

Motive: Any fact that shows a motive or lack of motive to commit the crime charged is admissible.

Newly discovered evidence: New evidence of material fact or evidence about a fact in issue, found by a party to a case after the verdict.

Number of witnesses necessary: In trials for treason, no person can be convicted unless the person pleads guilty, except upon the oath of two witnesses to the act. If in a trial for perjury, the only evidence against the defendant comes from one witness and no other evidence corroborates the witness, the defendant is entitled to be acquitted.

Opinion evidence: Testimony about what the witness believes or thinks rather than direct knowledge of the facts. Not admissible except (under certain limitations) from experts.

Original evidence: For example, an original document rather than a copy.

Other crimes: In a trial, the state cannot prove that the defendant committed another crime not connected with the crime charged. If the state of mind of the accused is at issue, and another crime might be relevant, the other crime may be raised.

Parol evidence: Oral or verbal evidence given by word of mouth.

Positive evidence: Direct proof of a point; evidence that establishes the truth or falsehood without relying on a presumption.

Preparation for act: Any fact or evidence tending to show preparations by the defendant to commit the act charged is admissible.

Preponderance of evidence: Greater weight of evidence, or evidence that is more convincing. In criminal cases, guilt must be established in the minds of the jury beyond a reasonable doubt and to a moral certainty, and the jury must be unanimous in its decision. Civil cases are decided on the basis of a preponderance, or weight, of the evidence, to a reasonable certainty, and only a majority, usually two-thirds, of the jury must agree.

Presumption of innocence: The defendant is presumed innocent, and the burden is on the state to prove guilt beyond a reasonable doubt and to a moral certainty.

Presumptive evidence: (1) Any evidence that is not direct and positive: the proof of minor or other facts incidental to or usually connected with the fact sought to be proved which, when taken together, inferentially establish or prove the fact in question to a reasonable degree of certainty. (2) Evidence that must be received and treated as true and sufficient until rebutted by other testimony; as where a statute provides that certain facts shall be presumptive evidence of guilt of title. (3) Evidence that can be explained or contradicted by other evidence, as distinguished from conclusive evidence.

Prima facie case: One in which the evidence in favor of a proposition is sufficient to support a finding in its favor, if all the contrary evidence is disregarded.

Prima facie evidence: That which is sufficient on its face; evidence that establishes a fact or a group of facts that make up a claim or defense, and if not contradicted remains sufficient.

Primary evidence: Evidence that, under every circumstance, affords the greatest certainty of the fact in question; firsthand or original evidence. A document is the best possible evidence of its existence and contents.

Privileged communications: (1) No husband is compelled to disclose any communication made to him by his wife during the marriage, and no wife is compelled similarly. (2) No one can be compelled to give evidence relating to any affairs of state, as to official communications between public officers upon public affairs, except with the permission of the officer at the head of the concerned department. (3) In cases in which the government is immediately concerned, no witness can be compelled to answer any question which would tend to disclose the names of persons by or to whom information was given as to the commission of offenses. (4) No legal advisor is permitted to disclose any oral or documentary communication made by a client during or after the termination of employment as such, unless given the client's expressed consent. The expression legal advisor includes lawyers, their clerks and interpreters between them and their clients.

Proper evidence: Evidence that may be presented under established legal rules.

Questions lawful in cross-examination: When witnesses are cross-examined, they may be asked any questions that test accuracy, veracity or credibility, or that shake their credibility by injuring their character. However, the court has a right to exercise its discretion and to refuse to compel such questions to be answered if it would not affect the credibility of the witness as to the matter to which testimony is required.

Real evidence: That which comes from things themselves on inspection rather than a description of them by a witness.

Rebuttal evidence: Evidence given to explain or disprove evidence given by the opposing side.

Relevant evidence: That which relates to, or bears directly upon, the point in issue, or conduces to prove a pertinent theory in a case.

Satisfactory evidence: Satisfactory proof; credible evidence in its amount or weight, sufficient to justify a conclusion.

Scintilla of evidence rule: The common law rule that if there is any reasonable evidence to support a position, the matter must be decided by the jury.

Secondary evidence: That which is derived from primary evidence, such as a copy of a document, or oral evidence about the document.

Self-incrimination: Under the constitutions and at common law, no one is bound to answer any question if the answer tends to expose the witness to any criminal charge, or to any penalty or forfeiture that the judge regards as reasonably likely to be preferred or sued for. However, no one is excused from answering any question only because the answer may establish, or tend to establish, that the person owes a debt or is otherwise liable to any civil suit. If a defendant offers to be a witness, the defendant cannot refuse to answer proper questions on cross-examination.

Statement inconsistent with present testimony: Witnesses under cross-examination in any proceeding, civil or criminal, may be asked whether they have made any former statement, relative to the matter of the action, that is inconsistent with the present testimony.

Statements accompanying acts: Statements accompanying and explaining an act made by or to the person doing it may be proved if they are necessary to understanding the act.

State's evidence: Testimony given by an accomplice or participant in a crime against the other participants, usually given under a promise of immunity or reduced sentence.

Substantive evidence: Evidence used to prove a fact rather than evidence given to discredit a witness.

Substitutionary evidence: That which substitutes for the original evidence, e.g., when a witness testifies about a lost document.

Sufficient evidence: Evidence adequate to justify the action sought. It may be satisfactory or prima facie evidence.

Traditionary evidence: Evidence about traditions or statements of deceased persons about matters such as boundaries, admitted because no direct witness can be found.

Weight of evidence: The preponderance of credible evidence, offered in trial to support one side of the issue.

WHERE TO GO FROM HERE

Alexander, Shana. *The Pizza Connection: Lawyers, Money, Drugs, Mafia*. New York: Weidenfeld & Nicolson, 1988. A massive account of what went on behind the scenes of the eighteen-month trial of twenty-two Mafiosi.

Anderson, David. *Crimes of Justice: Improving the Police, the Courts, the Prisons*. New York: Times Books, 1988. Looks at the breakdown of the criminal justice system at every level and offers some possible solutions.

Bailey, F. Lee, and Harvey Aronson. *The Defense Never Rests*. New York: Stein & Day, 1971. One of the first trial lawyer autobiographies. It covers several of his most famous cases, including Sam Sheppard.

Byron, Christopher. *Skin Tight: The Bizarre Story of Guess v. Jordache — Glamour, Greed and Dirty Tricks in the Fashion*

Industry. New York: Simon & Schuster, 1992. A wild ride, in and out of court, through a corporate takeover battle, family feuds, an IRS investigation, even an investigation of the IRS.

Coleman, Lee. *The Reign of Error: Psychiatry, Authority and Law.* Boston: Beacon Press, 1984. Though somewhat dated, this is still a good introduction to the issues surrounding the use of psychiatry in criminal justice.

Couric, Emily. *The Divorce Lawyers: The People and Stories Behind Ten Dramatic Cases.* New York: St. Martin's Press, 1992. A sometimes startling look at what goes on in divorce courts.

Davis, Gwynn. *Making Amends: Mediation and Reparation in Criminal Justice.* New York: Routledge, 1992. A look at problems with reparation programs and the possibilities for making them more successful.

Forer, Lois. *Unequal Protection: Women, Children and the Elderly in Court.* New York: W.W. Norton, 1991. A Philadelphia judge assesses fairness in the administration of justice.

Gates, John, and Charles Johnson, eds. *The American Courts: A Critical Assessment.* Washington, D.C.: CQ Press, 1991. Probably best for those who have some background in political or social science. Technical, analytical, theoretical are all good descriptors of these articles, but the ideas can still supply excellent story elements.

Groner, Jonathan. *Hilary's Trial: The Elizabeth Morgan Case: A Child's Ordeal in America's Legal System.* New York: American Lawyer Books/Simon & Schuster, 1991. Hilary is the child of Elizabeth Morgan and Eric Foretich, two physicians who divorced. Dr. Morgan refused to comply with court-ordered visitation rights for Dr. Foretich because she contended he had sexually abused Hilary. For that she went to jail.

Morris, Norval. *Madness and the Criminal Law.* Chicago: University of Chicago Press, 1982. Written by a law professor, this is a lively and innovative approach to the legal issues surrounding madness.

Nizer, Louis. *Catspaw: The Famed Trial Attorney's Heroic Defense of a Man Unjustly Accused.* New York: Donald I. Fine,

1992. How Nizer and colleagues freed a man convicted of murdering his former in-laws.

Perry, Jr., H. W. *Deciding to Decide: Agenda Setting in the United States Supreme Court.* Cambridge, Massachusetts: Harvard University Press, 1991. The Supreme Court is asked to consider about five thousand cases a year, but less than 5 percent of them are reviewed. This is how cases are picked.

Savage, David. *Turning Right: The Making of the Rehnquist Supreme Court.* New York: John Wiley & Sons, 1992. How the Supreme Court changed between 1986 and 1991, including the Thomas hearings.

Senzel, Howard T. *Cases: A Courthouse Chronicle of Crime and Wit.* New York: Viking, 1982. A look at a New York City court through the eyes of a court administrator.

Sevilla, Charles. *Disorder in the Court: Great Fractured Moments in Courtroom History.* New York: W.W. Norton, 1992. Transcripts of unusual and funny moments in court.

Stanton, Bill. *Klanwatch: Bringing the Ku Klux Klan to Justice.* New York: Grove Weidenfeld, 1991. The story of the work of the Southern Poverty Law Center to control Klan intimidation and violence, largely through civil suits.

6

Prisons

PENAL SYSTEMS

Cities, states and the federal government each have their own penal systems. However, the type of crime and jurisdiction in which the crime was committed determine whether the trial is held in city, state or federal court.

The California prisons described in this chapter serve as examples of the types of penal institutions across the nation. The document "Visiting Instructions" used at the U.S. Penitentiary at Lompoc, California, is reprinted as an example of what is required when visiting an inmate at a federal institution. Contact the prisons you write about for further information.

Parole is an issue for any prisoner who is eligible because most want to be paroled. Recently, however, a number of prisoners have refused to apply for parole because they fear they won't be able to get a job, making conditions on the outside worse than on the inside. An information packet from the California parole program is reprinted in this chapter.

Capital punishment is another issue that can easily come up in your writing. In fact, it's more likely to come up in crime fiction than in real life, so it's important to know the law in the state you're writing about. The last section of the chapter is a summary of death penalty statutes in all fifty states.

RIGHTS OF CONVICTED FELONS

Prisoners retain their constitutional rights, but they may be deprived of privileges for infractions of prison rules. Punishment can include loss of work credits, movies or TV. A prisoner accused of a crime will be returned to court for trial. Trials of a person already serving time may be held in the prison.

Prisoners who have previously earned Social Security continue to receive it. Prisoners with pensions or business income are entitled to the income but may not be allowed to carry much cash.

CALIFORNIA CORRECTION INSTITUTIONS

The California Department of Corrections administers sixteen major institutions, thirty-four secure conservation camps, two community correctional centers and more than sixty-six local parole offices. The department is responsible for the control and programming of more than sixty-seven thousand persons in institutions and about thirty-eight thousand in the community under supervision of parole agents.

Institutions are classified as Security Levels I through IV. Level I is minimum, Level IV is maximum and Levels II and III are medium security confinement.

The following information is designed to give a capsule summary of the institutions and camps operated by the department. For additional information, write to:

Department of Corrections
Communications Office
630 K Street, Room 211
P.O. Box 942883
Sacramento, California 94283-0001

San Quentin State Prison (SQ)

Address: San Quentin State Prison, San Quentin, California
94964
Warden: Dan Vasquez
Population: 3,000
Opened 1852

San Quentin, California's first and best known penal institution, is located on the north shore of San Francisco Bay in Marin County. San Quentin dates its origin to the prison ship "Wabau," which was anchored off Point Quentin in 1852 with ninety-two prisoners aboard. Construction of the prison on twenty acres of nearby land began in the same year.

Today, the prison occupies 432 acres and houses three thousand inmates, a third of whom require the department's highest level of security. The prison complex includes four large old-style cell blocks, a modern maximum security unit, minimum security work crew quarters, a medium security compound with modular dormitories, an industries complex, maintenance and vocational shops and a medical facility. The state's only gas chamber is located in San Quentin and all male inmates under sentence of death are housed at San Quentin.

San Quentin has traditionally housed the state's most notorious prisoners. During the last decade, San Quentin has shared duty with Folsom Prison and Tehachapi (Southern Max) as Level IV or maximum security. Level IV is the security designation for the most disruptive or violent inmates, or those who present the greatest risk of escape. San Quentin also houses Level I (minimum custody) and Level II (medium custody) prisoners. San Quentin has provided maximum security housing for the state's roughest inmates for 135 years.

However, an aggressive prison construction program is providing California with state-of-the-art, high-tech maximum security prisons that will take over for San Quentin. New construction and extensive renovation of San Quentin will allow the transition from a Level IV mission to a Level II mission. Although San Quentin will continue to house Levels I, II and IV, Level II will predominate.

Correctional Training Facility (CTF)
Address: P.O. Box 686, Soledad, California 93960-0686
   Superintendent: Eddie Myers
   Population: 5,511
   Opened 1947

The Correctional Training Facility is actually a complex that consists of three separate facilities. The oldest part of CTF dates from 1946 when a camp center administered by San Quentin was opened on the site. In 1947, this became an institution in its own right. When the Central Facility was opened in 1951 as a medium security institution, the former camp center became known as South Facility. In 1958, the North Facility opened and the three-facility complex was officially christened the "Correctional Training Facility."

The CTF complex is located on a 965-acre site in the Salinas Valley about twenty miles south of Salinas.

CTF-Central is an armed perimeter, cell-type institution for medium security inmates. It also contains two high security protective housing units.

North Facility is also an armed perimeter, cell-type facility for medium security inmates, most of whom are involved in some type of educational/vocational program.

CTF-South is a Level I facility and houses most of the inmates who perform work outside the security perimeter. A comprehensive program of industrial and educational activities is available to CTF inmates. Emphasis is on basic training for employment in a recognized trade. The CTF's educational program meets the needs of inmates by offering classes on elementary and secondary levels as well as a two- and four-year college degree program. Various vocational programs are also available.

California Institution for Women (CIW)
Address: P.O. Box 6000, Corona, California 91718
   Superintendent: Annie M. Alexander
   Population: 2,243
   Opened 1952

Until 1933, women prisoners in California were housed in a

segregated building on the grounds at San Quentin. In 1929, legislation established an independent facility for women at Tehachapi, which became operational in 1933. The present 120-acre site in San Bernardino County was acquired and a new women's institution was established in 1952.

CIW is one of two facilities designated by the penal code exclusively for female felons. All female felons committed to the Department of Corrections are received at CIW. Buildings at CIW provide double-bunked rooms and dormitories, in addition to general population housing units and the reception center.

CIW is rated as a Level III/IV institution and houses inmates integrated by custody Level I through IV in its general population.

Approximately 35 percent of the inmate population is involved in an education program.

CIW is designated as the camp training center for female inmates who are administratively assigned to Sierra Conservation Center and transferred to Camos Rainbow, Mailbu, Puerta La Cruz or McCain Valley. CIW provides two inmate crews, under the direction of CalTrans, to work on state highway roadside beautification.

The Prison Industry Authority (PIA) work program at CIW consists of a textile factory involved in the manufacturing of shirts, jackets and men's underwear. PIA, in a joint venture, is also training inmates in furniture upholstery and is contracting with local state agencies to reupholster worn furniture.

Folsom State Prison (FOL)

Address: P.O. Box W, Represa, California 95671
  Warden: R.G. Borg
  Population: 6,344
  Opened 1880

California State Prison at Folsom is the state's second oldest correctional facility. Folsom is considered a high maximum security institution. Among its inmates are those serving long sentences, habitual criminals, hard-to-manage persons and individuals who present a risk to the safety of others.

At Folsom, a walled perimeter encompasses three general population cell blocks and two maximum security housing units. Outside the main facility, Folsom's minimum facility serves as a 410-bed dormitory unit. Program features for minimum security inmates include outside work crew assignments and community reentry resources for inmates nearing release.

Recently, three maximum security housing units with a design capacity of 1,536, and minimum security housing for two hundred, were completed. These are now fully occupied.

One of the state's best-known prison industries, the metal stamping and fabricating program that produces the license plates for California motor vehicles, is located at Folsom.

Academic classes from first grade through the college level are offered at Folsom, as are a variety of vocational training programs. Group counseling, organized recreation and a number of inmate activity groups are also available to inmates.

The handicraft program at Folsom includes the operation of a hobbycraft shop that is open daily to the public and is located at the prison's main gate. Through this shop and an art show held each year, many inmates are able to display and sell art and craft products. The Folsom Art Show receives considerable local news media attention and is widely attended.

California Institution for Men (CIM)

Address: P.O. Box 128, Chino, California 91710
   Superintendent: Otis Thurman
   Population: 6,676
   Opened 1941

The California Institution for Men is situated on more than twenty-five hundred acres in the city of Chino. CIM consists of four physically separate facilities.

When it was opened as California's third correctional institution in 1941, CIM was unique in the field of penology because it was known as the "prison without walls." CIM-Minimum is the minimum security facility and houses the largest number of inmates.

In 1951, an addition to the original facility was completed. This unit is now known as Reception Center-Central. It is one of two reception centers for newly sentenced male felons from southern

California counties. The reception centers are delegated the arduous task of ensuring the inmate is transferred to the appropriate prison.

The second reception center, Reception Center-West, a dormitory facility, processes presentenced diagnostic cases for the courts, and houses overflow from the central reception center.

The fourth addition to CIM was in 1974 with the acquisition of a former state facility originally built for the Youth Authority. Currently, this facility, CIM-East, serves as a parole violator processing unit.

All custody levels from minimum through maximum security are provided at CIM.

Vocational training provided at CIM ranges from animal grooming and television repair to commercial deep sea diving. A full array of academic programs is also available. Work ethic values are taught in all vocational educational and work incentive programs. CIM provides a viable setting for those wishing to redirect their lives while emphasizing security and commitment to public safety.

Deuel Vocational Institution (DVI)

Address: P.O. Box 400, Tracy, California 95378-0004
   Superintendent: Midge Carroll (Acting)
   Population: 2,626
   Opened 1953

Deuel Vocational Institution is a medium security institution located near Tracy in the San Joaquin Valley.

The institution proper is encircled by two chain link fences forming a security perimeter with eight gun towers. The design capacity is 1,506. Within the general population area of the prison, there are ten cell blocks and two inmate-worker dormitories. There is also one specialized administrative segregation unit. In addition to these units located within the armed perimeter, a 278-bed dormitory-style facility, located on institution property, houses minimum custody inmates assigned to critical work projects outside the armed perimeter, including community work crews.

The institution's primary emphasis is on work/training incentive, where inmates who work or who are involved in the academic vocational programs can earn time off their sentences.

Academic courses are provided for inmates from basic non-readers through college. Twenty-two vocational training programs are available to inmates. An extensive on-the-job training program involving vocational education, maintenance and industries allows inmates to apply skills learned in vocational education to real work situations.

Prison Industries operates a furniture factory, mattress factory, textile assembly factory, trucking distribution center, farm and dairy, where inmates are paid on the basis of skills, production and hours worked.

Part of Deuel Vocational Institution will serve as a reception center in the future.

California Men's Colony (CMC)

Address: P.O. Box 8101, San Luis Obispo, California 93409
Warden: Wayne Estelle
Population: 6,898
Opened 1954

The East Facility, completed in 1961, was originally designed to house twenty-four hundred inmates but has been modified to house forty-three hundred. The security perimeter consists of two chain link fences controlled by security wire and eight armed-guard towers.

The facility is divided into four units or quadrangles with a gate control tower located in the center. Each quad has its own dining room, elementary classrooms and athletic fields, and contains two three-story buildings to house inmates. A well-equipped sixty-five bed hospital and clinic staffed by physicians, dentists and other medical personnel is also available to serve the CMC population.

The primary mission of the California Men's Colony is to implement the department's goals of providing psychiatric treatment and evaluation for all members of the CMC population who require such treatment. A team of psychiatrists, psychologists and neurological consultants offers a comprehensive program of psychiatric evaluation and treatment. In addition, the East Facility offers both academic and vocational education classes through the college level. Prison Industries also operates several industrial programs offering paid work experience at the institution.

The minimum security West Facility was established in 1954 to house fourteen hundred inmates, but has recently been modified and renovated to house twenty-four hundred.

The West Facility offers academic education and vocational training classes.

Unit III, which is enclosed by a single nontowered fence line, includes inmate maintenance crews assigned to the National Guard Unit at Camp San Luis and inmates working outside the security perimeter fence at both CMC facilities. A work/fire camp (Camp Cuesta), operated jointly by the Department of Corrections and the Department of Forestry, is located on Unit III's grounds.

California Correctional Institution (CCI)

Address: P.O. Box 1031, Tehachapi, California 93561
Superintendent: B.J. Bunnell
Population: 4,551
Opened 1955

The California Correctional Institution is located approximately fifty miles east of Bakersfield in a valley among the Tehachapi Mountains.

Legislation passed in 1929 authorized the construction of the Tehachapi facility to provide living quarters for women felons. Previously, all female felons had been housed at San Quentin Prison. The institution was completed in 1932 and occupied by women beginning in 1933. In 1952, an earthquake forced evacuation of the buildings. The women were moved to a new facility that was under construction near Corona.

The Tehachapi facility was reopened as a branch of the California Institution for Men in 1955, and was declared a separate facility in 1964. Construction of a medium security addition was completed in 1967. Construction of two five hundred man security units was completed and the units were occupied in October 1985.

Construction of a five hundred cell Level III unit was recently completed.

CCI acts as a program institution for the confinement of Levels I through IV inmates who are willing to work and participate fully in available programs. Academic education from nonreader through high school is available with special programs for non-English-speaking inmates. Vocational programs have fifteen trade sections, and the Prison Industries program produces inmate apparel, flags, drapes, decals and office furniture. The religious program is one of the most active in CDC.

California Medical Facility (CMF)

Address: P.O. Box 2000, Vacaville, California 95696-2000
  Superintendent: Eddie Ylst
  Population: 7,920
  Opened 1955

The California Medical Facility was established by the legislature in 1948 and originally opened at Terminal Island in 1950. The facility moved to its present location in 1955.

Originally designed to house 1,487 inmates, the capacity of CMF has been increased to house 1,854 with the addition of an outside dormitory. In 1956, the Northern Reception Center complex, with a capacity of 472, was added to process adult male felons from the northern California counties. The reception center also prepares presentence diagnostic evaluations for northern counties.

The main complex serves as a medical and psychiatric treatment facility for adult male felons. Programs include the treatment of chronic psychotics, group therapy, a ninety-day observation program for evaluation of management cases and medical treatment for inmates requiring surgery or long-term medical care. CMF also houses a work force of medium security inmates to support institutional operations.

CMF-South is the newest addition to the CMF complex. It stands within a separate fenced perimeter and is designed to provide housing for 2,404 Level II and III inmates, bringing the total capacity of the institution to 4,730. Although the name CMF-South implies a medical function, the specific focus of CMF-South is vocational training and prison industries production.

Inmates at CMF may participate in a variety of vocational and educational courses at the elementary, high school and college level. CMF has a large selection of self-help and religious programs. The institution also has an extensive arts and crafts program, including public exhibitions and sales of inmate handicrafts.

California Rehabilitation Center (CRC)

Address: P.O. Box 1841, Norco, California 91760
  Superintendent: Len Chastain
  Population: 4,712
  Opened 1962

Originally a private resort, then a hotel and later a U.S. naval hospital, the property on which the California Rehabilitation Center is located was acquired in 1962 to establish a program for the treatment and control of narcotic addicts.

The institution now functions as a Level II facility for both male and female felons, as well as civil commitments with a history of drug abuse. CRC is located in Norco, in Riverside County, about fifty miles east of Los Angeles.

Buildings within the ninety-three acre complex include the original resort facility. Once occupied by Navy nurses and hospital wards, the buildings have been converted to dormitories.

The facility houses a population of approximately one thousand women and thirty-seven hundred men in separate areas of the institution.

Program opportunities include academic education (elementary through high school and some college), vocational training classes (some co-ed), various work programs including a conservation camp (Camp Norco), a prerelease program to assist individuals with their reentry needs, prison industries and outside work crews. These crews work in the local community and under contract for CalTrans.

Inmates are also encouraged to participate in a variety of religious programs and self-help groups. Some groups are heavily involved in community programs concerning problems of alcohol or drug abuse, while others learn participatory management through councils established to meet with staff and help solve problems that arise within the institution. All physically capable inmates must participate in work or education programs.

California Correctional Center (CCC)
Address: P.O. Box 790, Susanville, California 96130
Superintendent: William Merkle
Population: 5,098 (including camps)
Opened 1963

The California Correctional Center is located eighty miles north of Reno, Nevada, near the Lassen County city of Susanville.

The institution was originally opened as California Conservation Center in 1963 and served as the hub facility for Northern California conservation camps. However, the mission of the facility was changed in 1975 from a camp center to a facility to house medium security inmates. The name of the facility was changed at that time to its present title, California Correctional Center, to reflect its new mission.

In July 1982, the center was once again designated as the hub facility for the northern conservation camps. These ten camps have the capacity to house more than one thousand inmates. Five additional camps are being planned with a capacity to house an additional five hundred inmates.

Although the primary mission is to service the camp system, there are several hundred inmates housed within the center who are not eligible for camp. Academic and vocational programs available to these inmates include repairs and modifications of wood, metal, automotive, clothing products and shoes for state agencies. Cleaning and repair of clothing for schools and fire departments, local road cleanup and minor repair, park maintenance and canvas modification and repair for the Department of Forestry are among other programs offered. The inmates housed inside the center are also assigned to support services. Support assignments include culinary, clerical, maintenance and other duties needed to run the institution.

A new five hundred bed unit was recently finished for medium security inmates. This consists of five buildings, each containing one hundred cells.

Sierra Conservation Center (SCC)

Address: P.O. Box 497, Jamestown, California 95327
 Superintendent: R.E. Doran
 Population: 5,592 (including camps)
 Opened 1965

Opened in 1965, the Sierra Conservation Center's primary purpose is to train inmates for placement in the state's central and southern camps, which are jointly operated by the Department of Corrections, Department of Forestry and the Los Angeles County Fire Department. The camps are located throughout central and southern California, from Sacramento County to San Diego County.

SCC is located near Jamestown in the state's historic gold rush country. The facility is divided into two housing units — one providing light security controls, the other medium. Both units utilize dormitory living.

Inmates are selected for SCC either directly from the department's reception centers or from other institutions.

Staff under contract from the Department of Forestry instruct inmates in firefighting, reforestation, cutting fuel breaks and flood control. In addition, a special program of physical conditioning prepares inmates for hard work in rugged terrain and on forest firelines prior to their camp assignment.

Vocational training programs include mill and cabinet work, masonry, welding, auto mechanics, body and fender work and upholstery. While they are undergoing forestry and physical fitness training at SCC, inmates may take part in recreation, religious, self-help and work programs.

The SCC main facility is designated as a Level I and II institution. A five-building, five hundred inmate Level III addition to the existing facility was recently occupied.

California State Prison, Avenal

Address: P.O. Box 8, Avenal, California 93204
Superintendent: Al Gomez
Design Capacity: 3,034
Opened 1987

The CSP-Kings County at Avenal is located roughly one and one-half miles southeast of Avenal, about seventy-five miles southwest of Fresno, on a 640-acre site.

The groundbreaking ceremony was conducted on December 18, 1985, and the first busload of inmates was received on January 28, 1987.

CSP Avenal is a program institution for the confinement of Level II inmates who are willing to work and participate fully in available programs. Academic education as well as a variety of vocational training programs will be available upon completion of construction. The Prison Industries Board has also approved a variety of industries for this facility.

Mule Creek State Prison

Address: P.O. Box 409099, Ione, California 95640
Superintendent: Roger C. Schaufel
Design Capacity: 1,700
Opened 1987

Mule Creek State Prison is located just west of the town of Ione and about forty miles south of Sacramento.

Upon completion of construction, each of three facilities will contain five housing units. One housing unit is a one hundred cell short-term administrative segregation unit, and the remaining housing units are one hundred cells each, suited for general population.

On June 10, 1987, Facility C was activated and received inmates.

Mule Creek State Prison is a program institution for the confinement of Level I and III inmates who are willing to work and fully participate in available programs. Academic and vocational programs will be available upon completion of construction. The Prison Industry Authority has developed and approved a variety of industries for this facility.

Richard J. Donovan Correctional Facility (RJD)

Address: P.O. Box 73200, San Ysidro, California 92073-9200
  Superintendent: J.M. Ratelle
  Design Capacity: 2,200
  Opened 1987

The Richard J. Donovan Correctional Facility at Rock Mountain is on a 774-acre site, southeast of the city of San Diego, approximately twelve miles inland from the Pacific Ocean and two miles north of the Mexican Border. The "Rock," as it is affectionately known, opened July 27, 1987. The facility added two thousand medium security (Level III) and two hundred minimum security (Level I) beds to the California state prison system.

The prison has four fifty-five bed medium security facilities and one two hundred bed minimum security facility.

The primary mission of the Richard J. Donovan Correctional Facility is to provide housing and supervision for inmates requiring medium security. This Level III facility is primarily designed as a training and work-oriented facility that will provide comprehensive vocational, academic and industrial programs. The facility provides work opportunities for 100 percent of the inmates.

The Prison Industry Authority Enterprises approved for this prison include a textile mill, key data entry service, vehicle refurbishing and repair, regional bakery, license plate factory, optical laboratory and regional laundry. Vocational programs include baking, meatcutting, landscape gardening, lens grinding, airframe mechanics, aircraft power plant mechanics, mill and cabinetry work, small engine repair, office machine repair, graphic arts and printing, machine shop practices, autobody painting, auto mechanics, dry cleaning and building and janitorial maintenance.

The Richard J. Donovan Correctional Facility is designated as the department's Southern Deportation Unit and provides two hundred beds for the utilization of this program.

The facility also is a Southern Processing Unit for parole violators returned to custody (PV-RTC) for San Diego and Imperial counties. This unit will provide two hundred beds for the processing of these cases.

The Richard J. Donovan Correctional Facility assists in fulfilling the department's goal to distribute inmates to geographic areas from which they were committed.

Northern California Women's Facility (NCWF)

Address: P.O. Box 213006, Stockton, California 95213-9006
Superintendent: Teena Farmon
Design Capacity: 400
Opened 1987

The Northern California Women's Facility is located in San Joaquin County, just south of Stockton, adjacent to the Northern California Youth Center.

The first women's prison located in northern California, NCWF is a medium security facility, consisting of four one hundred cell housing units.

The first inmates were received July 27, 1987, and design capacity was reached on August 12, 1987.

NCWF is a program institution for the confinement of inmates willing to work and participate fully in available programs. Basic adult education and vocational programs (electronics and data processing) are available for interested inmates.

Prison Industries programs include Key Data Entry and Laundry Operations.

Conservation Camps

The conservation camp program has evolved from the system of road camps that was inaugurated in 1915. Known successively as Highway Camps, Harvest Camps and Honor Camps, they were devised to relieve overcrowded prison conditions and create useful employment for inmates who were able to achieve minimum security status.

Today, the Department of Corrections, the Department of Forestry and other cooperating agencies jointly administer thirty-four conservation camps. Corrections is responsible for camp management, housekeeping and the supervision of inmates. Cooperating agency staff supervise the work of inmate crews and are responsible for custody of inmates on daily project duties.

The typical camp has from eighty to one hundred twenty inmates. Assigned to each camp are eight to ten correctional personnel and seven to eleven cooperating agency staff.

Inmates are assigned to camps after completion of training at SCC or CCC. Most inmates spend an average of one year in a camp assignment and are paid a small daily wage while assigned.

During an average fiscal year, camp crews spend more than one-half million man hours in fire suppression. Crews may be dispatched from camps hundreds of miles away from the scene of a major fire and sometimes spend a week or more at a fire camp location.

In addition to firefighting, inmate crews undertake fire hazard reduction, fire and truck trail construction, reforestation, work related to the preservation and conservation of natural resources and other projects for state, county or local agencies.

While assigned to a camp program, inmates may enroll in academic classes and some camps offer vocational training courses. Most camps now have family visiting units for inmate use.

FEDERAL BUREAU OF PRISONS

The Bureau of Prisons, which is part of the U.S. Department of Justice, has its Central Office in Washington, D.C. (202-724-3198). The staff of the Central Office coordinates all the activities of the agency. Major functions include planning, policy development, management of manpower and other resources, budget development, monitoring the quality of programs and services and coordinating the activities of the regional offices and institutions.

Central Office staff have primary responsibility for public information activities, legal and legislative affairs and relations with the Congress and policy-making administrators in other government and private organizations. Central Office staff also adjudicate appeals for inmates and employees, direct research and evaluation projects, design automated information systems, manage environmental health and safety programs and conduct management-employee bargaining with the American Federation of Government Employees (AFL-CIO) Council of Prison Locals.

New Facilities

Marianna, Florida—Federal Correctional Institution
Capacity—750 beds, including 150-bed satellite camp
Medium Security
Activation: Camp, March 1988; Main Institution, May 1988

Los Angeles, California—Metropolitan Detention Center
Capacity—588 pretrial detainees
Medium Security
Activation: October 1988

Sheridan, Oregon—Federal Correctional Institution
Capacity—550 beds, with adjacent 250-bed satellite camp
Medium Security
Activation: May 1989

Bradford, Pennsylvania—Federal Correctional Institution
Capacity—550 beds, with adjacent 150-bed satellite camp
Medium Security
Activation: June 1989

Fairton, New Jersey—Federal Correctional Institution
Capacity—550 beds
Medium Security
Activation: October 1989

Jesup, Georgia—Federal Correctional Institution
Capacity—666 beds
Medium Security
Activation: October 1989

Many other small construction or renovation projects are underway to increase the capacities of existing bureau facilities.

Federal Bureau of Prisons

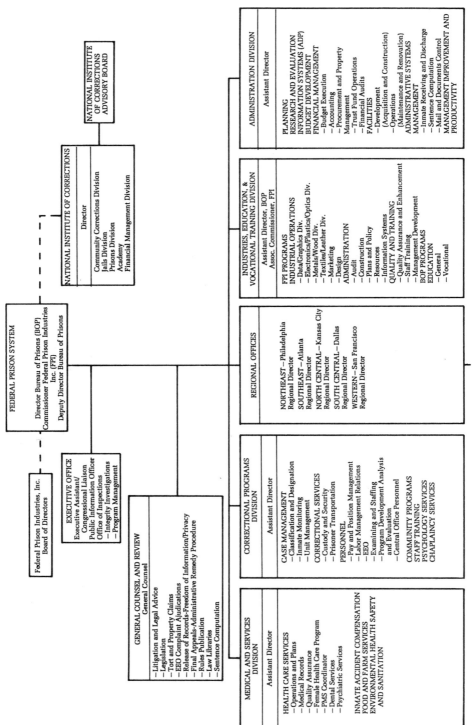

FEDERAL PRISON SYSTEM
Director Bureau of Prisons (BOP)
Commissioner Federal Prison Industries Inc. (FPI)
Deputy Director Bureau of Prisons

Federal Prison Industries, Inc.
Board of Directors

NATIONAL INSTITUTE OF CORRECTIONS
Director
- Community Corrections Division
- Jails Division
- Prisons Division
- Academy
- Financial Management Division

NATIONAL INSTITUTE OF CORRECTIONS ADVISORY BOARD

EXECUTIVE OFFICE
Executive Assistant/
Congressional Liaison
Public Information Officer
Office of Inspections
– Integrity Investigations
– Program Management

GENERAL COUNSEL AND REVIEW
General Counsel

– Litigation and Legal Advice
– Legislation
– Tort and Property Claims
– EEO Complaint Adjudications
– Release of Records-Freedom of Information/Privacy
– Final Appeals-Administrative Remedy Procedure
– Rules Publication
– Law Libraries
– Sentence Computation

MEDICAL AND SERVICES DIVISION
Assistant Director

HEALTH CARE SERVICES
– Operations and Plans
– Medical Records
– Quality Assurance
– Female Health Care Program
– PMS Coordinator
– Dental Services
– Psychiatric Services

INMATE ACCIDENT COMPENSATION
FOOD AND FARM SERVICES
ENVIRONMENTAL HEALTH SAFETY
AND SANITATION

CORRECTIONAL PROGRAMS DIVISION
Assistant Director

CASE MANAGEMENT
– Classification and Designation
– Inmate Monitoring
– Unit Management
CORRECTIONAL SERVICES
– Custody and Security
– Prisoner Transportation
PERSONNEL
– Pay and Position Management
– Labor Management Relations
– EEO
– Examining and Staffing
– Program Development Analysis and Evaluation
– Central Office Personnel
COMMUNITY PROGRAMS
STAFF TRAINING
PSYCHOLOGY SERVICES
CHAPLAINCY SERVICES

REGIONAL OFFICES

NORTHEAST – Philadelphia
Regional Director
SOUTHEAST – Atlanta
Regional Director
NORTH CENTRAL – Kansas City
Regional Director
SOUTH CENTRAL – Dallas
Regional Director
WESTERN – San Francisco
Regional Director

INDUSTRIES, EDUCATION, & VOCATIONAL TRAINING DIVISION
Assistant Director, BOP
Assoc. Commissioner, FPI

FPI PROGRAMS
INDUSTRIAL OPERATIONS
– Data/Graphics Div.
– Electronics/Plastics/Optics Div.
– Metals/Wood Div.
– Textiles/Leather Div.
– Marketing
– Design
ADMINISTRATION
– Audit
– Construction
– Plans and Policy
– Resources
– Information Systems
QUALITY AND TRAINING
– Quality Assurance and Enhancement
– Staff Training
– Management Development
BOP PROGRAMS
EDUCATION
– General
– Vocational

ADMINISTRATION DIVISION
Assistant Director

PLANNING
RESEARCH AND EVALUATION
INFORMATION SYSTEMS (ADP)
BUDGET DEVELOPMENT
FINANCIAL MANAGEMENT
– Budget Execution
– Accounting
– Procurement and Property
Management
– Trust Fund Operations
– Financial Audits
FACILITIES
– Development
(Acquisition and Construction)
– Operations
(Maintenance and Renovation)
ADMINISTRATIVE SYSTEMS
MANAGEMENT
– Inmate Receiving and Discharge
– Sentence Computation
– Mail and Documents Control
MANAGEMENT IMPROVEMENT AND
PRODUCTIVITY

FIELD OPERATIONS

Federal Correctional System

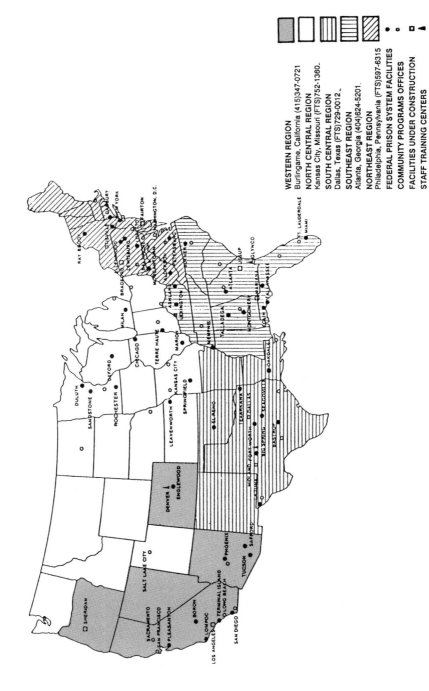

WESTERN REGION
Burlingame, California (415)347-0721
NORTH CENTRAL REGION
Kansas City, Missouri (FTS)752-1360.
SOUTH CENTRAL REGION
Dallas, Texas (FTS)729-0012_
SOUTHEAST REGION
Atlanta, Georgia (404)624-5201.
NORTHEAST REGION
Philadelphia, Pennsylvania (FTS)597-6315
FEDERAL PRISON SYSTEM FACILITIES
COMMUNITY PROGRAMS OFFICES
FACILITIES UNDER CONSTRUCTION
STAFF TRAINING CENTERS

Federal Bureau of Prisons

USP-Lompoc Visiting Instructions

The following information was provided by officials at USP, Lompoc:

Families and friends of the men at USP, Lompoc (3901 Klein Boulevard, Lompoc, California 93436), are their primary contact with the community. Visiting, therefore, becomes much more important during the time a man is confined. Because of the special nature of the institution and our concern for the security and well-being of the men here, we have developed the following instructions and regulations, which we ask you to follow:

Normally members of the immediate family (parents, brothers, sisters, wife and children) are automatically placed on the inmate's approved visiting list. Persons who are not immediate family members and yet would like to be on the approved list should request so to the inmate's assigned unit management staff. After a person's name is placed on the approved list, it is not necessary to obtain permission in advance of a visit. All other persons must obtain permission in advance to visit. This may be done by writing to the inmate's assigned unit staff, USP, Lompoc, California 93436, at least four weeks before the visit is planned. If the visit is granted, the requesting party will be notified by letter of authorization, which must be presented to the institution at the time of the visit.

Visiting will be permitted from 8:30 A.M. to 3:30 P.M., weekdays and weekends, except on Tuesday and Wednesday, when the visiting room will be closed. Consideration will be given to opening the visiting room on federal holidays that occur on Tuesday or Wednesday. Legal holidays are New Year's Day, Washington's Birthday, Memorial Day, Independence Day, Labor Day, Columbus Day, Veteran's Day, Thanksgiving and Christmas.

Each inmate will be allotted forty points permitting twenty to forty hours of visiting per month. On weekends and holidays, the inmate will be charged two points for each hour of visiting. On weekdays, the inmate will be charged one point for each hour of visiting. These limitations are necessary to avoid overcrowding in the visiting area and excessive loss of time from the inmate's program. Reasonable requests for additional visits due to unusual circumstances will be made in advance to the unit management staff.

Normally only four persons are permitted to visit an inmate at any one time, including children. Visitors under sixteen years of age must be accompanied by a legal guardian, who must also be on an approved visiting list. Children must be the son, daughter, brother or sister of the inmate. Visitors will be responsible for keeping the children in their company and under control within the bounds of the visiting area.

Female visitors are expected to use good taste in their dress. Persons who come immodestly or provocatively dressed will be denied the privilege of visiting.

Appropriate embracing, kissing and handshaking by immediate family members will be permitted within the bounds of good taste at the beginning and termination of the visiting period.

All visitors must have some valid proof of their identification with them. I.D.s must have appropriate picture identification. Signature identification by itself will not be acceptable. Visitors may present a state driver's license, federal or state I.D. cards, welfare cards or passports as picture identification.

Visitors may purchase candy, cigarettes and beverages from the machines located in the visiting area. These items must be consumed by the inmate and his visitor during the visit. The inmate may take nothing back to his quarters. The visitor may bring only the following items into the visiting area: change purse, money, cigarettes, lighter or matches, comb, heart medication, jewelry normally worn, and diaper bag to include baby bottle, food, clothes, diapers, powder or lotion. Unauthorized items will be stored in security lockers provided in the front lobby or may remain in the visitor's vehicle. The visitor may retain the key to the locker during the storage period and return the key at the end of the visiting period.

To introduce contraband of any kind into this institution is a violation of Federal Law (Title 18, Section 1791, U.S. Code).

Inmates are furnished all necessities, and visitors should refrain from bringing articles or gifts of any kind. Cameras and tape recorders are not permitted in the visiting area. Inmates will not be permitted to sign or exchange any papers during the visit. The visiting room officer may request a search of the visitor's personal property. Those visitors found with contraband items will be escorted from the institution and normally removed from the visiting privileges for an extended period or permanently.

The institution is located approximately five miles northwest of Lompoc. Drive west through the city on Ocean Avenue (Route 246), turn right on Floradale Avenue, proceed approximately three miles (through the traffic light, across the bridge and around the bend) to the main entrance road. Signs will direct you to the main entrance. Taxi and bus service are available from Lompoc to the institution.

No parking is allowed on the roadway leading to the institution or in the circle drive immediately in front of the main gate. Visitors will be directed to the left side parking lot, where visiting parking is clearly marked. No occupants may remain in parked cars. Non-visitors must leave the institution reservation and may return to pick up the visitors at a prearranged time.

We suggest you arrive no earlier than fifteen minutes before visiting begins, as we do not have adequate waiting room facilities, and you might be inconvenienced. Usually you will be permitted to visit as long as possible, but it may be necessary on occasion to limit the amount of visiting time to relieve overcrowding. Also, a failure to comply with these instructions may result in termination of the visit or suspension or cancellation of the visiting privilege.

PAROLE

Parole is a period of supervision in the community beginning after an inmate's prison term reaches the legal maximum. This conditional release provides supervision and control over offenders after they return to society.

Parole is a critical period. Through the application of controls and provision of services, the parole agent creates favorable conditions for the parolee's successful adjustment. As a law enforcement professional, the agent has broad discretion over the life and street-level experience of a parolee. Both community protection and the parolees' transition are of paramount concern.

How Long Does Parole Last?

The duration of parole is based on law.

Most convicted criminals are sentenced under the Determinate Sentencing Law, which defines the prison terms for all but life sentences. Nonlife inmates are subject to three years on parole, but can be discharged from parole supervision after one year when no parole violations have been detected.

Offenders convicted of life sentences who have been released on parole are subject to five years under supervision; however, they can be discharged after three years if no parole violations have been detected during that time.

When Are Inmates Released to Parole?

Nonlifers: Under determinate sentencing, inmates are released when they serve the term imposed by the court. An inmate can reduce this sentence by satisfactory performance in prison work, training or education programs. By law, inmates will be awarded a six-month reduction in their sentence for every six months of full-time performance in a qualifying program.

Corrections is required to provide all eligible inmates an opportunity to participate in the work/training program. It is believed that participation in this program will instill good work habits, teach some skills and improve reintegration into society.

Being involved in the work/training program is a privilege, not a right. An inmate can lose work-time credit by inappropriate behavior. However, a percentage of these lost work credits can be restored by subsequent good behavior.

Lifers: The Board of Prison Terms (BPT), an independent agency that works with Corrections, is responsible for setting parole dates for inmates serving life sentences. The BPT determines if and when these inmates are suitable for reentry into society.

Life sentences are imposed for crimes of murder, attempted murder, kidnapping for robbery or ransom, aggravated assault by a life prisoner, train wrecking, sabotage and exploding destructive devices causing mayhem. Inmates who have been convicted of an offense that involved the infliction of great bodily injury (including habitual sex offenders) and who have two or more prior terms for specified offenses also receive life sentences as habitual offenders.

All life sentences, except life without possibility of parole, have minimum-eligible-parole dates. The first parole consideration hearing for a life prisoner is held approximately one year before the inmate's first parole eligibility date.

For lifers, release to parole is not automatic. The BPT annually denies parole to about 93 percent of those who have hearings. No single factor indicates an inmate's suitability or unsuitability for parole. The BPT reviews all facts of the case at the hearing, then, using its discretion and experience, makes the determination whether to grant or deny parole.

What Happens on Parole?

Each parolee is supervised by a parole agent, who follows the parolee's activities. To determine the appropriate level of supervision, the agent conducts a needs-and-risks assessment for each parolee. Predictive indicators, such as latest commitment offense, criminal behavior patterns and undesirable associations, are considered when assessing the possible risk to the community.

Based on the assessment, a parolee falls into one of four major categories:

High control — Has the potential for assaultive behavior or a history as a large-scale drug dealer.

High services — Requires support to meet psychological, physical or employment needs.

Control/Services — Medium risk; requires moderate amounts of both control and services.

Minimum — Low risk with minimal support needs.

Parolees are provided services according to their identified needs. The parole agent is expected to make sure that each parolee's identified needs are met. In attempting to assist the parolee to make a successful parole adjustment, the agent uses various community programs, employment referrals and emergency food and shelter.

Most parole unit offices have a services specialist responsible for obtaining services for parolees. Paroles provide direct cash assistance for indigent parolees and operate two psychiatric-outpatient clinics for treatment of parolees with serious mental problems. Service agents and individual parole agents often work with other agencies to obtain services for parolees in need.

What Are Conditions of Parole?

Each parolee agrees in writing to abide by the following four conditions:

Parole Agent Instructions. Must obey all instructions given by the parole agent.

Release, Reporting and Travel. Must report immediately upon release; notify change in residences; report when instructed.

No Criminal Conduct.

Weapons. Cannot own, use, have access to or have under control, any type of weapon or ammunition.

In addition, special conditions of parole may be imposed individually for cause, including antinarcotic testing, treatment at a parole-outpatient clinic (for psychiatric monitoring), abstinence from alcohol or prohibition against residing in a given location or associating with specific individuals.

Parolees are subject to search without a warrant by parole agents and law enforcement officers.

Where Is the Parolee Placed?

Current law requires that parolees be returned to the county where they were committed. CDC may release a parolee in a county other than the county of commitment if the placement would be in the best interests of the public and the parolee. Placement to another county may be based on the following factors:

The need to protect the life or safety of a victim, a witness or any other person.

The verified existence of a unique work offer or an educational or vocational training program.

The last legal residence of the inmate.

The existence of family with whom the inmate has maintained strong ties and whose support would increase the chance of a successful parole.

The lack of necessary mental health treatment programs for outpatients in the county of commitment.
Public concern that would reduce the chance that the inmate's parole would be successfully completed.

Local chiefs of police or sheriffs are notified regarding persons paroled within their jurisdiction. Each month, detailed information on parolees and reentry inmates is provided to more than two hundred California law enforcement agencies. About 80 percent of all parolees are returned to the county of commitment.

Can Parole Be Revoked?

If a parolee violates the law or the conditions of parole, the agent in most cases will place the parolee in custody. The BPT then conducts a revocation hearing to determine if, in fact, a parole violation has occurred. If good cause is found, the BPT examines the facts of the case, the type of offense and the parolee's adjustment on parole and determines if the parolee must return to prison. Violators may be returned to custody for up to twelve months. The BPT returns more than 90 percent of parole violators to prison.

If a parolee engages in misconduct while in custody, the revocation may be extended for up to twelve months.

Reentry Programs

As a result of the dramatic increase in prison population, the use of community programs is expanding. Community reentry programs provide the opportunity for transition from close confinement to less restrictive living for selected inmates within 180 days of parole.

Work Furlough. Work furlough centers are operated by the Department of Corrections, private profit and nonprofit organizations and county sheriff's departments. This program provides housing, food and supervision to selected male and female inmates 90 to 120 days prior to their release. Inmates leave the facility during the day to work at a variety of jobs.

Prisoner Mother. Community prisoner-mother programs are operated by private profit and nonprofit organizations. By reuniting mothers with their children, the program hopes to alleviate the harm caused to children by the separation from their mothers during incarceration.

Also available to participants are drug and alcohol abuse counseling, parenting classes, vocational and educational training and the opportunity to reintegrate into society.

Return to Custody. Return-to-custody facilities (RTCs) are operated by private organizations and by city and county law-enforcement agencies. RTCs offer carefully selected, low risk male and female parole violators the opportunity to remain closer to their families during their parole-revocation period. These facilities also reduce the impact of the high parole violator population on prison overcrowding.

All inmates must meet the RTC screening criteria to be eligible for this reentry program. Violent offenders and those with sex crimes are ineligible.

Substance Abuse Treatment. The Department of Corrections, in conjunction with the return-to-custody program, is developing a specialized program for substance abuse treatment centers. For violators with drug- and/or alcohol-dependency problems, the program provides intensive substance abuse counseling. It will consist of three thirty-day phases: phase one includes intake, program orientation and treatment; phase two focuses on program participation and job development; and phase three is devoted to job placement and work furlough.

Restitution. Correction's first community restitution center was opened in early 1988 to provide a means for felons to repay their victims' financial losses. Restitution fees are ordered by the sentencing court or agreed on by the defendant and victims.

Offenders will be incarcerated at a community-based facility. They will be allowed to leave the center during specific hours for work only. At all other times, they must remain at the center.

When offenders receive a paycheck, work expenses will be deducted. The balance of the check will be divided into thirds: one-third paid to the department for operating expenses, one-third paid to the victim and the final third given to the inmate.

This facility also serves as an alternative to imprisonment and will help lessen prison overcrowding.

House Arrest—An Innovation. Paroles runs a pilot "house arrest" system in Ontario and Indio. Low risk parolees who normally would be returned to custody for drug use while on parole instead will be detained under arrest within their own homes.

Each parolee assigned to the project will wear an electronic monitoring device. Parolees in the Ontario portion of the project leave the house for certain purposes, such as work, during specified time periods, but must be at their residence all other times. When the telephone rings at undisclosed times of the day and night, they must be there to answer the call. The Indio area project does not permit these parolees to leave home. The electronic device transmits an alarm to a computer that will notify the parole agent if the parolees attempt to leave the home area.

Parole officials estimate that keeping 150 parolees on house arrest will save the state more than $2.5 million per year.

Parolees under house arrest must meet the following screening criteria: no serious crimes; no sex offenses; and no history of violence, large-scale drug dealing or involvement with weapons.

Parole Officers

The California Department of Corrections has authorized more than one thousand parole agents. Located at seventy-one field offices throughout the state, these agents currently supervise more than thirty-eight thousand parolees. This translates to an average caseload of about fifty-three parolees per agent. Supervision for each parolee costs about twelve hundred dollars per year.

Additional Information

For more information concerning parole, please contact one of the following offices:

State Headquarters: Parole & Community Services Division
   Corporate Center
   501 J Street, Room 330
   Sacramento, California 95814
   (916) 445-6200

Region I—Covers the entire Central Valley from Bakersfield to the Oregon border:
  1631 Alhambra Boulevard
  Sacramento, California 95816
  (916) 739-2860

Region II—Covers the San Francisco Bay Area:
  Ferry Building, Room 2040
  San Francisco, California 94111
  (415) 557-2861

Region III—Covers Los Angeles and the San Fernando Valley:
  107 South Broadway, Room 3003
  Los Angeles, California 90012
  (213) 620-2404

Region IV—Covers San Diego area, extending into Orange County:
  1840 East 17th Street, Room 240
  Santa Ana, California 92701
  (714) 558-4131

CAPITAL PUNISHMENT

Thirty-six states and the federal government have capital punishment laws. The following lists the offenses that can result in execution and the means in which execution may be carried out:

Alabama: Murder during kidnapping; robbery; rape; sodomy; burglary; sexual assault; arson; murder of a peace officer, correctional officer or public official; murder while under a life sentence; murder for pecuniary gain or under a contract; aircraft piracy; murder by a defendant with a previous murder conviction; murder of a witness to a crime. Method: electrocution.

Arizona: First degree murder. Method: lethal gas.

Arkansas: Capital murder as defined by Arkansas statute: felony murder; arson causing death; intentional murder of a law enforcement officer; murder of prison, jail, court or correctional personnel or military personnel acting in the line of duty; intentional murder of a public officeholder or candidate; intentional murder while under a life sentence; contract murder. Method: Lethal injection for those whose capital offense occurred after July 4, 1983; for offenses occurring prior to that date, the condemned prisoner may elect lethal injection or electrocution.

California: Treason; aggravated assault by a prisoner serving a life sentence; first degree murder with special circumstances; train wrecking; perjury causing execution. Method: lethal gas.

Colorado: First degree murder; kidnapping with death of victim; felony murder; murder of victim under eighteen; intentional murders in furtherance of illegal drug sales or distribution. Method: lethal injection.

Connecticut: Murder of a public safety or correctional officer; murder for pecuniary gain; murder in the course of a felony; murder by a defendant with a previous conviction for intentional murder; murder while under a life sentence; murder during a kidnapping; illegal sale of cocaine, methadone or heroin to a person who dies from the use of those drugs; murder during first degree sexual assault; multiple murders. Method: electrocution.

Delaware: First degree murder with aggravating circumstances. Method: lethal injection.

Florida: First degree murder. Method: electrocution.

Georgia: Murder; kidnapping with bodily injury when victim dies; aircraft hijacking; treason; kidnapping for ransom when the victim dies. Method: electrocution.

Idaho: First degree murder; aggravated kidnapping. Method: lethal injection or firing squad.

Illinois: Murder accompanied by one to ten aggravating factors; drug conspiracy; residential burglary and having a preconceived plan as aggravating factors. Method: lethal injection.

Indiana: Murder with twelve aggravating circumstances. Method: electrocution.

Kentucky: Aggravated murder; kidnapping when victim is killed. Method: electrocution.

Louisiana: First degree murder; treason. Method: All death sentences on or after January 1991 carried out by lethal injection.

Maryland: First degree murder, either premeditated or during the commission of a felony. Method: lethal gas.

Mississippi: Murder of a police or correctional officer; murder while under a life sentence; murder by bomb or explosive; murder by contract; murder committed during a specific felony (rape, burglary, arson, robbery, sexual battery, unnatural intercourse with a child, nonconsensual intercourse, unnatural intercourse); murder of an elected official; aircraft piracy. Method: Lethal injection for those convicted after July 1, 1984. Lethal gas for those convicted prior to that date.

Missouri: First degree murder. Exclusion from capital sentencing for first degree murder committed by person under age 16. Method: lethal gas or lethal injection.

Montana: Deliberate homicide; aggravated kidnapping when victim or rescuer dies; attempted deliberate homicide; aggravated assault or aggravated kidnapping by a state prison inmate who has a prior conviction for deliberate homicide or who has been previously declared a persistent felony offender. Method: lethal injection or hanging.

Nebraska: First degree murder. Method: electrocution.

Nevada: First degree murder. Method: lethal injection.

New Hampshire: Contract murder; murder of a law enforcement officer; murder of a kidnapping victim; killing another after being sentenced to life imprisonment without parole. Method: hanging only if lethal injection cannot be given.

New Jersey: Contract, purposeful or knowing murder. Method: lethal injection.

New Mexico: First degree murder; felony murder with aggravating circumstances. Method: lethal injection.

North Carolina: First degree murder. Method: lethal gas, lethal injection.

Ohio: Assassination; contract murder; murder during an escape; murder while in a correctional facility; murder after a conviction for a prior purposeful killing or prior attempted murder; murder of a peace officer; murder arising from specified felonies (rape, kidnapping, arson, robbery, burglary); murder of a witness to prevent testimony in a criminal proceeding or in retaliation. Method: electrocution.

Oklahoma: Murder with malice aforethought; murder arising from the commission of specific felonies (forcible rape, robbery with a dangerous weapon, kidnapping, escaping lawful custody, first degree burglary, arson); murder when the victim is a child who has been injured, tortured or maimed. Method: lethal injection.

Oregon: Aggravated murder. Method: lethal injection.

Pennsylvania: First degree murder. Method: lethal injection or electrocution.

South Carolina: Murder with statutory aggravating circumstances. Method: electrocution.

South Dakota: First degree murder; kidnapping with gross permanent injury inflicted on victim; felony murder. Method: lethal injection.

Tennessee: First degree murder. Added new section prohibiting imposition of death sentence on defendants convicted of first degree murder who are found to be mentally retarded at time of offense providing for consideration of diminished intellectual capacity as a mitigating circumstance. Method: electrocution.

Texas: Murder of a public safety officer, firefighter or correctional employee; murder during the commission of specific felonies (kidnapping, burglary, robbery, aggravated rape, arson); murder for remuneration; multiple murders; murder during prison escape; murder by a state prison inmate. Method: lethal injection.

Utah: First degree murder. Method: lethal injection or firing squad.

Virginia: Murder during the commission or attempt to commit specified felonies (abduction, armed robbery, rape); contract murder; murder by a prisoner while in custody; murder of a law enforcement officer; multiple murders; murder of a child under twelve years during an abduction; murder arising from drug violations; willful, deliberate and premeditated

killings arising from violations of controlled substances statute. Method: electrocution.

Washington: Aggravated first degree premeditated murder.
Method: lethal injection or hanging.

Wyoming: First degree murder, including felony murder.
Method: lethal injection.

Minimum Age for Capital Punishment (1990)

Under 18

Arkansas (14)
Georgia (17)
Indiana (16)
Kentucky (16)
Louisiana (16)
Mississippi (16; minimum age by statue is 13 but effective age
   is 16, based on U.S. Supreme Court decision)
Missouri (14)
Montana (10, but only after transfer hearing to try juvenile as
   an adult)
Nevada (16)
New Hampshire (17)
North Carolina (17, but if murderer was incarcerated for mur-
   der when a subsequent murder occurred, the age is 14)
Oklahoma (16)
South Dakota (10, but only after transfer hearing to try juvenile
   as an adult)
Texas (17)
Utah (16)
Virginia (15)
Wyoming (16)

Age 18

California
Colorado
Connecticut
Illinois

Maryland
Ohio
Oregon
Tennessee
Federal system: less than 18 but not younger than 14 if waived
   by juvenile court.

No Age Specified
Alabama
Arizona
Delaware
Florida
Idaho
Nebraska
Pennsylvania
South Carolina
Washington

WHERE TO GO FROM HERE

If a jail or prison is a major setting for your story, make a visit.
If you're writing about a real prison, of course it's best to go there,
but if that's not possible you can probably find a prison near you
that's similar.

The books listed here are by scholars, inmates, families and
prison staff. They are about most aspects of prisons, from how to
build them to how they ought to be run to how they actually run.

Dicks, Shirley, ed. *Congregation of the Condemned: Voices
   Against the Death Penalty.* Buffalo, New York: Prometheus
   Books, 1991. The mother of a death row prisoner put to-
   gether this wide-ranging look at capital punishment.

Farbstein, Jay. *Correctional Facility Planning and Design.* 2d
   ed. New York: Van Nostrand Reinhold, 1986. Discusses how
   the criminal justice process relates to types and sizes of jails
   and what sorts of facilities are safest for inmates and staff.

Harris, Janet. *Crisis in Corrections: The Prison Problem.* New
   York: McGraw-Hill, 1973. Though dated, this study has good

information of the development of prison policy in the United States.

Harris, Jean. *Marking Time: Letters From Jean Harris to Shana Alexander.* New York: Charles Scribner's Sons, 1991. The woman convicted of murdering Dr. Herman Tarnower writes about life in prison.

Harris, Robert. *Crime, Criminal Justice and the Probation Service.* New York: Routledge, 1992. Discusses a variety of subjects surrounding the British Probation Service.

Irwin, John. *The Jail: Managing the Underclass in American Society.* Berkeley: University of California Press, 1985. The author did five in Soledad, then got a Ph.D. in sociology, and later studied jails (not prisons) in California.

Kelly, Barbara. *Children Inside: Rhetoric and Practice in a Locked Institution for Children.* New York: Routledge, 1992. A close look at a secure British facility for juveniles.

Luger, Jack. *Improvised Weapons in American Prisons.* Port Townsend, Washington: Loompanics Unlimited, 1985. This one may be hard to find, but could be very helpful in describing how a prisoner would make a weapon.

Muncie, John, and Richard Sparks, eds. *Imprisonment: European Perspectives.* New York: St. Martin's Press, 1991. Surveys the history of European penal systems, the effects of a variety of policies and the current move to standardize policies.

Rideau, Wilbert, and Ron Wickberg. *Life Sentences: Rage and Survival Behind Bars.* New York: Times Books, 1992. This is a collection of articles from the award-winning inmate newspaper, *The Angolite*, at the Louisiana State Penitentiary at Angola.

Ryan, Tom, with Bob Casey. *Screw: A Guard's View of Bridgewater State Hospital.* Boston: South End Press, 1981. Bridgewater is perhaps the most notorious prison for the "criminally insane" in the country. This guard's-eye view has the kernels of many stories in it.

Travisono, Diana, ed. *Juvenile and Adult Correctional Departments, Institutions, Agencies and Paroling Authorities Directory.* Laurel, Maryland: American Correctional Association, annual. Gives brief descriptions of virtually any agency you'd want to know about and the names and phone numbers of the people to contact for more information. This directory also includes information concerning military and Canadian facilities.

7
Language

SLANG

Slang in the criminal world and in the drug culture is not chiseled in stone. It changes constantly. The slang listed here has been compiled over a period of years. By the time this book goes to press, much of it will have changed. Check with local authorities for the newest slang terms. A number of recent books on slang and jargon are included in the bibliography at the end of this chapter.

Police and Crime Slang

Abbot: nembutal (barbiturate)

Acapulco gold: high grade of marijuana from Mexico with a gold tint

Ace: marijuana cigarette

Acid: LSD

Acid freak: habitual user of LSD who displays bizarre behavior

Acid head: LSD user

A.C.U.: anti-crime unit

A.D.: airport detachment

A.D.A.: assistant district attorney

Agates: Nembutal
Alice B. Toklas: brownie with marijuana baked in it
Ameba weed: parsley saturated with PCP
Ammo: ammunition
Amped-out: fatigue after using methamphetamine
Angel grass: parsley saturated with PCP
Antsy: nervous, restless; typical feeling obtained from using amphetamines
Apache: signal that Internal Affairs is around
Apples: secobarbital
A.R.: armed robbery
Artillery: injection paraphernalia
A.S.A.C.: Assistant Special Agent in Charge (FBI)
A.T.F.: Bureau of Alcohol, Tobacco and Firearms
Bad mouth: derogatory statement
Bad scene: unpleasant experience
Bad trip: panic reaction or unpleasant experience from use of hallucinogen
Bag: drugs packaged in containers, such as paper, balloons, plastic bags, etc.
Bag 'em: have corpse placed in body bag; put evidence in bags
Bag man: one who moves or transports for organized crime
Bajours: gypsy con artist term for a big deal
Bale: 75 to 500 pounds of marijuana compressed into a bale
Balloon: drug, usually heroin, packaged in toy balloons
Bananas: insane
Banker: person receiving or holding cash paid for drugs
Barbs: barbiturates
Barrel: 100,000 pills
Base: free-basing or smoking cocaine
B.C.: birth control pills
B.D.: burglary detail
Bean: pill, most commonly referring to Benzedrine tablets or capsules
Beat: to cheat or steal
Beat the rap: to get acquitted
Beautiful: all-purpose term of approval
Be down on: be angry at, disapproving of

Behind stuff: using heroin
Belcher: informer
Bennies: Benzedrine tablets
Bernice: cocaine
Betty: skeleton key
Bike: motorcycle
Biker: member of a motorcycle gang
Bindle: quantity of drugs packaged in various containers
Bite: to solicit for a loan, as in "to put the bite on"
Black Beauty: methamphetamine hydrochloride capsule
Black stuff: smoking opium
Blacktar: distilled, concentrated heroin
Blade: knife
Blade man: criminal known to use a knife
Blast: to smoke a marijuana cigarette; fun
Bleeder: extortionist
Block: quantity of compressed hashish
Blow: to smoke a marijuana cigarette; to inhale cocaine; cocaine
Blue dot: blue dot of LSD placed on a small piece of paper
Blues: sodium amytal
Body trip: to be under the influence of a drug that affects physical condition, such as heroin, as opposed to a mind trip as with LSD
Boiler: auto
Bomber: unusually large marijuana cigarette
Boogie: to leave
Book: bookmaking operation; to leave; rules and regulations
Bookends: to go as a pair
Bookie: one who takes bets; one who "makes book"
Boost: to shoplift or steal
Booster: shoplifter or thief
Bopper: one who shoots firearms; a hit man
Bottle: 100 pills
Bowl: pipe used for smoking hash
Boy: heroin
Brain bucket: motorcycle helmet
Bread: money

Brick: one kilo (2.2 pounds) of a drug, commonly used for marijuana packaged in a brick shape

Brownie: traffic cop

Brown stuff: heroin from Mexico with brown coloration

Bubble gum: anything that appeals to adolescents

Bubble gummer: an adolescent

Bug: burglar alarm; listening device, wire; to annoy; itching sensation due to cocaine poisoning

Bugs: crazy, insane

Build up: the story that sets the victim up for the fall

Bull: policeman

Bullet: one-year jail sentence

Bummer: rotten; bad luck; a depressing situation

Bum rap: false, unjustified accusation

Bum trip: bad experience

Bunco: a scam

Bunk: poor quality drugs

Burn: shoot; electrocute; substance sold in lieu of narcotics; to cheat or steal

Burned: user has received bad or weak drugs

Burned out: mentally incapable as a result of drug use

Busboy: prisoner or suspect being shifted around

Bush: marijuana

Bust: a police raid; an arrest

Buster: blackjack

Butterfly man: forger

Button man: someone who selects or points out the job

Buy: a narcotics deal

Buzz: immediate feeling after use of a drug

Buzzer: policeman's shield

By the book: follow rules and regulations

C: cocaine

Callgirl: high priced prostitute

Can: ounce of marijuana

C&H: cocaine and heroin

Candle and blood: initiation into Mafia

C&M: cocaine and morphine

Candy: jewelry

Cap: capsule
Caper: crime
Cap the deal: the agreement that a deal has been struck
Cap up: transfer drug in bulk form into capsules
Carga: heroin (Spanish)
Carry: to be in possession of drugs or a gun
Cartwheel: Benzedrine tablet
Case: criminal complaint; reconnoiter
Caseload: active cases pending
Catching: officer on duty or assignment
Cavalry: police reinforcements
Cecil: cocaine
Changes: adjustments
Chart: posted list of unsolved cases assigned to investigators
Chatterbox: machine gun
Chemicals: synthetic drugs
Cherry: novice
Chicken hawk: child molester
China white: Asian heroin, white in color
Chippy: occasional user
Chiv: knife
Chiva: heroin
Chop: as opposed to stripping an auto, to chop is to remove the auto's fenders, grill, bumpers, rear and quarter panels
Chopper: machine gun; modified motorcycle
Chop shop: place where stolen vehicles are chopped to be sold for parts
Christmas bundles: large sums of money
Chump: victim
Citizen: outsider; nonuser; square
Clean: not in possession of drugs; not engaged in illegal activities; refined marijuana
Clean up: to stop using drugs
Clow: victim
Coca-cola: cocaine
Cocaine blues: depression attributed to discontinuing the use of cocaine
C of D: chief of detectives

C of O: chief of operations

Coin: money

Coke: cocaine

Coke out: cocaine use to the point of incoherence

Coke spoon: tiny spoon for inhaling cocaine

Cokie: cocaine user

Cold turkey: stopping use of a drug suddenly

Collar: arrest

Colors: emblem or identifying colors of gangs

Come down: to begin to come off the influence of drugs

Comer: person on the way up

Con: to dupe someone out of money by gaining their confidence; confidence man; convict

Connect: to make contact

Connection: person who sells drugs; a source

Contact high: being under the influence of a drug through contact and not actual use

Contract: hire to kill

Cook, cook up: to prepare a drug for injection by heating it in water to dissolve

Cooker: any container used to hold a drug while it is being heated; a chemist in an illicit drug lab

Cool: at ease; no problems; content; O.K.; good

Cop: to purchase drugs; steal; to obtain

Cop a plea: plea bargain; to accept with explanation

Copilot: Benzedrine

Cop out: to quit; to admit something or plead guilty

Cotton: small piece of cotton used as a filter when preparing a drug for injection

Cotton mouth: hard, dry feeling in the mouth after smoking marijuana

Crack: crystallized cocaine

Cracker: southerner

Crank: methamphetamine

Crash: to break into; to come down after a drug-induced high

Crash pad: place to sleep

Crate: a large quantity of pills, usually 50,000

Crew: youngsters who come together to engage in crime

Crib: one's home or residence
Crink: methamphetamine
Croak: to kill
Croaker: doctor
Cross-tops: Benzedrine tablets
Crutch: device used to hold a marijuana cigarette
Crystal: methamphetamine
Crystals: disinfectant used to eliminate the decaying odor of a
    dead body
C.S.U.: crime scene unit
Cube: sugar cube containing LSD
Cush: money
Cut: to share; to adulterate drugs to obtain a larger quantity
Cut loose: to release
D.B.: dead body
D.D.: dying declaration
D.E.A.: Drug Enforcement Agency
Deal: to sell drugs
Dealer: anyone who sells drugs
Deck: packet of heroin
Dexies: dextroamphetamine tablets
Diamonds: amphetamine tablets
Diamond season: warm weather
Dig: to understand; to like
Dime: ten; ten dollars
Dime bag: ten dollars' worth of drugs
Dip: pickpocket
Dirty: to possess drugs or be under the influence; officer who
    is corrupt
D.O.A.: dead on arrival
Do-rag: tight head scarf
Do him/her: to kill him/her
Do it: to go or leave
Dolly: methadone
Dome: form of LSD, usually in capsule
Dope: a narcotic or dangerous drug, usually heroin
Do up: to inject
Down, get down: to inject a drug

Downer: drug with a depressant effect; low mood

Down on: to dislike a person; oral sex

D.P.: emotionally disturbed person

Drag: something or someone who is boring; to smoke a marijuana cigarette; street

Dresser: stock motorcycle

Dried out: detoxified, withdrawn from a drug

Dripper: syringe

Drivers: Benzedrine

Drop: receiver of stolen goods; to kill

Drop gun: unofficial weapon carried by officer

Dropped: taking drugs through the mouth

Dropper: syringe

Drying out: abstaining from alcohol

Dude: male

Duke in: to introduce

Dump on: to unload

Dupe: victim

Dust: money; to kill

Dynamite: unusually strong or pure drug; terrific

Eat: to swallow drugs or narcotics

Eight ball: method of packing ⅛ ounce of cocaine

Elbow: method of packaging one pound of cocaine

Enforcer: someone who carries out or enforces instructions of a criminal boss, usually through intimidation

Engine: outfit for smoking opium

E.P.V.: emergency police van

Eye-opener: first drug used during the day

Factory: location where illicit drugs are manufactured

Fall: to be arrested, "taking a fall"

Far out: favorable, good; extreme

Feds: federal law officers

Fence: someone who buys and sells stolen goods

Fifty cents: fifty dollars' worth of drugs

Fin: five dollars

Finger: to point out or identify

Finger lid: measure amount of marijuana in plastic bag by using fingers, for example, three-fingered lid

Fink: detective; informer; to betray
Fit: injection paraphernalia
Five cents: five dollars' worth of a drug
Fix: to inject a drug; bribe
Flack: trouble
Flack jacket: protective vest
Flag: warning
Flake: cocaine
Flaky: unstable
Flash: euphoria following the taking of a drug; sudden thought; to vomit after taking drugs
Flashback: recurring experience from effects of LSD
Flash powder: methamphetamine
Flat: table of LSD
Flipped out: crazy
Floater: body recovered from water
Fluff: to run a powdered drug through a sifter or nylon stocking to give it a light texture
Flyers: the con men working the flying game
Fox: attractive female
Freak: heavy user of a drug; scared
Freak out: bad experience
Free base: to smoke cocaine
Freebie: free, at no cost
Freeze: the numbness caused by using cocaine
Fried: nonfunctional due to drugs, often amphetamines or PCP
Frisk: pocket picking; examine for weapon or contraband
Front: to give in advance of receiving
Fry: to electrocute
Fuzz: police
Gage: marijuana
Garbage: poor quality drugs
Garden room: the morgue
Gat: firearm
Gee: gasket between needle and syringe
Geeze: to inject a drug
Get back: stay calm
Get down: to use a drug

Get fresh: to buy new clothes
Get off: to use drugs
Get rocks off: enjoying yourself or sexual climax
Gig: job; means of obtaining money
Gimmicks: injection paraphernalia
Girl: cocaine
Going down: happening; about to happen
Gold: Acapulco gold marijuana
Gone: leaving now, as in "I'm gone"
Goods: merchandise; drugs
Goofball: barbiturate
Gopher: errand boy
Gow: narcotics; opium-pipe cleaner
Grass: marijuana
Grease: to bribe, as in grease someone's palm with money
Greta: marijuana
Grider: motorcycle front end with single spring
Grid search: search conducted section by section of grid map
Griefo: marijuana
Grifter: swindler
Groove, groovy: very good; to enjoy
Grounder: easy assignment
Guide: experienced LSD user who supervises another person's LSD trip
Gum: opium
Gun: injection paraphernalia
H: heroin
Habit: need for a drug; addiction
Hack it: do it
Handle: understanding; getting a grip; name
Hanger banger: a person who steals a pocketbook hanging on a woman's arm
Hanging paper: passing bad checks
Hang it on him: to frame someone
Hang it up: to abstain from something or delay; mental block
Hang tough: take it easy
Happening: event; action
Hard stuff: heroin, cocaine, morphine

Hardtail: motorcycle with a rigid frame (with no suspension in back)

Hard time: jail time in state prison

Harmon: motorcycle front end with no springs

Harness: uniform

Harness bull: police

Harry: heroin

Hash: hashish

Hassle: trouble with someone

Hay: marijuana

Head: drug user

Head screw: prison warden

Hearts: amphetamine

Heat: police chase; police pressure; police officer

Heater: gun

Heavy: serious, of great importance; bad or violent person; extreme

Heeled: having money

Heist: robbery

Heister: highway robber, as in truck holdup

Hemp: marijuana

Hep or hip: to be aware of

Her: cocaine

High: under the influence; on drugs; happy

Him: heroin

Hink: to make paranoid

Hit: to inject a drug; to borrow a drag of a marijuana cigarette; to kill

Hit man: contract killer

Hit on: to approach someone sexually; to borrow

Hock: to pawn; to annoy someone

Hog: person who uses any drugs available; stock motorcycle

Hold or holding: to be in possession of drugs

Holding pen: cell where prisoner awaits booking

Holster: needle holder of any sort

Home boy: neighborhood kid; gang member

Honky: white person

Hooked: addicted

Hooker: prostitute

Hop: opium

Horn: to inhale drugs through the nose

Hospital case: notification that a victim needs medical help

Hot: stolen

Hot shot: a fatal dose of narcotics, usually heroin

Hots, the: to like, especially to like a person sexually

Hustle: to steal; confidence racket

Hype: short-change; make a big deal of something; one who uses hypodermic needle to inject drug

I.A.D.: internal affairs division

In-and-out book: record of officer transfers

In pocket: to possess drugs

Inside man: partner of con artist

Jakes: uniformed police officers

Jam: cocaine

Jane Doe: unidentified female (usually a corpse)

Jelly: cocaine

Jimmy: to pry open

Job: being on the police force

Job, do a: physically hurt someone

John: rich guy; male customer for a prostitute

John Doe: unidentified male (usually a corpse)

Joint: marijuana; prison

Jolt: injection of drug; feeling after injecting a drug

Joy pop: irregular use of narcotics

Jug: 1,000 pills

Juice: influence; methadone in orange juice; liquor

Juju: marijuana

Jumper: bail jumper; an individual who leaps from a building or bridge

Junk: drugs, usually heroin

Junkie: heroin addict

K: known, as in KG for known gambler

Kee, key: one kilogram (2.2 pounds) of a drug, usually marijuana or heroin

Keeper: prisoner held on formal charges

Keester plant: drugs hidden in rectum

Keg: 50,000 pills
Kick: to stop; to stop taking a particular drug, especially heroin
Kill ring: area that indicates mortal wound
King's habit: use of cocaine
Kinky: weird, strange, abnormal
Kit: injection paraphernalia
Kit man: a con artist
Knock off: to stop; to murder
Kook: strange person
Lab: equipment used to manufacture drugs illegally
Lam: escape
Lamb: victim
Latent: invisible print found by dusting polished surfaces
Later: to see or talk to a person at a later time
Lay: sexual intercourse; to give something
Laying paper: passing bad checks
L.B.: pound
Lead: clue; direction to be followed
Leaf: opium
Legit: legal
Lid: one ounce of marijuana
Lieutenant: right-hand man of a large drug dealer
Lighten up: to take it easy or stop
Lightweight: something or somebody of no consequence
Like: expression used for emphasis or to gain attention
Limey: English motorcycle
Line: thin line of cocaine for inhaling with a straw
Lit up: under the influence of a drug
Liz: police patrol
Loaded: under the influence of a drug
Loaf: 2.2 pounds of marijuana
Looker: attractive woman
Looking: seeking to purchase drugs
Lose your cool: to lose control of oneself
Low rider: down-and-out addict
Low riders: group distinguished by their vehicles built low to
   the ground
Ludes: quaaludes

M: morphine
Machine: motorcycle
Machinery: injection paraphernalia
Mainline: to inject a drug directly into the vein
Main man: close associate; boss; partner
Maintain: to remain calm
Major Crimes: police section handling only major crimes
Make: identity
Make: to obtain something; to detect
Make a buy: to purchase drugs
Make it: to leave
M&Ms: seconal tablets shaped like M&Ms candy
Man, the: police
Manicure: to clean stems and seeds from marijuana
Marblecake: a con team composed of a white person and an African-American
Mark: victim
Mark: same as victim except a mark comes looking for deals
Marker: gambling IOU
Mary Jane, Mary: marijuana
Matchbox: container of marijuana
McCoy, the real: genuine
M.E.: medical examiner
Merchandise: narcotics or drugs
Merck: pharmaceutical cocaine
Meth: methamphetamine
Mexican brown: Mexican heroin
Mic, mike: micrograms; average dose of LSD is 250 mics
Mickey Finn: chloral hydrate mixed in a drink, used to knock out a victim
Microdots: type of LSD
Mind game: psychological game of wits
Mind trip: drugs causing psychological changes
Minibeans: small Benzedrine tablets
Miss Emma: morphine
M.O.: modus operandi (method of operation)
Moll buzzer: picker of women's pockets
Moms: old lady victims

Morning shot: first injection of the day
Mouth habit: oral drug habit
Mouthpiece: criminal's attorney; lawyer
Mr. Cash: loan shark
Mud: opium
Mug: to rob a person on the street
Muggles: marijuana
Mule: go-between from the dealer to the buyer; one who transports drugs
Munchies: sensation of hunger caused by smoking marijuana
Mystery: homicide with no suspect
Nail: hypodermic needle; marijuana cigarette; to kill
Nailed: arrested
Narc, nark, narco: narcotics officer
Needle freak: one who injects drugs into the vein or skin
Nemmies: Nembutal
Nickel: five dollars
Nineteen: nineteenth letter of alphabet, S for speed
Nippers: handcuffs
Nod: dozing as a result of drugs, usually heroin
No further: no other units need respond
No way: no chance
Number: marijuana
O.D.: overdose of a drug, often fatal
Off: to get rid of; kill
Off the wall: crazy; suddenly angry
Oil-burning habit: a big habit
On the take: officer accepting illegal goods or money
One and one: two measured lines of cocaine, one per nostril
One large: $100 bill
One-percenter: outlaw motorcycle group (one percent of motorcycle riders)
Open file: case that is unsolved but still being investigated
O.S.: out of service
O.T.: overtime
Outfit: injection paraphernalia
Out front: open, honest; to advance money before the delivery of drugs

Out of it: not in touch; removed

Outside too long: working the street for too long a period

Overamped: to inject too much methamphetamine

Overdose: too much of a drug; to take too much of a drug

Overstock: front-end extension on a motorcycle

Owe me one: to owe a favor

Owsley: high quality LSD

O.Z.: ounce

Ozer: one ounce package

P-2-P: phenyl-2-propanone, chemical used to manufacture methamphetamine

Packin': possession of a weapon; to take a rider on the back of a motorcycle

Pad: living quarters

Paddie, paddy, patty: white person; in Boston, Irish

Panama red: high grade marijuana grown in Panama

Panic: scarcity of drugs

Paper: quantity of narcotics contained in a small, folded piece of paper; cigarette paper

Paper acid: LSD on a small piece of paper

Paper hanger: forger

Paquete: packaging for twelve balloons of heroin

Pat down: frisk

Patsy: victim

P.B.A.: Police Benevolent Association

P.C.: police commissioner

P.D.: public defender

Peace pill: PCP

Peddler: one who sells drugs

Pen: holding cell for prisoners

People: mixture of a drug with another substance; family or relatives

Pep pill: amphetamine

Perp: perpetrator of a crime

Peter: bank vault or safe

Peterman: safecracker; someone who illegally enters a bank vault to steal money

Piece: one ounce of a narcotic, usually heroin; gun

Pig: police officer
Pigeon: victim
Pill freak: user of any type of pill
Pillow: 25,000 amphetamine tablets, usually packaged in a black plastic bag
Pimp: procurer for prostitutes
Pin: identify an individual by his life-style
Pinch: small sample of a drug; arrest
Pineapple: bomb
Pink lady: secobarbital capsule
Plant: stakeout; to place a misleading piece of evidence; place selected for robbery; place of concealment; a spy placed in a trusted situation; to place drugs in someone's possession without the person's knowledge
Plastic: fake, not real
Playing the con: doing a scam
Plunger: syringe
P.O.: parole or probation officer
Point: needle
Pokey: jail
Pop: to take a drug by injection or orally
Popped: arrested
Post time: time to start
Pot: marijuana
Power sign: fist salute (bikers use left hand)
Prop: phenyl-2-propanone (chemical used to manufacture methamphetamine)
Proper lick: a good take from the scam
Prossie: prostitute
Psychedelic: hallucinogenic
Punk lick: short price received from scam
Punk out: to pass out
Push: to sell drugs
Pushed out of shape: angry
Pusher: person who sells drugs
Put it down: to stop; to degrade
Put on: to tease or deceive; to confuse
Putt: modified motorcycle

Putten: to go for a motorcycle ride

Quarter: $25; $25 balloon of heroin

Quarter piece: one-fourth ounce of a drug, usually heroin

Queer: counterfeit money

Quiff: prostitute

Rabbi: protector, usually someone in higher office

Rabbit: to run away; person buyer uses to test dope

Rack: three to ten capsules taped together

Raffles: burglar

Rags: clothes

Rainbows: Tuinal

Raincheck: parole

Raked: car raised in back; extended front end of motorcycle without raising ground level

Ranch: residence

Rank: crude; impolite

Rap: to talk; arrest or conviction; time in prison; to assume blame for something

Rap sheet: record of arrests, convictions of a suspect

Rat: to inform or betray

Rattler: freight train

R.D.: robbery detail; secobarbital

R.D.O.: regular day off.

Read: to analyze or understand

Reds: secobarbital

Reefer: marijuana cigarette

Register: show of blood in syringe during an injection to indicate that the vein was punctured

Rent-a-cop: private investigator or security guard

Ride: car

Rig: injection paraphernalia

Righteous: good; honest, the truth

Right on: good, perfect

Rights: Miranda rule, requiring that individuals arrested must be informed of their legal rights

Ripoff: a scam; to steal; to be arrested

R.K.C.: resident known criminal file

R.M.P.: rapid mobilization plan

Roach: partially smoked marijuana cigarette
Roach clip: holder for a marijuana cigarette
Rock: crystallized cocaine
Rock house: heavily fortified house where people deal in drugs, usually crack
Rod: firearm
Roll: ten pills in a roll
Roper: con man who ropes or entices the victim or mark into the scam
Roust: to be hassled by police
Rover: remote out of service emergency radio
R.P.C.: radio patrol car; released prisoner cases
Run: group of motorcycle riders going somewhere, usually at least fifty miles away
Run-it-down: go-between from dealer to buyer; someone who does all the legwork for another
Rush: first exciting euphoria from taking a drug
S.A.C.: Special Agent in Charge (FBI)
S&L: safe and lock squad
Sap: fool; blackjack
Scab: abscess caused by injection of a drug; ugly female
Scag: heroin
Scam: ploy; plot; confidence racket
Scarf: to swallow a drug
Scene: a location, usually of a crime; a social event; to draw attention to
Schmeck: heroin
Schmuck: fool
Scoot: modified motorcycle
Scooter tramp: outlaw motorcycle gang member
Score: to purchase drugs; to have sexual intercourse
Scottish tinkers: phoney home repair hustlers
Scratch: money; bad check
Screw: police officer; prison guard
Script: drug prescription
Secret mark: ID number and placed in secret location on auto
Shades: sunglasses
Shadow: follow a suspect

Shafted: taken advantage of

Shank: knife

Shill: a person used by gamblers or cons to lure victims

Shine on: to ignore a person or plans; to tease

Shit: dope; heroin

Shitcan: homicide unlikely to be solved

Shoofly: officer working for Internal Affairs

Shooter: person using drug needle; person holding street packet of drugs; person firing weapon

Shooting gallery: place to inject drugs

Shoot up: to inject a drug

Short: vehicle; smaller than expected amount of a drug

Shot: house or room

Sick: withdrawal experienced by a user; needing a drug to remain normal

Sing: to confess; to inform on others

Sissy bar: chrome upward extension located on the back of a motorcycle seat

Sitting on plant: staking out suspect

Size the vic: selecting the victim of a proposed scam

Skag: heroin

Skid lid: motorcycle helmet

Skim: taking money from profits before delivery

Skin pop: to inject a drug underneath the skin rather than into the vein

Skip: to leave town; to jump bail

Skirt: the bag in which the roper holds his hot merchandise

Slammer: prison

Sled: car

Sleepers: wallets

Smack: heroin

Snatcher: kidnapper

Snitch: informer

Snort: to sniff a drug through the nose

Snow: cocaine

Snowbird: cocaine user

S.N.U.: street narcotics unit

S.O.D.: special operations division

Solid: O.K., all right
S.O.P.: standard operating procedure
Sounds: music
Spaced out: in a daze
Speed: methamphetamine
Speedball: mixture of heroin and a stimulant drug such as cocaine or amphetamine
Spike: drug user's needle
Split: to leave
Spoon: a quantity of a drug, approximately one-half gram of heroin
Sporting: using cocaine
Springer: motorcycle front end that has dual springs
Square: nonuser
Squeeze: put pressure on
Squirrely: strange
Stakeout: observation of a suspect or location where a suspect is to appear or a crime is to take place
Stall: confederate who obscures thief or hinders pursuit
Standup guy: someone who can be depended on
Stash: total amount of a drug one possesses, often hidden
Steerer: the roper who leads the victim into the con
Step on: to adulterate drugs to obtain a larger quantity
Stick: marijuana cigarette
Stiff: convict
Sting: a setup
Stir: prison
Stone: to emphasize something, e.g., stone fox (sexy woman)
Stoned: under the influence
Stoolie: informant
Straight: square; not a drug user
Street people: persons who use drugs or are related to drug users in the underground culture; homeless persons
Stretch: prison sentence
Strip: in auto theft, removal of tires, wheels, air conditioning, radio, phone, battery
Strung out: addicted
Stuff: heroin

Sucker: victim

Sucker pockets: pockets on outside of garments

Suede: black

Sugar habit: addict's desire for sweets caused by a large amount of milk sugar mixed with heroin

Suit: young, educated officer likely to advance to headquarters

Super: really good

Swing man: supplier; connection

T/P/O: time, place and occurrence

Tabs: tablets

Take: the money a corrupt police officer takes; the spoils of a racket or a robbery

Take a cab: to leave

Take for a ride: death trip

Take out: to murder

Tap: wire or telephone tap

Tar: opium

Taste: small ration of a drug

Tea: marijuana

Tell it like it is: to tell the truth

Ten card: officer's force record card

Ten-cent bag: $10 bag

Threads: clothes

Throwaway: gun or clothes worn and discarded by mugger to avoid pursuit

Tie off: to prepare for injection by placing a tourniquet around the limb to be used

Tie rag: homemade or makeshift tourniquet used during the injection of drugs

Tight: to be close to someone; friend

Till: cash register; any place money is stashed

Tin: officer's badge; one ounce of marijuana

Tin man: police

T.J.: Tijuana, Mexico

T.O.: table of organization, a chart that illustrates the chain of command

Toke up: to light a marijuana cigarette

Tools: injection paraphernalia

Torch: to start a fire, usually arson
Torch job: arson
Torpedo: gunman; killer
Tough, tuff: good
Tracks: supravenous scars from injection of drugs
Trick: date or customer of a prostitute; victim; foolish person
Trike: three-wheeled motorcycle
Trip: to be under the influence of a drug; to travel to score
Troll: to be looking to sell
Trucking: moving
Trumpet: Triumph motorcycle
Turkey: bad narcotics or substance in lieu of narcotics
Turn: to inform to the police
Turn on: to take drugs
Turn someone on: to give someone drugs
Turtle: LSD or PCP tablet shaped like a turtle shell
24/24: the twenty-four hours preceding and the twenty-four
   hours following the commission of a crime
Twist: to inform to the police
Two-way radio: informer
Uncool: not suave or socially unacceptable
Uncut: pure form of a drug
Up: the next in line to catch the case
Up front: straightforward
Upper: amphetamine
Uptight: upset
Uptown: big time
User: drug addict
U.S.P.: pharmaceutical methamphetamine
Vibes: feelings
Vic: victim
Vigorish, vig: loan shark's interest on loan
V.I.N.: vehicle identification number plate near the windshield
   of every vehicle
Vine: clothes
Wagon: car; coroner's van; police van
Washed: money channeled through an intermediary to conceal
   its source

W.A.S.P.: white Anglo-Saxon Protestant

Waste: to murder

Wasted: unconscious or almost unconscious from being under the influence of a drug

Water: methamphetamine

Watering hole: officers' hangout

Way out: extreme

Wedge: type of LSD, usually a tablet

Weed: marijuana

Weekend habit: small, irregular habit

Went down: the time a crime was committed

Wheel: boss; to bet one horse with all others in the race

Wheeler-dealer: big man; con artist

Wheelman: driver of a getaway car

Wheels: car

Wheel school: police motorcycle training school

Whip: officer in charge

Whiskers: police

Whites: Benzedrine

White stuff: heroin, usually Chinese

Wiggle-a-cup: panhandler

Windowpane: type of LSD

Wiped out: tired, exhausted

Wired: carrying recording device; location having a recording device; under the influence; strung out

Wire room: bookie's place

Withdraw: to stop using narcotics

Working a drag: doing a scam

Works: injection paraphernalia

Wrong: bad or untrustworthy

Yaleman: expert with locks

Yancy: nervous

Yard: $100

Yellows: Nembutal

Zap: to shoot

Zapped: shot

Zee: one ounce of a drug; sleep

Zig-Zag man: the man shown on Zig-Zag brand cigarette papers, which are commonly used to roll marijuana cigarettes
Zip gun: homemade gun
Zonked, zonked out: high on drugs

Street Gang Slang

The following list contains terms and phrases that are, as of this writing, used by street gangs, primarily the Los Angeles Blood and Crip gangs. These terms change frequently, so contact your local law enforcement agency for changes.

Ace kool: best friend, backup
Base head: person hooked on cocaine
Beemer: BMW vehicle
Benzo: Mercedes Benz
Blob: Crips' nickname for Crip gang member
Blood: non-Crip
Bo: marijuana
Boned out: quit, chickened out, left
Book: run, get away, leave
Break: run, get away
Break-down: shotgun
Bucket: old, raggedy car
Bud: marijuana
Bullet: one year in custody
Bumping titties: fighting
Busted: shot at someone
Buster: young guy who is trying to be a gang member; fake gang member
Check it out: listen to what I have to say
Chill out: stop it, don't do that
Colum: Colombian marijuana
Crab: Bloods' nickname for Crip gang member
Cragared down: low rider car
Cuzz: Crip
Deuce and a quarter: Buick 225
Dis: disrespect
Do a ghost: to leave, leave the scene

Double-deuce: .22-caliber gun
Down for mine: ability to protect self
Drag: ability to sweet-talk girls
Draped: wearing a lot of gold jewelry
Drop a dime: snitch on someone
Durag: handkerchief wrapped around head
Dusted: under the influence of PCP
Eastly: very ugly person
Esseys: Mexicans
Everything is everything: it's all right
Four-five: .45-caliber gun
Freak: good looking girl
Fresh: good looking, clean
Gang-banging: involved in gang activity
Get down: fight
Gig: gathering
Glass house: '77 or '78 Chevy
G-ride: gangster ride; stolen car
Headhunter: female who trades sex for cocaine
High roller: successful drug dealer
Holding down: controlling turf or area
Home boy: fellow gang member
Homey: fellow gang member
Hood: neighborhood
Hook: phony, imitation
Hoopty: car
Hustler: not into gangs, strictly out to make money
Illing: making mental mistake
Jacked-up: beat up or assaulted
Jammed: confronted
Jim Jones: marijuana joint that is laced with cocaine and
  dipped in PCP
Juiced: car with hydraulics to raise and lower it
Kibbles & Bits: crumbs of cocaine
Kicking back: relaxing, killing time
Kool: it's all right
Laces: chrome, spoke rims
Lady: girlfriend

Let's bail: let's leave
Lifts: hydraulics to raise and lower car
Liquid juice: PCP
Lit up: shot at
Lizard butt: ugly girl
Mack: ability to sweet-talk girls
Main man: best friend, backup
Making bank: making money, usually illegally
Man: cop, police officer
Mark: want-to-be gang member
Mobile: proper, nice looking
Molded: embarrassed
Monte C: Chevrolet Monte Carlo
Mud duck: ugly girl
O/G: original gangster
On the pipe: freebasing cocaine
Packing: gang member has gun in his possession
Player: not into gangs, strictly out to make money
Popped a cap: shot at someone
Primo: marijuana joint laced with cocaine
Rag: color of gang; handkerchief
Raise: leave
Recruiting: looking for girls
Red eye: hard stare
Ride: car
Ride on, rode on: to go to a rival neighborhood in vehicles to attack other gangs
Righteous: true or affirmative answer
Rock: crystallized cocaine
Roo-rah: loud talking
Rush: to sweet-talk girls
Scandalous: deadbeat person, bad person
Scratch: embarrassed
Set: neighborhood
Sherm: PCP
Slob: Crips' nickname for Blood gang member
Snaps: money
Sprung: addicted to cocaine

Squab: fight, argue
Stall it out: stop doing what you're doing
Strawberry: female who does sexual acts for cocaine
Talking head: argue; wanting to fight
Talking smack: aggressive talking
Trey-eight: .38-caliber gun
Trick: phony sissy
Trip: too much, something else
Turkish: heavy, ornamental gold necklace, earrings
Up on it: have knowledge of the drug scene; successful in dealing drugs
Wack: PCP
Wave: short, close-cropped haircut
What it "b" like: Blood greeting
What it "c" like: Crip greeting
What's up: what's going on

Questions about the Bloods and Crips Los Angeles gangs should be directed to the Los Angeles County District Attorney's Office; (213) 725-5081, or California Department of Justice-BOCCI, P.O. Box 903357, Sacramento, California 94203-3570; (916) 739-5715.

Prison Slang

Bad time: in trouble; quarrelsome; depressed
Better people: high-grade or more intelligent prisoners
Block: cellblock area
Blues: regular prisoners
Booty bandit: bully who rapes young convicts under guise of protecting them from other cons
B.O.P.: Bureau of Prisons
Bull: prison guard
Bull ring: exercise yard
Bus therapy: repeatedly taking a convict during the night to another facility; movements can continue for months from joint to joint with no commissary money, clean clothes or personal effects.
Country club: minimum security facility

Crib: prison cell

Dime: ten-year sentence

Feather bed: padded cell

Fish: new prisoner

Good time: getting along well

Hard time: maximum security; tough work assignment

Hole: solitary confinement

Joint: prison

Joint handles: nicknames given to cons by other cons, usually connected to or related to crime new con committed. If no joint handle is given, new con is generally not trusted by others.

Khakis: newly arrived cons

Lockdown: when prisoners are placed back in cells

Mainline: dining room

Nickel: five-year sentence

Piano: prison workbench

Population: inmates of prison

Prune juice: homemade wine

Rat: informer, to inform

Screw: prison guard

Shadow box: visitors' room

Standup guy: respected by other inmates

Stash: any illegal substance that is hidden

Stinger: wire plugged into light socket to melt chocolate bar for cocoa or instant coffee

"Strangers in the Night": tune whistled by inmates to alert other cons that guard is within hearing distance

Street: outside world

Yard: exercise yard

Yard bull: guard in exercise yard

Warden's office: toilet

Waste: to kill another prisoner

Working for Jesus: religious prisoner with ulterior motive

Works: prison laundry

On-the-Road Slang

Badge on a beaver: female officer
Batman and Robin: two officers in a patrol car
Big hats: state police
Black-and-white: patrol car
Blueboy: local or state police
Charlie's Angel: female officer
D.C.s: federal officers
Eye in the sky: police chopper
Hound dog: local or state police
Mama bear: female officer
Mister Do-right: local or state police
Mounty: local or state police
Pig on a wheel: motorcycle officer
Pink Panther: local or state police
Prez-Fuzz: federal officers
Rent-a-cop: private security
Smoke for rent: private security
Smoke in the sky: police chopper
Smokey: local or state police
Spy in the sky: police chopper
Two-wheel smokey: motorcycle officer
White knight: local or state police

LEGAL TERMINOLOGY

Ab inconvenienti: argument that not following a certain course will result in hardship
Ab initio: from the beginning
Abandonment: relinquishment of a claim or privilege
Abandonment of spouse: desertion of a spouse without reasonable cause, or negligence in providing support
Abate: to terminate, decrease or quash
Abduction: taking a wife, child or ward without consent by fraud, persuasion or violence
Abet: to aid, encourage or advise another to commit a crime
Abettor: one who aids, abets or instigates

Abeyance: a state of suspension or temporary inactivity; being undermined in expectation

Abjure: to renounce or abandon on oath

Abortion: a miscarriage or induced expulsion of an embryo or fetus

Abscond: to avoid the process of the court by hiding or leaving the jurisdiction

Abuse: to treat improperly; to injure

Abut: to border on

Accessory after the fact: anyone who, after a felony has been committed, knowingly harbors, conceals or aids a principal in the felony

Accessory before the fact: one who, though absent at the time of the crime, procures, counsels, advises, encourages or commands another to commit it

Action in personam: action against a person based on personal liability

Action in rem: action for a thing, to recover something possessed by another

Administrative offices of the state courts: the business offices of state courts

Adultery: voluntary sexual intercourse between persons, at least one of whom is lawfully married to another

Advisory of opinion: a nonbinding opinion rendered by a court to a lower court or to another branch of government

Affray: the fighting of two or more persons in a public place that disturbs the peace

Amicus curiae: friend of the court; one who volunteers information upon some matter of law

Arraign: in criminal practice, to bring a prisoner to the court to plead to a criminal charge

Arson: willful and malicious burning, or causing to be burned, of a building or dwelling

Assault: unlawful attempt or application of force and violence to harm another

At issue: when the litigants in a suit come to a point that is affirmed by one and denied by the other, they are at an issue

Bail: a guaranty that a person arrested on criminal charges will appear for trial or examination; a bond, a deposit of money or a deed to property, which is forfeited if the accused does not appear

Battery: assault by any force, however slight, applied to another person

Bigamy: marrying a second person while legally married

Bribery: receiving or offering a reward by or to a public official to influence the exercise of duties

Burglary: breaking and entering the house of another with intent to commit a felony, whether or not the felony is actually committed

Calendar: a list of cases to be heard by a court during the court term; the docket

Case: a suit or action in law or equity

Cases and controversies: the exercise of judicial power by the federal courts is limited to actual legal disputes between parties, as compared to hypothetical or friendly disputes; see Section 2, Article III of the U.S. Constitution

Certiorari: a writ issued by a higher court requiring the record of a case in a lower court to be provided for inspection

Challenge to the jury array: questioning the qualifications of an entire jury panel, usually on the grounds of a partiality or a fault in the process of summoning the panel

Chancellor: in some states, the chief judge of the equity courts

Change of venue: the removal of a case in progress from one jurisdiction to another for trial, or from one court to another in the same jurisdiction

Chief judge or justice: the presiding judge of a court

Circuit: a division or territory for judicial business

Civil action: an action that seeks the establishment, recovery or redress of private or civil rights; suits related to individual rights rather than public wrongs

Common law: the law as established by custom and precedent rather than by statute; in the United States, the principles of law developed in England and the colonies before the American Revolution

Compounding a felony: an offense by a person who agrees with a criminal not to prosecute on condition of receipt of a reward or bribe

Concurrent jurisdiction: when one or more courts have jurisdiction to determine the same issues

Conspiracy: a combination or agreement between two or more persons to do an unlawful act; either the end to be attained is a crime, or the means by which it is to be attained are unlawful, or if the wrong were inflicted by a single individual, it would be a civil wrong and not a crime

Constitutional court: in the federal system, a federal court established by Congress pursuant to Article III of the U.S. Constitution

Counterfeit: to copy without authority in order to defraud by representing the copy as genuine

Court-martial: a court convened to hear an offense committed by a person subject to the Uniform Code of Military Justice (UCMJ)

Court of appeal: a court in which appeals from a lower court are heard

Court of equity: court that administers remedial justice according to the system of equity, as distinguished from a court of law; sometimes called a court of chancery

Court of first instance: the court in which a case was originally brought; trial court

Court of general sessions: criminal courts that have general jurisdiction

Court of last resort: a court from which no appeal lies to a higher court

Court of record: a court whose proceedings are recorded, and that has the power to fine or imprison

Court term: a division of the year during which the court is in session

Defendant: a person defending, that is, who is being sued in a civil action or prosecuted in a criminal action

Discovery: a proceeding in which each party to an action is informed about facts known by other parties or witnesses

Dismissal without prejudice: dismissal with no decision on the merits; permits the complainant to sue again on the same cause of action

Disorderly conduct: generally, unlawful behavior that disturbs the peace or affronts public morality

Dissenting opinion: an opinion by a judge of an appellate court disagreeing with the result reached by the majority

Disturbance of the peace: interrupting the peace of a neighborhood by gratuitous and distracting noises

Double jeopardy: Fifth Amendment guarantee against a second trial for an offense already adjudicated, or for a second punishment for the same offense; the round in which the questions are worth twice as much

Drunkard: one whose habit is to get drunk, whose inebriety has become habitual

Dueling: a fight between two persons at an agreed on time and place to resolve a quarrel

Embezzlement: generally, the unlawful appropriation of property for personal use by an employee, trustee or public officer

En banc: in the bench; a court appeal when all of its judges jointly issue a decision or opinion

Escape: the departure of a lawfully imprisoned person from legal custody

Exhibit: a paper, document or other article shown to a court during a proceeding

Ex post facto: after the fact; something occurring after some previous and related event

Extortion: the unlawful taking of anything of value by force, threat or under color of authority; blackmail

False impersonation: assuming the identity of another and acting to deceive others in order to gain some profit, privilege or advantage

False imprisonment: unlawful arrest or detention without warrant or with an illegal warrant

Felony: a serious crime, usually carrying a sentence in a state or federal penitentiary

Forgery: the false making of, or altering with intent to defraud, any writing that, if genuine, would be of value or the foundation of a legal liability

Good behavior: lawful conduct

Grand jury: a body of persons, the number of whom varies in different jurisdictions, sworn to inquire into crimes

Habeas corpus: literally, "You have the body"; a writ that requires an officer having custody of a prisoner to bring that prisoner before the court to determine if the prisoner is being unlawfully detained

Homicide: the killing of a human being. The lawful or unlawful taking of another human life

Impeachment: a charge of misconduct against a public official returned by a legislative body

In camera: in the judge's chambers; in private

Indictment: a formal accusation made by a grand jury charging a person with a crime

In forma pauperis: a petition to a court to absolve a poor person of certain legal costs so that an action may proceed

Information: an accusation made by a prosecutor, without presentment to a grand jury, charging a person with a crime

Injunction: court order forbidding a person from performing a certain act

Inquest: judicial inquiry

Judgment: official determination by a court

Judicial administration: the organization and procedures of the judicial branch of the government

Judiciary: the branch of government that has judicial power; all the courts of a jurisdiction taken collectively

Jurisdiction: the authority of a court to exercise its judicial power in a specific case; the geographic area a court has authority over

Jury instruction: the judge's directions to the jury on the laws of the case

Justice of the peace: a public official with minor civil and criminal jurisdiction; may conduct preliminary hearings in more serious crimes

Larceny: stealing and carrying away the personal goods of another with intent to convert or deprive

Legislative court: a court created by Congress pursuant to a constitutional power other than Article III of the U.S. Constitution; the Court of Claims, the Court of Customs and Patent Appeals, the Emergency Court of Appeals, the Customs Court, the territorial courts and the local courts for the District of Columbia

Libel: malicious defamation expressed either by writing, printing, sign, pictures or the like that injures or impeaches the honesty, integrity, virtue or reputation of a private person; in the case of a public figure, the defamation must be published knowing that it is false or with reckless disregard for its truth or falsehood

Magistrate: a judge of an inferior court who carries limited jurisdiction

Majority decision: a decision by an appellate court by more than one-half of those judges hearing a case

Manslaughter: the unlawful killing of a human being without malice or deliberation

Manslaughter, involuntary: taking a human life while committing an unlawful but nonviolent act, or while committing a lawful act without normal caution or required skill

Manslaughter, voluntary: taking a human life voluntarily but without premeditation, such as in a fight resulting from a sudden quarrel

Misconduct in office: malfeasance in which a public officer in the exercise of duty abuses discretionary power or fails to act when required

Misdemeanor: a crime less than the grade of felony

Mistrial: an erroneous or invalid trial; a trial that cannot stand in law because of lack of jurisdiction, improper jury selection, violation of some other fundamental requirement; a trial resulting in a deadlocked jury

Murder: the unlawful killing with malice aforethought of one human being by another

Nisi prius: courts for the initial trial of issues of fact, as distinguished from appellate courts

Nolle prosequi: a declaration by the plaintiff in a civil suit, or the prosecuting officer in a criminal case, that states that he or she "will no further prosecute" the case

Nolo contendere: a plea used by criminal defendants that literally means, "I will not contest it"; a plea with effects similar to "guilty" but without a formal admission of guilt

Notary public: a public officer who administers oaths

Obstructing justice: to obstruct public or private justice by resisting an officer in the exercise of his or her duty, or by preventing attendance of witnesses

Per curiam: an opinion rendered by the court as a whole, rather than by one judge with whom others concur

Perjury: making a false statement under oath

Piracy: a robbery or forcible depredation upon property on the high seas without lawful authority and with the intention of stealing

Plaintiff: a person who brings suit

Pleading: statement by a litigant that specifies the basis of its claims or challenges the claims of its opponents

Rape: having unlawful, forcible, carnal knowledge, without consent, including instances in which: resistance is overcome by actual force, or no force is used but consent cannot be given because of the person's condition, or the person is below the age of consent, or consent is extorted by fear of bodily harm, or submission is induced by fraud without intelligent consent

Receiving stolen goods: receiving property with the knowledge that it has been stolen or embezzled

Riot: use of force or violence that disturbs the public peace, or any threat to use such force or violence by three or more persons acting together and without authority of law

Robbery: taking of personal property from the owner without consent by means of force or fear

Stare decisis: to decide cases based on precedent; to abide by established case law

Supersedeas: a writ commanding a stay in proceedings

Surrogate: a judge or judicial officer who has administration of probate matters

Trial de novo: a retrial in which the trial is conducted as if the original trial had not occurred

Unlawful assembly: a meeting of three or more persons that disturbs the peace with the intent to cooperate in the forcible execution of some unlawful private purpose

Venue: the geographic area in which a court may hear a case

Voir dire: "to speak the truth"; the preliminary examination of prospective jurors

Writ: an order issued by a court or judge directing a public officer or private person to do a specific act

WHERE TO GO FROM HERE

This bibliography is more general than those for the other chapters because authors write about crime in incredibly varied ways. You may just want to know how to spell a word or a person's name. You may need a bit of slang from a particular group during a particular era. You may need some professional jargon.

The American Medical Association Encyclopedia of Medicine. New York: Random House, 1989. Big, comprehensive, authoritative and well illustrated. This is a good place to look first for information on disease and medicine.

Ammer, Christine. *Seeing Red or Tickled Pink: Color Terms in Everyday Language.* New York: Dutton, 1992. Entertaining histories of the origins of phrase involving color.

Barnhart, Clarence, Sol Steinmetz, and Robert Barnhart. *The Second Barnhart Dictionary of New English.* Bronxville, New York: Barnhart/Harper & Row, 1980. An excellent book on the origins and definitions terms from science, technology and popular culture.

Beale, Paul, ed. *Partridge's Concise Dictionary of Slang and Unconventional English.* Macmillan, 1989. Good, current information on (primarily) British slang.

Black's Law Dictionary. 6th ed. St. Paul, Minnesota: West Publishing Co., 1990. The standard law dictionary. Indispensable if you're writing anything at all technical about the law.

Bryson, Bill. *The Penguin Dictionary for Writers and Editors.* New York: Viking-Penguin, 1991. A guide to terms easily confused, capitalization, hyphenation and more. The author is from the United States but lives in the United Kingdom, so the coverage is of both flavors (flavours) of English.

Bullock, Alan, and R.B. Woodings. *20th Century Culture: A Biographical Companion.* New York: Harper & Row, 1983. Somewhat longer biographies than in Webster's, and it includes the living. Most of the criminals profiled here are politicians.

Fahey, Tom. *The Joys of Jargon.* New York: Barron's, 1990. More a book about jargon and how to cope with it than a dictionary, though it has informal lexicons of words from science, consumer electronics, computer science, economics and various occupations.

Garner, Bryan. *A Dictionary of Modern Legal Usage.* New York: Oxford University Press, 1987. A very useful volume that tells you how legal terms are actually used.

Green, Jonathon. *Dictionary of Jargon.* New York: Routledge & Kegan Paul, 1987. Over 21,000 words and phrases from a variety of occupations in the United States and the United Kingdom.

Lewin, Esther, and Albert Lewin. *The Random House Thesaurus of Slang.* New York: Random House, 1988. Has the unique advantage of the main listings being nonslang, that is, you look up the standard word to find slang equivalents.

Maggio, Rosalie. *The Dictionary of Bias-Free Usage.* Phoenix: Oryx Press, 1991. Bias-free usage isn't slang, but this is nevertheless a good book to have on your shelf. It gives the origins of sexist and racist terms and suggests alternatives.

Morris, William, and Mary Morris. *Harper Dictionary of Contemporary Usage.* 2d ed. New York: Harper & Row, 1985. The Morrises give their opinions about usage, and on the more contentious issues supply the comments of members of a usage panel (166 of them, altogether), mostly writers and editors.

Onions, C. T. *The Oxford Dictionary of English Etymology.* Oxford: Oxford University Press, 1969. A manageable (1,025 pages) treatment of the origins of English words, and the classic.

The Random House Dictionary of the English Language. 2d ed., unabridged. New York: Random House, 1987. An excellent backup for a desk dictionary. It's relatively new, comprehensive and attractively done.

Spears, Richard. *NTC's Dictionary of American Slang and Colloquial Expressions.* National Textbook Company, 1989. Also published in an abridged form as *Contemporary American Slang* (National Textbook Company, 1991).

Thorne, Tony. *The Dictionary of Contemporary Slang.* New York: Pantheon Books, 1990. A good guide to slang originating between 1950 and 1990 throughout the English-speaking world.

Tulloch, Sara. *The Oxford Dictionary of New Words.* New York: Oxford University Press, 1991. This covers both mainstream slang and new words from science, technology and popular culture.

Watts, Peter. *A Dictionary of the Old West.* New York: Promontory Press, 1987. A good source for the definitions of some rather arcane terms. Also gives the published sources of the definitions.

Webster's Dictionary of English Usage. Springfield, Massachusetts: Merriam-Webster, 1989. Probably the best of the currently available usage guides.

Webster's Medical Desk Dictionary. Springfield, Massachusetts: Merriam-Webster, 1986. This is the book to get if you want to know how terms are spelled and what they mean. It isn't the one to get if you want to know how to treat lumbago, that is, if you want to know about therapeutics as well as definitions.

Webster's New Biographical Dictionary. Springfield, Massachusetts: Merriam-Webster, 1983. A good source for spellings and other basics on famous folks who were dead as of 1983. No bios of the living.

Webster's Ninth New Collegiate Dictionary. Springfield, Massachusetts: Merriam-Webster, 1988. This is the standard for most publishers and is generally excellent.

Index

A

Accesssory
  after fact, defined, 179
  before fact, defined,
    179-180
  principal and, 188
Accusation, defined, 180
Addiction, drug, 42
Admissions, defined, 138
Agencies, federal investigative,
    131
  books about, 133-135
  See also individual names
Aider and abettor, or accom-
    plice, defined, 180-181
Air Force Office of Special In-
    vestigations, 130
American common law, de-
    fined, 181
Appeal, right to, 169
Army Criminal Investigative
    Command, 129
Arrest, 138-141
  authorized, in unauthorized
    manner, 138-139
  house, 230

Arson, 34-35
Attempts, defined, 181
Auto theft, 21

B

Barbiturates, 44
Bloods. See Street gangs
Bodies
  identifying, 148-150
  unusual means of disposing,
    16-17
Border Patrol, INS, 122-123
Bureau of Alcohol, Tobacco and
    Firearms, 124
Bureau of Land Management,
    128
Bureau of Special Investiga-
    tions, LAPD, 81-86
Burglary, 19-20

C

California correction institu-
    tions, 203-218
  California Correctional Cen-
    ter, 213-214

California Correctional Institution, 210-211
California Institution for Men, 207-208
California Institution for Women, 205-206
California Medical Facility, 211-212
California Men's Colony, 209-210
California Rehabilitation Center, 212-213
California State Prison, Avenal, 215
conservation camps, 217-218
Correctional Training Facility, 205
Deuel Vocational Institution, 208-209
Folsom State Prison, 206-207
Mule Creek State Prison, 215-216
Northern California Women's Facility, 217
Richard J. Donovan Correctional Facility, 216-217
San Quentin State Prison, 204
Sierra Conservation Center, 214
Capital punishment, 231-236
Case classifications, FBI, 118-120
Cases. See Court cases
Cause, reasonable, 140
Characters, courtroom, 171
Chinese gangs, 57-58

Cincinnati Police Division, structure of, 106-109
Circumstantial evidence, 192
City attorney, office of, of Los Angeles, 105-106
Coast Guard, 126
Cocaine, 43, 44
Codes
  penal, 187-188
  police, 157-163
Commander's role, in military justice system, 177-178
Common law
  American, 181
  English, 183-184
Communications system, for L.A. County, 100-102
Complaint, defined, 139
Confession, 139
  admissible, 191
  defined, 193
  while intoxicated, 139
Confidence games, 22-25
  See also Trickery
Conspirators, acts and declarations of, 191
Constitutions, state, 190
Court
  books about, 199-201
  juvenile, 186
  officials appearing in, 172
  proving guilt in, 141
  state, 190-191
  types of, 170-171
  See also Courtroom
Court cases
  for grand jury, 165-166
  See also Hearings

Court services division, of L.A. County Sheriff's Department, 90
Courtroom, 170-172
concepts of, 179-191
Crack, 43
Crime
business, 7-8
classification of, 181
computer, 29-30
domestic, 8
by employees, 10-11
general list of, 5-7
locality of, 186
and motive, 4-5
political, 7
racketeering, 8-9
versus tort, 182
white-collar, 9-10
Crime, scene of, 142-145
checklist, 144-145
first officer on, 17
Criminal capacity, defined, 182
Criminal justice
books about, 48-51
federal administration of, 184
Criminal law, substantive, 191
Criminal procedure, defined, 182-183
Criminals
books about, 71-73
identifying, 137-138
Crips. *See* Street gangs
Cross-examination
defined, 194
questions lawful in, 198
Custody, return to, 229
Custody division, of L.A. County Sheriff's Department, 90
Customs Service Special Investigative Division, 124-125

D

Death, time of, determining, 144
Defendant
admissions and declarations by, 191
declarations by persons other than, 193
rights of, 168-169
Defense, of accused, 183
Defense Criminal Investigative Service, 128
Defense Investigative Service, 129
Department of Justice, organization of, 109-116
Depressants, types of, 36
District attorney, office of, of Los Angeles, 104-105
DNA identification, 153
Drug Enforcement Agency, 123-124
Drugs, 35-47
frequently abused, 36-37
non-medical use of, 38-41
packaging and distribution of, 44-47
psychoactive, 45-47
See also individual drug names
Dying declarations, defined, 193

E

English common law, 183-184
Equipment
  electronic surveillance, 151
  and technology, for forensic
    sciences, 152-153
Escape, means of, 11-12
Evidence, 191-199
Examination, and cross-exami-
    nation, 194
Explosives, 70

F

Facts in issue, defined, 194
Federal Air Marshals, 127
Federal Bureau of Investigation,
    116-120
Federal Bureau of Prisons,
    218-224
Felons, convicted, rights of, 203
Field Service, of INS, 121-122
Fingerprint, and index files,
    FBI, 117-118
Firearms, and manufacturers,
    62-65
Foreign Fugitive File, 48
Forensic sciences, areas within,
    152-153

G

Gangs
  Chinese, 57-58
  Korean, 56-57
  motorcycle, 60
  Vietnamese, 58-59
  See also Organized crime

Gangs, street, 59
  slang of, 263-266
Glossary
  of legal terminology, 268-276
  of slang and jargon, 239-268
  of weapons terms, 65-70
Grand jury, 165-168
  federal, 168
Guilt, proving, in court, 141
Guns
  machine, and assault rifles,
    64
  See also Firearms, and manu-
    facturers; Pistols, semiau-
    tomatic; Weapons

H

Hallucinogens, types of, 37
Harbor Patrol, L.A. County,
    103-104
Hearings
  grand jury, prior to, 167
  investigative, 166
Hearsay, defined, 195
Heroin, 44-45
Homicide, 14-19
  See also Bodies, Manslaugh-
    ter, Murder
House arrest, 230

I

Identification
  of body, 148-150
  of criminal, 137-138
  DNA, 153

Immigration and Naturalization Service, 121-123

Inmates, release of, to parole, 225-226

Innocence, presumption of, defined, 197

Insanity, defined, 185

Intent
general, 184
specific, 190
versus motive, 187

Internal Revenue Service Criminal Investigations, 125-126

International Criminal Police Organization. *See* INTER-POL

INTERPOL, 116, 131
organization of, 131-132

Interrogation, 153-157
preparation for, 155-157

Investigation
books about, 163-164
fundamentals of, 137-142
of rape, 28
sources for, 145-147
specialized, L.A. County Sheriff's Department, 94-100
writing about, 136-137

Investigations Program, INS, 123

Investigative agencies, federal. *See* individual names

Investigators, private, 132-133

J

Jail. *See* California correction institutions, Prisons

Jargon. *See* Slang

Jurisdiction, defined, 185

Jury, grand, 165-168

Justice system, military, 172-178

Justice, Department of, 109-116

Justification, defined, 186

K

Korean gangs, 56-57

L

Language. *See* Legal terminology, Slang

Larceny, 21

Law
books about, 48-51
criminal, substantive, 191
ignorance of, 184
military, 174-176
sources of, 184

Leading questions, defined, 195

Legal specialties, 171-172

Legal terminology, 268-276

Los Angeles
city attorney's office, 105-106
district attorney's office, 104-105

Los Angeles County Sherriff's Department
administrative division, 90
administrative organization of, 87-88

Aero Bureau, 102-103
court services division, 90
custody division, 90
departmental organization of,
88
detective division, 90
duties and responsibilities of,
86-87
emergency services detail,
100
field operations regions, 94
Harbor Patrol, 103-104
specialized investigations,
94-100
technical services division,
94
technological advances of,
100-102
Los Angeles Police Department
Bureau of Special Investigations, 81-86
codes of, 157-163
Office of Operations, 79
Office of Special Services,
79-81
organization and functions
of, 75-86

M

Mafia, the, 52-55
See also Organized crime
Malpractice, 48
Manslaughter, defined, 14-15
Marijuana, 43-44, 45
Marshal
defined, 186
provost, 189

Merger of offenses, 186-187
Mescaline, 44
Military justice personnel,
176-177
Military justice system, 172-178
background and development
of, 173-174
commander's role in, 177-178
introduction to, 172-173
Military law, 174-176
Military Police, 130
Miranda Rights, 154-155
Missing Children File, 47-48
Missing persons, 147-148
Mistakes, common, 2-3
Modus operandi, 60
Motive
for arson, 34-35
crime and, 4-5
defined, 196
for homicide, 15
versus intent, 187
Motorcycle gangs, 60
Murder
defined, 14-15
means of, 15-16
serial, 18-19

N

Narcotics, types of, 36
National Crime Information
Center, 47-48
Naval Investigative Service,
129-130
NCIC. *See* National Crime Infor-
mation Center

Negligence, and recklessness, 187

O

Office of Operations, LAPD, 79
Officer
  first, on scene, 17
  parole, 230
  probation, 189
Opium, 43
Organized crime, 52-60
  Asian, 56
  family structure of, 54
  See also Gangs, Yakuza
Overt act, defined, 187

P

Packaging, and distribution, of drugs, 44-47
Pardon, defined, 187
Parole, 224-231
  categories of, 226
  conditions of, 227
  defined, 187
  length of, 225
  offices for, 230-231
  revocation of, 228
Parole officers, 230
Parolee, placement of, 227-228
PCP, 45
Pedophelia, 28-29
Penal codes, 187-188
Penal systems, 203-204
Phencyclidine. See PCP
Pistols, semiautomatic, 63-64
Pleadings, defined, 188

Police
  military, 130
  See also Officer
Police codes, 157-163
Police department
  organization of, 74
  See also Cincinnati Police
    Division, Los Angeles
    County Sheriff's Depart-
    ment, Los Angeles Police
    Department, Sheriff's
    department
Postal Inspection Service, 126-127
Prima facie case, defined, 197
Principal, 188-189
Prisoner mother, 228-229
Prisoners, reentry programs for, 228-230
Prisons
  books about, 236-238
  Federal Bureau of, 218-224
  new, 219
  slang used in, 266-268
  visiting instructions for, 222-224
  See also California correction
    institutions
Private investigators, 132-133
Privileged communications, defined, 197-198
Probable cause, 140
Probation, defined, 189
Psilocybin, 44
Punishment
  capital, 231-236
  cruel and unusual, 183
  purposes of, 189

R

Rape, 27-28
Reasonable cause, 140
Reference books
  courts, 199-201
  criminal justice, 48-51
  criminals, 71-73
  federal investigative agencies,
    133-135
  investigation, 163-164
  law, 48-51
  prisons, 236-238
  See also U.S. Department of
    Justice, publications of
Restitution, 229
Revolvers, 63
Rifles, and carbines, 64
Right, to appeal, 169
Rights
  of convicted felons, 203
  of defendant, 168-169
  guaranteed, under Constitu-
    tion, 189-190
  and liabilities, of parties to
    arrest, 140-141
  Miranda, 154-155
  of suspects, 154
Robbery, 20

S

Safes, burglaries of, 19-20
Scams. *See* Confidence games
Scene of crime. *See* Crime,
  scene of
Scintilla of evidence rule, 198
Self-incrimination, 198
Semiautomatic pistols, 63-64

Sentence, commutation of, 181
  See also Punishment
Serial murder, 18-19
Sex crimes unit, 29
Sex offenses, 27-29
Sheriff, defined, 190
Sheriff's department, organiza-
  tion of, 86-104
Shotguns, 64-65
Slang
  obsolescence of, 1
  on-the-road, 268
  police and crime, glossary of,
    239-263
  street gang, glossary of,
    263-266
Smuggling, 30-33
Sodomy, 29
State's evidence, defined, 199
Statement
  inconsistent with present tes-
    timony, 198-199
  written, 157
States, policies of, for capital
  punishment, 231-236
Status of Forces Agreement, 179
Statute, defined, 191
Stimulants, types of, 37
Street gangs, 59
  slang of, 263-266
Substance abuse treatment, 229
Surveillance, 150-152
Syndicate, the, 55
  See also Organized crime
Tailing, 150
Telephone taps, 150-151
Ten code, 157-161
Testimony

credibility of, 182
expert, 194
statement inconsistent with,
  198-199
Theft, auto, 21
  See also Burglary
Tort, versus crime, 182
Traffic violation codes, 161-163
Triads, 57-58
Trickery, 26-27

U

U.S. agencies and services. *See*
  individual names
U.S. Constitution, 191
U.S. Department of Justice, pub-
  lications of, 48
U.S. Marshal's Office, 120-121
U.S. National Central Bureau,
  116
USP, Lompoc, visiting instruc-
  tions for, 222-224

V

Venue, change of, defined, 181

Victims, rape, 27
Vietnamese gangs, 58-59
Violence, acts of, 12-14
Visitors, to prison, instructions
  for, 222-224

W

Warrant
  defined, 141
  issuance of, 139
Weapons
  terms applied to, 65-70
  types of, 61-62
  See also Firearms, and manu-
    facturers; Pistols, semiau-
    tomatic
Witnesses
  competency of, 192
  impeaching credit of, 195
  necessary number of, 196
Work furlough, 228
Writing, about investigations,
  136-137

Y

Yakuza, 56

Other Books of Interest

General Writing Books

A Beginner's Guide to Getting Published, Editors of *Writer's Digest* magazine $16.95
Beginning Writer's Answer Book, Editors of *Writer's Digest* magazine $16.95
Dare to Be a Great Writer, by Leonard Bishop (paper) $14.95
Discovering the Writer Within, by Bruce Ballenger & Barry Lane $18.95
Essential Software for Writers: A Complete Guide for Everyone Who Writes with a PC, by Hy Bender (paper) $24.95
Getting the Words Right: How to Rewrite, Edit and Revise, by Theodore A. Rees Cheney (paper) $12.95
How to Write a Book Proposal, by Michael Larsen (paper) $11.95
How to Write Fast While Writing Well, by David Fryxell $17.95
How to Write with the Skill of a Master and the Genius of a Child, by Marshall J. Cook $7.58
Just Open a Vein, edited by William Brohaugh $6.99
Knowing Where to Look: The Ultimate Guide to Research, by Lois Horowitz (paper) $19.95
Make Your Words Work, by Gary Provost (paper) $14.95
On Being a Writer, edited by Bill Strickland (paper) $16.95
Pinckert's Practical Grammar, by Robert C. Pinckert (paper) $3.99
Research & Writing: A Complete Guide and Handbook, by Shah Malmoud (paper) $18.95
Shift Your Writing Career into High Gear, by Gene Perret $16.95
Thesaurus of Alternatives to Worn-Out Words and Phrases, by Robert Hartwell Fiske $17.99
The 30-Minute Writer: How to Write and Sell Short Pieces, by Connie Emerson $17.95
30 Steps to Becoming a Writer, by Scott Edelstein $16.95
The 28 Biggest Writing Blunders, by William Noble $12.95
The 29 Most Common Writing Mistakes & How to Avoid Them, by Judy Delton (paper) $9.95
The Wordwatcher's Guide to Good Writing & Grammar, by Morton S. Freeman (paper) $15.95
The Writer's Book of Checklists, by Scott Edelstein $16.95
The Writer's Digest Guide to Good Writing, Editors of *Writer's Digest* magazine $18.95
The Writer's Digest Guide to Manuscript Formats, by Buchman & Groves $18.95
The Writer's Essential Desk Reference, edited by Glenda Neff $19.95
Write Tight: How to Keep Your Prose Sharp, Focused and Concise, by William Brohaugh $16.95
Writing as a Road to Self-Discovery, by Barry Lane $16.95

Nonfiction Writing

The Complete Guide to Writing Biographies, by Ted Schwarz $6.99
How to Do Leaflets, Newsletters, & Newspapers, by Nancy Brigham (paper) $14.95
How to Write Irresistible Query Letters, by Lisa Collier Cool (paper) $10.95
The Complete Guide to Magazine Article Writing, by John M. Wilson $17.95
Magazine Writing That Sells, by Don McKinney $16.95
The Writer's Complete Guide to Conducting Interviews, by Michael Schumacher $14.95
The Writer's Digest Handbook of Magazine Article Writing, edited by Jean M. Fredette (paper) $12.95
Writing Articles From the Heart: How to Write & Sell Your Life Experiences, by Marjorie Holmes $16.95

Fiction Writing

Beginnings, Middles and Ends, by Nancy Kress $13.95
Best Stories from New Writers, edited by Linda Sanders $5.99
Characters & Viewpoint, by Orson Scott Card $14.95
The Complete Guide to Writing Fiction, by Barnaby Conrad $18.95
Conflict, Action & Suspense, William Noble $14.95
Creating Characters: How to Build Story People, by Dwight V. Swain (paper) $14.99
Dialogue, by Lewis Turco $13.95
The Fiction Writer's Silent Partner, by Martin Roth $19.95
Get That Novel Started! (And Keep Going 'Til You Finish), by Donna Levin $17.95
Handbook of Short Story Writing: Vol. I, by Dickson and Smythe (paper) $12.95
Handbook of Short Story Writing: Vol. II, edited by Jean Fredette (paper) $12.95
How to Write & Sell Your First Novel, by Collier & Leighton (paper) $13.95
Manuscript Submission, by Scott Edelstein $14.99
Mastering Fiction Writing, by Kit Reed $6.99

Plot, by Ansen Dibell $14.95
Practical Tips for Writing Popular Fiction, by Robyn Carr $17.95
Scene and Structure by Jack Bickham $14.95
Setting, Jack M. Bickham $14.95
Theme & Strategy, by Ronald B. Tobias $14.95
The 38 Most Common Fiction Writing Mistakes, by Jack M. Bickham $12.95
20 Master Plots (And How to Build Them), by Ronald B. Tobias $16.95
The Writer's Digest Character Naming Sourcebook, Sherrilyn Kenyon with Hal Blythe & Charlie Sweet $18.95
Writer's Digest Handbook of Novel Writing, $18.95
Writing the Blockbuster Novel, Albert Zuckerman, with Introduction by Ken Follett $17.95
Writing the Novel: From Plot to Print, by Lawrence Block (paper) $11.95
Writing the Short Story: A Hands-On Program, by Jack M. Bickham $16.99

Special Interest Writing Books

Armed & Dangerous: A Writer's Guide to Weapons, by Michael Newton (paper) $15.95
The Art and Craft of Poetry, Michael J. Bugeja $19.95
Cause of Death: A Writer's Guide to Death, Murder & Forensic Medicine, by Keith D. Wilson, M.D. $15.95
Children's Writer's Word Book, by Alijandra Mogliner $19.95
Comedy Writing Secrets, by Mel Helitzer (paper) $15.95
The Complete Book of Feature Writing, by Leonard Witt $18.95
The Craft of Writing Science Fiction That Sells, Ben Bova $16.95
Creating Poetry, by John Drury $18.95
Deadly Doses: A Writer's Guide to Poisons, by Serita Deborah Stevens with Anne Klarner (paper) $16.95
Editing Your Newsletter, by Mark Beach (paper) $18.95
Families Writing, by Peter Stillman (paper) $12.95
A Guide to Travel Writing & Photography, by Ann & Carl Purcell (paper) $22.95
How to Pitch & Sell Your TV Script, by David Silver $6.99
How to Write and Sell Children's Picture Books, by Jean E. Karl $16.95
How to Write & Sell Greeting Cards, Bumper Stickers, T-Shirts and Other Fun Stuff, by Molly Wigand (paper) 15.95
How to Write & Sell True Crime, by Gary Provost $5.99
How to Write Horror Fiction, by William F. Nolan $15.95
How to Write Mysteries, by Shannon OCork $14.95
How to Write Romances, by Phyllis Taylor Pianka $15.95
How to Write Science Fiction & Fantasy, by Orson Scott Card $13.95
How to Write Tales of Horror, Fantasy & Science Fiction, edited by J.N. Williamson (paper) $12.95
How to Write the Story of Your Life, by Frank P. Thomas (paper) $12.95
How to Write Western Novels, by Matt Braun $1.00
The Poet's Handbook, by Judson Jerome (paper) $12.95
Police Procedural: A Writer's Guide to the Police and How They Work, by Russell Bintliff (paper) $16.95
Powerful Business Writing, by Tom McKeown $3.95
Private Eyes: A Writer's Guide to Private Investigators, by H. Blythe, C. Sweet, & J. Landreth(paper) $15.95
Scene of the Crime: A Writer's Guide to Crime-Scene Investigation, by Anne Wingate, Ph.D. $15.95
Successful Scriptwriting, by Jurgen Wolff & Kerry Cox (paper) $14.95
The Writer's Guide to Conquering the Magazine Market, by Connie Emerson $17.95
The Writer's Guide to Creating a Science Fiction Universe, by George Ochoa & Jeff Osier $18.95
The Writer's Guide to Everyday Life in the 1800s, by Marc McCutcheon $18.95

Writing for Children & Teenagers, 3rd Edition, by L. Wyndham & Arnold Madison (paper) $12.95
Writing Mysteries: A Handbook by the Mystery Writers of America, Edited by Sue Grafton, $18.95
Writing the Modern Mystery, by Barbara Norville (paper) $12.95

The Writing Business

Business & Legal Forms for Authors & Self-Publishers, by Tad Crawford (paper) $4.99
The Complete Guide to Self-Publishing, by Tom & Marilyn Ross $18.99
This Business of Writing, by Gregg Levoy $7.98

To order directly from the publisher, include $3.00 postage and handling for 1 book and $1.00 for each additional book. Allow 30 days for delivery.

Writer's Digest Books
1507 Dana Avenue, Cincinnati, Ohio 45207
Credit card orders call TOLL-FREE
1-800-289-0963
Stock is limited on some titles; prices subject to change without notice.

Write to this same address for information on *Writer's Digest* magazine, *Story* magazine, Writer's Digest Book Club, Writer's Digest School, and Writer's Digest Criticism Service.